LA GENTE

HISPANO HISTORY AND LIFE IN COLORADO

LA GENTE

HISPANO HISTORY AND
LIFE IN COLORADO

VINCENT C. DE BACA

EDITOR

COLORADO HISTORICAL SOCIETY

1998

Colorado History
Number 2
1998

ISSN 1091-7438

COLORADO HISTORICAL SOCIETY

Research and Publications Office
David Fridtjof Halaas and David N. Wetzel, *directors*

Publications Director
David N. Wetzel

Colorado History **Editor**
Steven G. Grinstead

Book Review Editor
David Fridtjof Halaas

Editorial Assistant
Ariana Harner

Book Design
Airiel Mulvaney

The Colorado Historical Society publishes *Colorado History* to provide a flexible scholarly forum for well-written, documented manuscripts on the history of Colorado and the Rocky Mountain West. Its twofold structure is designed to accommodate article-length manuscripts in the traditional journal style and longer, book-length works which appear as monographs within the series. Monographs and special thematic issues are individually indexed; other volumes are indexed every five years. The Colorado Historical Society disclaims responsibility for statements of fact or opinion made by contributors.

Contents

GROWING DIVERSITY, 1945–PRESENT

Cover: San Ysidro de Labrador, 1995, Carlos Fresquez.
Collection of Rick Manzanares.

Back cover: Valdez rug woven by Gilbert Fernandez for George M. Kirk, director of the Colorado Fuel and Iron Company's Valdez Rug Project. Private collection.

To the Memory of RICHARD CASTRO

"Castro's commitment to the city of Denver and
the state of Colorado is an example for all Chicanos."

— *Virginia Castro*

Preface

CCORDING to the 1990 U.S. Census, the Hispano population of Colorado had increased about 24 percent over the
previous decade. It was found that 424,000 "Hispanics"
lived in Colorado, about 23 percent of them in Denver, the
state's capital and largest city. It is likely that the census of 2000 will show
continued growth of the Mexican American population across the state.

The tremendous growth of the Hispano population in Colorado and
throughout the nation has provoked controversy and, in some cases, measures designed to curtail the full expression and diversity of *la Gente*—
demands for immigration restriction, English-only laws, an end to bilingual
education, abolition of Cinco de Mayo festivities, and strict policing of
Chicano youth. Yet in the face of what seems to be a degenerating national
discourse on race relations, it is well to remember that the *Declaration of
Independence* promises all Americans the same right to "life, liberty, and
the pursuit of happiness" and that the most important issue for discussion
is whether or not this nation will pursue its commitment to civil, political,
and social justice for all.

Historically, in 1848, the United States and Mexico signed the Treaty
of Guadalupe-Hidalgo and guaranteed Hispano civil, property, and cultural rights one hundred fifty years ago. Despite guarantees that are still in
force, Hispanos in Colorado and elsewhere were displaced, marginalized,
and treated like "foreigners in their native land." They were tolerated
here only if they remained unseen and silent about their place in society.
However, over time, Hispano/Chicano/Mexicano citizens of this nation
consistently asserted their rights and demanded full equality. Here in
Colorado, the Mexican American struggle for rights and respect has been
particularly noteworthy.

This collection of essays is a major step toward explaining the dynamic
experience of *la Gente* in Colorado. Colorado Hispanos' regional traditions differentiate them among members of their own ethnic group
throughout the American Southwest. As a whole, these eleven essays
show why Hispanos are significant in our region, thereby bridging a gap in
understanding Colorado history. Years in the making, this work includes

a cross-section of scholars and experts from across the state who write on various Hispano lifestyles and historical events. It is hoped that this anthology will stimulate the writing of a comprehensive survey of Hispano history in Colorado.

The editor, Vincent C. de Baca, begins the anthology with an introduction about Spanish-Mexican exploration, conquest, and settlement of the Colorado region. His essay demonstrates that Hispanos have been familiar with the region since the sixteenth century. Taken together, all eleven essays in this collection span a time frame extending over the last hundred fifty years. The essays are organized into three parts reflecting periods of continuity and change coinciding with the Hispano experience in Colorado and reflecting the organization of the exhibition *La Gente: Hispanos in Colorado*, on permanent display in Denver's Colorado History Museum.

Part one, "Settlement in the North, 1800–1900," includes three essays describing Hispanos who sought opportunities in Colorado after the United States assumed control of the vast western part of the continent once belonging to Spain. Although each of the subjects was born and raised in a Hispano cultural context, these three people had both positive and negative contracts with Anglo American culture. In the first essay, Deborah Mora-Espinosa shows how nineteenth-century accounts of Hispanic women by male writers seldom described them in detail or in a favorable way. Through an analysis of archival sources, she profiles one of the founders of Pueblo, Teresita Sandoval—an influential woman who was tellingly ignored in most writings of her day. In the second essay, Richard Louden provides the personal memoir of Elfido Lopez, Sr., who worked as a cowboy (*vaquero*) most of his life. Lopez also describes the communal labor activities of rural Hispanos near Trinidad, Colorado. Third, Vincent C. de Baca offers a bilingual version of an autobiography written by Pablo Cabeza de Baca, his great-grandfather. Cabeza de Baca recalls the values of his youth and his days at Denver's Sacred Heart College (the precursor of Regis University) in 1891, the school's first year of operation.

Part two, entitled "Displacement and Adaptation, 1900–1945," includes four essays about an era when Hispano economic self-sufficiency had disintegrated. Desperate native-born Hispanos and Mexican immigrants competed by the thousands for cash-paying jobs at Anglo-owned mining and agricultural corporations throughout Colorado. Mexicans and Hispanos entered the American capitalist system and the working class, side by side, earning the lowest wages and under the worst conditions. In the first essay of this section, M. Edmund Vallejo recalls how his family survived the infamous Ludlow coal strike of 1913–14. He writes that the violent labor dispute divided family and friends into warring factions, supporting either Rockefeller's company or the miners' union. In the second essay, José Aguayo discusses how his family emigrated from Mexico and came to work in Colorado's sugar beet industry. Aguayo relates that his family constantly faced discrimination as beet pickers employed by the Great Western Sugar Company in the 1930s. The third essay, by Tanya W. Kulkosky, analyzes the development of the state's sugar industry as epitomized by monopolistic practices. She notes that the collapse of Colorado sugar production devastated Mexicans, who had become the preferred labor force in the field. Fourth, Katie Davis Gardner tells how hundreds of Hispanos were laid off when Colorado Fuel and Iron (CF&I) closed its smelting plant in Pueblo during the Great Depression. In a New Deal–era experiment, unemployed workers were trained to weave Río Grande–style blankets, in the process revitalizing a dying Hispano folk art.

Part three, "Growing Diversity, 1945–Present," contains four essays that encompass the political integration and cultural rebirth of Hispanos in recent times. In rural and urban settings, the Hispano community has mobilized to protect its traditions and rights. In the first essay, Ernesto Vigil interprets the origins of the Crusade for Justice, Denver's leading Chicano rights organization founded in the 1960s. Based on declassified FBI documents, Vigil proves that government agencies tried to suppress the Crusade, its popular leader Corky Gonzales, and the Chicano movement. The next selection, co-authored by George Rivera, Jr., Aileen F. Lucero, and the late Richard Castro, applies the "Internal Colonialism" model to Chicano experience in Colorado. In constructing a case study in decolonization, the authors cite efforts by Denver's Westside Coalition to end the community's dependency and assert control over its own affairs. Thirdly, Ramon Del Castillo studies the historic synthesis of Indian and Spanish folk medicine known as *curanderismo*. He interviews a practicing *curandera* named Diana Velazquez, who is currently a licensed mental health professional in Colorado. The essay strives to explain that modern medicine cannot discount indigenous medical tradition as superstition in Indian or Hispano culture. In the final essay, Devon G. Peña analyzes Hispano land use patterns in southern Colorado. The author argues that traditional Hispano practices like communal land tenure, irrigation, and crop rotation maintain ecological and social balances disrupted by modern agribusiness. He cites the town of San Luis as an example of a Hispano community trying to preserve its communal self-sufficiency and the environment against greedy forces.

In summary, *La Gente: Hispano History and Life in Colorado* embraces the proud heritage of a people who have worked and loved this land for centuries. The scope of these essays broadly extends over Colorado's written history, and this ambitious volume advances knowledge about Hispanos in this part of the country. Of particular value for scholars, the book introduces two significant Hispano autobiographies and a pair of family histories. Likewise, two other essays have been written by participant observers, who give clarity and depth to their subjects. Recognized scholars and authorities shared their original research and expertise. The authors have done justice to their subject.

This anthology shows that the Hispano past and present are woven of the same cloth. It is hoped that readers will find the work both informative and provocative. These essays also convey a timely, serious message that may reduce misunderstandings and conflicts among Hispanos and between them and Americans of other ethnic backgrounds. Like their fellow Americans, Hispanos shed blood, sweat, and tears to enjoy citizenship. In Colorado and elsewhere, Hispanos have proven their loyalty to this country countless times, and they will not be denied the right to practice their own cultural traditions or honor their heritage. Hispanos add an important dimension to the democratic American experiment.

The following provided invaluable assistance in the preparation of this volume: the Hispanic Advisory Council of the Colorado Historical Society, José Aguayo, Anne Bond, Christopher Gerboth, Andrew E. Masich, and Dr. Luis Torres. Early contributors to the planning of this book and the evaluation of submitted essays were Juan Espinosa, Dr. David Fridtjof Halaas, Dale Heckendorn, Rick Manzanares, Deborah Mora-Espinosa, Arnold A. Valdez, and Maria A. Valdez.

Vincent C. de Baca

Introduction

T SEVENTY-NINE years old, Major Rafael Chacón proclaimed his unending affection for God, family, and his former Mexican homeland. He loved both Mexico and the United States. His new American homeland had nationalized him and eighty thousand Mexicans living in the Southwest after the Mexican-American War (1846–48). He had served in the Mexican army, traveled the Santa Fé Trail, fought Indians, and defended the Union in the Civil War. He spent the last fifty-five years of his life in Colorado supporting a family as a farmer, rancher, merchant, sheriff, and politician. Looking back on his exciting life, Chacón wrote in his memoirs: "We have done our duty for our country, for our family, and for our fellow men, and upon passing from this scene we do not leave property of great wealth but we do leave for our children a clean and honorable name."[1] In 1925, Chacón died at ninety-two years of age in Trinidad, Colorado. Unsurprisingly, his beliefs and life reflect the experience of his Hispano people—*la Gente*—in Colorado, who are collectively the subject of this anthology.

In ethnic context, the blood of Apaches, Spaniards, Mexicans, and American forty-niners is mixed together (*mestizaje*) in the veins of their modern Hispano descendants. For their own part, these cultural ancestors played a dynamic role in making the American Southwest a place where many millions now live. It was not by God's will alone that Hispanos currently inhabit the Southwest: for centuries, previous generations also worked this unforgiving land. Over the last four hundred years, Indians and Hispanos lived, fought, and mixed together; yet these two indigenous ethnic groups remain distinct and enduring cultures.[2]

In geographic context, the Spanish empire claimed Colorado as part of its New Mexico province. In the Adams-Onís Treaty of 1819, Spain and the United States set boundaries that placed most of modern Colorado within New Mexico's jurisdiction until the middle of the nineteenth century. When it became a U.S. territory in 1861, Colorado acquired northern New Mexico's land, south of the Arkansas River—much to the chagrin of local Hispano residents. When Colorado achieved statehood in 1876, many Hispano pioneers had already built adobe homes, Catholic churches, and traditional villages in the San Luis Valley and other settled areas in the state. Though separated politically, southern Colorado has remained a vital extension of New Mexico's cultural sphere. Therefore, the history of Hispanos in Colorado cannot be understood without first knowing New Mexico history.

During the Spanish Colonial Era (1598–1821), Spaniards first arrived in Colorado by way of New Mexico. In 1594, the Humaña-Bonilla expedition entered Colorado, and they named the Purgatory River. In 1596, Juan de Zaldívar illegally explored New Mexico and the San Luis Valley; he was later arrested for his unofficial efforts. From 1598 to 1608, New Mexico's first Spanish governor, Juan de Oñate, sent many authorized expeditions across the Southwest; some groups went north to Colorado and beyond. Lastly, in 1776, Friar Dominguez and Captain Escalante mapped the Spanish Trail to California along the Colorado River's west bank, where they reported encountering Hispano fur trappers and merchants trading with the Southern Utes in Colorado.[3]

The colonial militia led punitive expeditions against the Apaches, Utes, Navajos, and Comanches in Colorado. Ultimately, the Spaniards failed to adequately populate or exercise full sovereignty over their northern borderlands in Colorado because financial burdens, Indian resistance, and foreign intrusion constantly impeded them. But the Indians and Spanish colonists were both hurt by the endemic violent attacks and retaliations. Colorado was the battleground where Hispanos and Indians often fought. Juan Archuleta led Spanish militia in pursuit of Pueblo Indians who fled to modern Kiowa County.[4] During the 1690 reconquest of New Mexico, Governor Diego de Vargas repeatedly attacked Apaches and Pueblo efugees living in the San Luis Valley. Likewise, after mounted Comanches first raided New Mexico in 1704, Captain Juan de Ulibarrí, with forty Hispano volunteers and a hundred Pueblo allies, pursued them into Colorado. On the Arkansas River (east of the modern city of Pueblo), Ulibarrí discovered a series of Apache and Pueblo villages running downstream. The Indians wanted Spanish help against the Comanches, so Ulibarrí claimed the region for Spain and named it El Cuartelejo.[5]

Fifteen years later, the Spanish returned. In 1719, Governor Antonio Valverde led one hundred soldiers and six hundred Indians in chasing the Comanches to the Platte River. Returning through El Cuartelejo, Indians told Valverde that French explorers had been in the area. In 1720, he ordered Pedro de Villasur, forty-two soldiers, and sixty Indians to investigate possible French intrusion. In June, on the Platte River in Nebraska,

Pawnees armed with French weapons attacked and killed all but thirteen Spaniards.[4] As a result, the Plains Indians traded with the French for the next three decades without Spanish interference.

The harried New Mexicans continued fighting Indians, but the Utes and Jacarillas signed a peace treaty in the 1740s. The three then joined forces against the Comanches, their common threat. Finally, in 1779, Governor Juan de Anza's army cornered a large party of Comanches in the foothills between modern Walsenburg and Pueblo. Through some trickery, Chief Green Horn (Cuerno Verde) and sixteen Comanche leaders were killed by the Hispano force, while their Pueblo allies allegedly killed another one hundred four Comanche captives. After eight more years of warfare, the Comanches finally sued for peace, and the Hispano colonists enjoyed a generation of relative tranquility.

The region remained under Indian control throughout the Spanish and Mexican eras. In the 1780s, the Spanish built a town for the Comanches near the junction of the Arkansas and San Carlos rivers. But, the town was soon abandoned. When American trappers and traders arrived in the region in the next century, secure forts were built where Indians, Hispanos, and Americans traded goods and services. In 1833, the American commercial partnership of Ceran St. Vrain, Charles Bent, and William Bent constructed a large adobe trading post on the Arkansas River known as Bent's Fort, just beyond Mexican territory. They hired more than a hundred Taos laborers who worked and lived at the fort. Likewise, Louis Vasquez built a temporary trading post near modern Denver.

During the Mexican Republic Era (1821–48), the government issued suspicious land grants (*mercedes*) covering parts of southern Colorado, including the Sangre de Cristo, Conejos, Vigil St. Vrain, Nolan, Tierra Amarilla, and Baca grants.[7] In 1843, New Mexico's last Mexican governor, Manuel Armijo, granted the above land to foreigners of questionable loyalty like Americans Ceran St. Vrain and Stephen Lee and Canadians Gervais Nolan, Charles Beaubien, and his son Narciso. These large grants covered eight million acres in southern Colorado. Furthermore, the 2,680-square-mile Beaubien-Miranda grant in New Mexico included about 265,000 acres in Colorado.[8]

Under Spanish and Mexican law, such land grants stipulated that grantees recruit loyal Hispanos to settle on the sites. The government tried to protect its northern border with trustworthy citizens, but meanwhile New Mexico's burgeoning population also needed farmland to sustain itself. For instance, the last Mexican census of 1842 enumerated 46,988 Hispanos in New Mexico, while the first U.S. census of the territory in

1850 counted 58,415 Hispanos in the newly acquired territory—a 20 percent population increase in only eight years.[9] Ironically, the large land grants issued to foreigners provided New Mexico a safety valve to vent its surplus Hispano population, thereby creating Colorado's first enduring non-Indian communities.

In 1833, the Conejos grant in the San Luis Valley was the region's first communal land grant; but Utes and Navajos soon drove the New Mexicans back to Abiquiú. In 1843, Governor Armijo reissued the land as a private grant of one million acres to Charles Beaubien, who renamed it the Sangre de Cristo grant. Finally, in 1851, Beaubien assigned individual plots and common lands to fifty families from Mora and Chama counties in New Mexico. The settlers called their community San Luis; thus, Colorado's first permanent town was formally born. By the end of the decade, the valley contained a dozen villages and forty irrigation ditches (*acequias*) that watered the fields of two thousand settlers from New Mexico.[10]

About eighty miles northeast of San Luis, in the 1840s, the former trading post called El Pueblo had become a small Hispanic village. Tragically, in 1854, the Utes attacked Marcelino Baca's ranch and the fort at El Pueblo, killing seventeen Hispanos and capturing two boys who were later killed as well.[11] The survivors fled to Fort Union, New Mexico, for help. The U.S. Army sent three hundred regulars and five hundred New Mexican volunteers with orders to kill or capture those responsible for the deaths.

Rafael Chacón, quoted earlier, experienced his first taste of war during this campaign as a sergeant in St. Vrain's volunteer battalion. By March 1855, the volunteers had already won a minor battle against Apaches at Saguache, Colorado. The punitive expedition showed little mercy to any Indians encountered. In unflinching words, Chacón wrote that

> we again caught up with the Indians at what is now Long's Canyon in Las Animas County and we killed some of them. Here a soldier belonging to my company scalped an Indian who had a very luxuriant growth of hair. When we had made our camp he took the scalp to Colonel St. Vrain, and this officer became indignant and reprimanded him severely because he thought he had killed a woman. Then the soldier went back to where the dead Indian lay and castrated him and brought the parts to the colonel, tied to a stick, and the colonel was satisfied although surprised at such an unusual method of proving the dead Indian was a man and not a woman.
>
> We also took several women and children prisoners there and then

we followed the trail up to the place [where] the old house of Dick Wootton was afterward located. At Ponil, after having killed several Indians, we captured fifty squaws and their little ones. From that point the main force under Colonel St. Vrain went to Fort Union with the captives.[12]

Life on the Colorado frontier taught people very cruel lessons, and the uninitiated learned fast or paid the price. Such atrocities were common occurrences.

Ironically, St. Vrain led the New Mexico volunteers across the extent of his own Colorado land grant. He and Cornelio Vigil, who was killed in the Taos Revolt of 1847, acquired the large tract from Armijo. In 1843, Vigil and St. Vrain, a naturalized Mexican citizen born in Missouri, received the largest grant in Colorado (four million acres), including the sites of modern Trinidad, Walsenburg, and La Junta. In later years, the United States reduced the grant to 97,000 acres. For his part, St. Vrain gave away most of the land and made no effort to recruit settlers.

In 1862, wealthy New Mexican Felipe Baca and twelve compatriot families moved onto the grant and established the town of Trinidad as a farming and commercial venture.[13] In the waning years of the Santa Fe Trail, Baca and other Hispanic merchants profited from their location between New Mexico, the eastern railheads, and the Denver goldfields. These mercantile capitalists were able to transport crops, livestock, and lumber within the regional market. As a result of Hispano initiative, the U.S. Territorial Census of 1870 determined that "ninety percent of the 6,400 residents" in Las Animas and Huerfano counties had direct or indirect ties to New Mexico.[14] At the time, Anglo Americans casually referred to Trinidad as the largest "Mexican" town in Colorado. In 1877, the Anglos' misplaced insecurity was relieved when American railroads connected Trinidad to the rest of the nation.[15] Colorado historians have asserted that the railroads, lumber, and coal inevitably shifted demographics, political power, and economic wealth in favor of the Americans; but that story is only half true.

The other side of the story describes the dynamism of Hispanos and Mexican immigrants who carved a niche for themselves and their culture. *La Gente* did not disappear after Colorado became a state in 1876. They came to Colorado with strong traditions of religious faith, mutual assistance, civic activism, and local participatory democracy.[16] Hispano farming villages still practice a communal work ethic that extends from regulating grazing rights to cleaning irrigation ditches. Also, the ancient religious society known as the Penitentes and the mutual aid society known as the Sociedad Protección Mutua de Trabajores Unidos still enhance cultural survival and solidarity when others refuse to help. This Hispano spirit of cooperation and communal labor is an ancient tradition in the Southwest.

In state political history, Hispanos retained significant influence. For example, Casimiro Barela, native of Mora, New Mexico, served in the Colorado State Senate for thirty-six years, from 1876 until 1912.[17] And, in Las Animas County, Jesus Maria Garcia was secretary of the Democratic Party and power broker for thirty years. Republican Rafael Chacón was elected to a few county offices in his life. Historically, they acted on local and statewide interests of their community. But they also inspired recent politicians, like Polly Baca-Barragan, Federico Peña, and the late Richard Castro, who have given Colorado Hispanos a national presence.

When the American Era began in 1848, the New Mexico–Colorado region was the cultural homeland for Hispanos who migrated throughout the country. Hispano history and life in Colorado was not a simple event but a complex, dynamic process of evolution spanning centuries. Almost unconsciously, Hispano culture resisted complete assimilation into American society; however, adaptations that were mutually beneficial have freely occurred. Today's Hispano culture has developed from the unique interaction of Spanish, Indian, Mexican, and American frontiers.

In conclusion, Hispano traditions have preserved a way of life. Historian Olibama Lopez Tushar reminds younger Hispanos about the time-tested values that helped their ancestors survive in this country. Rhetorically, she concludes, "Perhaps, [morality] is a bit out of style, but then again, when are basic courtesy, good manners and honesty really out of style?"[18] In their struggle for self-determination, Chicano activists should remember these powerful traditions which served their antepasados so well. Significantly, four centuries of Hispano history in this region proved that human endurance, adaptability, and spirit will triumph over great odds. In Colorado, Hispanos are proud of their history and their vital way of life.

In the final analysis, only the land endures. On the dear lands, Hispano family ranches and farms inspired development of the American West and frontier icons. On the lonely lands, the *vaquero* tended herds of cattle. On the lush lands, the *pastor* grew crops in irrigated valleys. On the private lands, the *patrón* and *peón* bequeathed a dreamland that only tourists and rich city folk now imagine. On the communal lands, indigenous peoples revered "Mother Earth" and fought the greedy who pretended to own her. On the battle lands, too many people's blood fertilized a desperate, protracted revenge. On scholarly grounds, Hispano culture suffered a land tenure system that oppressed social relations. On dusty cactus lands, proud, weather-beaten survivors dug hands into dead *llanos* for dear life. On her grandfather's land, prima Fabiola Cabeza de Baca waxed prophetic in 1950 when she warned that

> . . . Papá had a full life.
>
> He is gone, but the land which he loved is there. It has come back. The grass is growing again and those living on his land are wiser. They are following practices of soil and water conservation which were not available to Papá. But each generation must profit by the trials and errors of those before them; otherwise everything would perish.[19]

The Hispano land nurtures *la Gente*, a lesson we ignore at our peril. The following essays prove that Hispanos make no excuses for being here; they earned the right to live in their homeland.

Notes

1
Jacqueline Dorgan Meketa, ed., *Legacy of Honor: The Life of Rafael Chacón, a Nineteenth-Century New Mexican* (Albuquerque: University of New Mexico Press, 1986), 333.

2
John R. Chavez, *The Lost Land: The Chicano Image of the Southwest* (Albuquerque: University of New Mexico Press, 1984), 21-3; Edward H. Spicer, *Cycles of Conquest: The Impact of Spain, Mexico, and the United States on the Indians of the Southwest, 1533–1960* (Tucson: University of Arizona Press, 1986), 283-4; Jack D. Forbes, *Apache, Navaho and Spaniard* (Norman: University of Oklahoma Press, 1982), 279.

3
Carl Abbott, Stephen J. Leonard, and David McComb, *Colorado: A History of the Centennial State* (Niwot: University Press of Colorado, 1982), 35.

4
Olibama Lopez Tushar, *The People of El Valle: A History of the Spanish Colonials in the San Luis Valley* (Pueblo, Colorado: El Escritorio, 1992), 14.

5
Abbott et al., *Colorado*, 27-8.

6
John L. Kessell, *Remote Beyond Compare: Letters of don Diego de Vargas to His Family from New Spain and New Mexico, 1675–1706* (Albuquerque: University of New Mexico Press, 1989), 190; Abbott et al., *Colorado*, 28.

7
Lopez Tushar, *The People of El Valle*, 27ff.

8
John R. Van Ness and Christine M. Van Ness, eds., *Spanish and Mexican Land Grants in New Mexico and Colorado* (Manhattan, Kans.: Sunflower University Press, 1980), 26.

9
Ramón A. Gutiérrez, *When Jesus Came, the Corn Mothers Went Away: Marriage, Sexuality, and Power in New Mexico, 1500–1846* (Stanford: Stanford University Press, 1991), 167.

10
Lopez Tushar, *The People of El Valle*, 36.

11
Ibid., 23; Abbott et al., *Colorado*, 39; Meketa, *Legacy of Honor*, 97.

12
Meketa, *Legacy of Honor*, 103.

13
Ibid., 306, 321.

14
Abbott et al., *Colorado*, 43.

15
Ibid., 46.

16
Sarah Deutsch, *No Separate Refuge: Culture, Class, and Gender on an*

Anglo-Hispanic Frontier in the American Southwest, 1880–1940 (New York: Oxford University Press, 1987), 26.

17
Abbott et al., *Colorado*, 48.

18
Lopez Tushar, *The People of El Valle*, 199.

19
Fabiola Cabeza de Baca, *We Fed Them Cactus* (Albuquerque: University of New Mexico Press, 1994), 178.

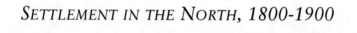

Settlement in the North, 1800-1900

Teresita Sandoval: Woman in Between

Deborah Mora-Espinosa

ABOUT THE AUTHOR

Deborah Mora-Espinosa is the director of El Pueblo Museum (a property of the Colorado Historical Society), a position she has held for ten years. She received her bachelor's degree in history and Chicano studies from the University of Southern Colorado. Under her administration, El Pueblo Museum was relocated to Pueblo's central historic district. She has expanded the museum's public history programs and exhibitions and continues to oversee the fund campaign for museum expansion.

HAD IT NOT been for the religious traditions that marked the milestones of their lives, any knowledge we might have of early frontier Spanish and Mexican women would be lost to time. Still, what we must settle for are mere glimpses, as if we are peering at ghosts, visions we can hold only for a second before the images fade: figures wrapped in rebozos, bent over their work in the garden, at the *hornos*, at the river.

Their names are recorded in church documents, as testimony to the work of Franciscans who officiated at the rites of baptism and marriage. Where they lived, who they married, their *compadres*, the children they baptized and buried—all are meticulously documented. These records are invaluable to researchers. They serve as an introduction to real people; they prove existence and trace the migration of families. They also bring to light the relationships of men and women who lived in a far more complex society than once imagined.

But these documents cannot reveal to us the personalities of the people who lived out these lives. What would these Spanish women, mixed-blood *mestizas*, and *genizaras* (Indian captives accepted into Spanish households) share with us if they could? What would they have told us of their marriages and love, or of the foreigners who traded in their villages? How did they view the Indian women that they routinely had contact with in the villages, or even those within their own families? What would they recount of American trade and the goods that stirred their imaginations about another life far away? What did their grandmothers tell them of coming north with Oñate, of births and deaths along the way? What was the female perspective of Pope's rebellion and the reconquest?

Indian raids, slavery, illness, fear, and death were not the experiences of men alone, but of entire families who were just as vulnerable to the treacheries of the frontier. Women—sisters, wives, daughters, mothers, aunts, and grandmothers—were the heart of extended families. Without them, the western frontier would have been devoid of the interactions of families, the routine of households, the children, the comfort, the traditions, and the celebrations of life.

The Southwest is a territory of conquests, of land taken and reclaimed. Yet, the experiences of the woman in these repeated conflicts are only beginning to be considered. Modern historians are compiling a "new women's history." But what is also "new" is the role historians are taking on: the authority, the scholarship, and the methodology to answer the questions never before asked.

The study of women becomes a study of family and relationships. As Elizabeth Jameson and Susan Armitage state,

> All people, then, are historical actors, and half of the actors are women. Among the most basic social interactions are those between men and women, parents and children.
> They create and re-create families, homes, and communities . . . . The mundane process of personal negotiation is fundamental to how people change their social roles and possibilities.[1]

The new research is also taking into account frontier marriage and mixed-race families of the nineteenth century. Some element of respectability is, at last, being given to Mexican and Indian wives of mountain men and early American settlers, many of whom, as it turns out, had long-lasting relationships. Better yet, contextual understanding is being given to the women of the West who stepped outside the norm.

This solid research is a relief from often-repeated accounts of *señoritas* smoking and dancing at fandangos. Descriptions of their clothing and grooming, though fascinating, are often the only things written about by the men, who were obviously captivated by these details. The relaxed social interactions the women enjoyed only served to shock Americans who based their judgments on Victorian standards. Add Hollywood's smoldering Jane Russell stereotype and any sense of the reality of the Spanish/Mexican frontier woman blows away like a tumbleweed.

To base interpretations of the Spanish/Mexican woman on these early descriptions alone is inadequate. Collectively, church and social records provide a composite of women, but only a few individuals rise above obscurity. Only a handful are described physically, and the comings and goings of even fewer are documented. Not even the gifted prophet John Brown could foresee that some day we would want to know more about his wife, Luisa Sandoval.

Brown resided at Fort Pueblo and Greenhorn and eventually went on to become a prominent lawyer in California. Yet he did not describe or write extensively of his wife in his book, *The Mediumistic Experiences of John Brown, the Medium of the Rockies*. Such entries as "Mrs. Brown entered with a comb and brush . . ." and "Mrs. Brown . . . asked me what was the matter" are typical.[2]

Yet, if we take more than a glimpse of this woman we find that she was once the wife of the famous African American mountain man James P. Beckwourth, and the mother to their daughter, Matilda. She herself was born in Taos and had lived within the walls of El Pueblo trading post. In California, she gave birth to ten more children and lived an affluent life unlike that of nearly anyone in her native New Mexico. Unfortunately, we have nothing in her own words.

This is true of all the women of El Pueblo. They were the first New Mexican women to arrive and live at the trading post, which was located where Fountain Creek flowed into the Arkansas River, the northern Spanish border. Janet Lecompte, author of *Pueblo, Hardscrabble, Greenhorn*, is the writer who first gave substance to the Indian and Mexican women at El Pueblo, and lightly examined their relationships.[3]

The women of El Pueblo were not the first to venture from their villages. Women, both Mexican and Indian, had been present at Bent's Fort for nearly ten years, and it is documented by Marian Meyer that Spanish and French women traveled the trail before the first women of U.S. citizenry—some of them more than once, such as Carmel Benevides, wife of Antoine Robidou.[4]

With so little attention given to women, when one stands out in description and memory we find ourselves asking, "Why is this so?" Why is it that one woman of El Pueblo, María Teresa "Teresita" Sandoval, made such a lasting impression? More interestingly, why were the feelings of one man, Alexander Barclay, so strong that he sketched her the first time he saw her? Who was this Teresita? What was her world like?

Taos had been established for nearly two hundred years when Teresita was born in 1811 to Gervasio Sandoval and Ramona Barela. Yet, compared to the centuries-old Pueblo villages, Taos was relatively new. Nevertheless, life within the colonies had not changed much since the first days of settlement.

Families raised sheep and spun, dyed, and wove the wool into a variety of products in abundance, selling them along with other items at *rescates*, or trade fairs, where Indian captives were also sold. Skilled *ciboleros* hunted on staked plains—hunting territories usually marked off by buffalo skulls. They brought back buffalo meat for the families in simple wooden *carretas*, the same kind used for hauling grain and firewood. Mothers' duties ranged from healing with herbs to replastering adobe walls. Vaqueros bred and broke horses, and families depended on the land, one another, and patrons for subsistence. From the church they received spiritual security.

A deceptively simple lifestyle emerges, yet there was also a complex interweaving of age-old Spanish and native traditions and dialects, peni-

Teresita Sandoval as sketched by Alexander Barclay in 1853. From Hammond, The Adventures of Alexander Barclay, *vi facing.*

tential practices and bicultural Catholicism, class designations, tribal lifestyles, Indian raids, and a system of captivity and slavery. Even before New Mexico was colonized, northern Spanish slavers raided along the Río Grande for Indian captives to supply the silver mines.[5]

After colonization, labor was exploited through the *encomienda* and *repartimiento* privileges granted to landowners, similar to the English system of feudalism.[6] Captives taken in native warfare gave strength to tribal populations, provided labor, and served as important pawns in trade.[7] The taking of horses, personal property, and captives must have seemed far more civilized to the people of the Plains than the mass killings of European warfare.

By the time Teresita Sandoval was born, the European and American traders living within colonial society were making their impact on commerce and government. Sandoval lived at a time when change was on the horizon: it was inevitable, and many welcomed it. While on the surface nothing had differed for centuries, the church, the borders, and the very fiber of life were on the verge of upheaval.

When the Mexican-American War ended in 1848 and the United States acquired the land south of the Arkansas River to the Río Grande, colonial descendants became separated from their countrymen. New laws and customs dictated a major change in lifeways for the New Mexicans, resulting in displacement and the loss of political power. Further dissection by territorial lines separated native populations from familiar and extended cultural regions. This was Sandoval's world. Life was not simple, nor was it always harmonious.

Unlike any time before the arrival of Sandoval's ancestors, new possibilities and opportunities existed. Like Sacagawea and countless other Indian women, Spanish/Mexican women too would play a major role in a cultural and economic transition. This transition would bring Sandoval and her children to the Arkansas River, where a site was chosen for the building of a trading post.

Trade had always been the connection that bound tribes and families and maintained a fragile peace. Wary of foreign intrusion, Spain had prohibited trade and contact to the north of the New Mexican colonies. But enforcement was weak, and the lure of new products and profits was much stronger. During the Mexican period (1821–48), foreign traders also circumvented the law by becoming naturalized citizens of Mexico. Citizenship gave them access to land grants, either by petition or by marriage.

Indian women long had contact with the trapper-traders. In an examination of frontier relationships, Jack Faragher writes,

> Indian women with white husbands often played influential roles within their societies, fortified by their powerful connections to a steady source of trade goods. Family members often rose in rank within the tribe . . . . Called "women in between," these wives often were the ones to introduce new products, techniques, and ideas into their tribes.[8]

The fur trade relied on the labor of Indian wives: they served as guides; cleaned and dressed pelts; pitched tents; made and mended clothing; gathered wild food and provided other foodstuff; fished and snared small game; manufactured maple sugar, pemmican, and various buffalo products; and made snowshoes and birch-bark boats. They were important economic partners, also involved as interpreters and negotiators.[9] The women of El Pueblo would play a similar role.

Teresita wed later than most girls in the New Mexican villages. In 1828, at the age of seventeen, she married Manuel Suaso. Three daughters and a son were born: the oldest was Juana María, followed by María de la Cruz, then Thomas. After the birth of the youngest, Rufina, the Suaso-Sandovals received a land grant at Mora.

It was at Mora that Sandoval's life departed from tradition. There she met a Kentuckian, Mathew Kinkead, a naturalized citizen and land grantee. An affair produced a child, Juan Andres, and thus Sandoval's marriage of seven years ended scandalously. A year later, she and Mathew had another child, a daughter they named Rafaela.

The details of the Suaso-Sandoval courtship and separation are unknown, as are any solid facts about Suaso's character. It is likely that Sandoval's affair brought Suaso great shame, in accordance with the beliefs and attitudes of the Spanish. The chastity of wives and daughters was to be protected. Girls were prepared for marriage as young as thirteen or fourteen to avoid the risk of pre-marital pregnancy. The honor of the family—primarily the men—was at stake.

However, the prescribed ideal for women did not necessarily reflect the reality. Lecompte has written that "sexual freedom and concubinage was taken for granted in New Mexico, where relatively few couples married. No shame or blame was attached to women bearing children out of wedlock, nor did the children carry a stigma for their illegitimacy."[10] For the Spanish, the rules of chastity did not apply to women in Indian villages. In his essay, "When Strangers Met: Sex and Gender on Three Frontiers,"

Albert L. Hurtado describes the tremendous abuses experienced by Indian women.[11] What emerges from analyses such as his is the powerlessness of women's sexuality within European attitudes.

Courtship, marriage, and sexual behavior varied from tribe to tribe, but generally conflicted with the idealistic behavior the Catholic church prescribed for women. Among Plains peoples, consent and cohabitation by the partners and the girl's family were usually the only requirements for marriage. Divorce was granted by simple removal of the man's belongings from the woman's tipi. The conflicting attitudes of American Indians, Spaniards, Mexicans, and Euro-American frontiersmen resulted in a complex arrangement of values and expectations.

As stated in the preface to Hurtado's essay, "We need to consider differences in the Europeans' enterprises, economies, and social expectations on various frontiers, as well as variations in Indian cultures, as we untangle what 'intimacy' meant in different circumstances."[12] All variables taken into account, one fact emerges: the women carried the burden of blame for perceived improprieties.

Lecompte's quotes of white frontiersmen who wrote of Spanish/Mexican women reflect the double-standard: "The standard of the female chastity is deplorably low"; "The women deem chastity no virtue"; ". . . [she was] mild and affable, if deficient in common chastity."[13] The male dominance, expectations, and misconceptions of both the Spanish and Americans greatly affected the life of the indigenous woman.

Adding to the complexity is the *mestiza*—the Spanish-Indian woman, a mixture of indigenous and European cultures and blood. She is a presence in both worlds, yet is unaccounted for in either. As defined in the Spanish-Catholic realm or the Protestant-Victorian vocabulary, her "Indian-ness" has been historically excluded.

In other words, part Indian, part Spanish, the mestizo carries the blood of both the conquered and the conquistador. The inner turmoil of self-definition is complex and confusing, often resulting in both love and hate for oneself. The mestiza must contend with the additional dilemma of sexual identity. Historically, in light of the conflicting duality of Indian and European sexual attitudes, the motives and actions of frontier women are often judged unfairly.

For Sandoval, the judgment—both then and now—has been harsh. What we do know, however, is that she and Kinkead seized their opportunity for love and partnership in an era when rules were being challenged by others who were also caught up in the social upheavals of the time.

For many, a game of sorts was taking place: that of double citizenship, which allowed the players to move freely between laws, tariffs, borders, and responsibilities. When it came to trade, women, and land, the benefits to be reaped by the men were plenty. Winning was easy and the penalties were few. Nor did the freedom to play belong to the *Americanos* alone. Manuel Alvarez, American Consul to Northern Mexico, for example, was a citizen of both Mexico and the United States. New Mexican governor Manuel Armijo was a player who bet away his country. The women of New Mexico, however, were both pawns *and* players, whether they knew it or not.

The erosion of Mexico's northern lands had begun, and anti-American feelings were rising among the established families of New Mexico. Texas already was the independent Lone Star Republic, and threats of an invasion by a Texas army increased tensions between New Mexicans and the Americans residing in the remaining northern Mexico territories. The Kinkead-Sandoval family's economically-motivated decision to leave Mora, and to resettle at a point on the Arkansas River on the American side, was timely.

The family's first occupation was an attempt to raise buffalo. Sandoval even participated in the capture of calves, but the plan was soon abandoned for the opportunity to form a trading partnership with other white naturalized Mexican citizens who wanted to trade on both sides of the border. Thus, the construction of El Pueblo trading post began in 1842.

By 1844, Sandoval was a grandmother. Isabel, the first child of Juana María and George Simpson, was born that year. Isabel's parents had married the year before at El Pueblo in an informal ceremony conducted with the residents as witnesses. Four months later Sandoval's family went to Taos to baptize the baby, sanctify the Simpson marriage, and hold the marriage ceremony of Sandoval's second daughter, María de la Cruz, and Joseph Doyle.

If Mexican citizens felt any tension or animosity toward the women at El Pueblo, it is not evident. Trade and socializing with the New Mexican villages was frequent. The women's religious devotion brought them back to Taos, where Father Antonio Martinez continued the Catholic traditions despite his own political uneasiness.

Father Martinez seemed to have two souls in one body. The first was that of a strong spokesman for the people who was unafraid of confrontation. He was a political man influenced by Father Miguel Hidalgo's philosophies, which had led to Mexico's independence from Spain in 1821. The second was that of a humble Franciscan who never denied services to the faithful. His love for the land and the New Mexican people helped shape both sides of his personality.

If Sandoval and the families of El Pueblo were ever treated coldly, it is not apparent. It is more likely that the Padre Martinez they encountered was the one they knew best—simply the man who performed baptismal and marriage ceremonies. As a "woman in between," Sandoval was not castigated; rather, she and her family, as well as the other families at El Pueblo, appear to have been full participants in the church and the New Mexican communities.

By 1843, Teresita Sandoval Kinkead was the matriarch of a grow-ing and influential family. She and her children had moved beyond the realm of her own upbringing and into the realm of the rapidly changing U.S./Mexican borderlands. Sandoval's evolution continued when she met a British man by the name of Alexander Barclay, who would prove to be the love of her life.

Barclay came from a working-class London background. He detailed his journey into the American West in letters to his family, the novelty of which they shared with others. He once wrote to his family that he might someday return to his native England if he could "relinquish this semi-savage life and endeavor to return to a civilized state if the restrictions of society were not too irksome after the unlimited independence I have so long indulged in."[14] In these letters and a sketchy diary he kept for years, Barclay also gave us more insight into Teresita Sandoval's personality.

Only the extreme circumstances of their lives could have brought two more diverse personalities and backgrounds together. Barclay was an edu-cated, single man, who believed he would marry a woman from his country. Sandoval was the "wife" of another man and mother of several children.[15] Together, they would risk another move and another enterprise.

Precisely when the two met is unknown. By the time the Sandoval-Kinkead family had become settled at Pueblo, Barclay had been employed by the Bent brothers as a bookkeeper. He had known for some time that he wanted a change in his life and had taken on the work of an indepen-dent trader, making two trips to St. Louis for goods between 1843 and 1844.

It was probably on one of his trading trips to El Pueblo that he first saw her. Her image never left his memory, and he captured it in a water-color sketch ten years after that first meeting—the only permanent portrait of her. In it she stands erect, holding a wooden bucket on her head. She is clad in the customary off-the-shoulder *camisa* and mid-calf skirt, her long, fringed *rebozo* hanging from her neck. Her eyes are dark and large, her black hair braided and looped around her ears. Her beauty and strength transcend time and Barclay's faded memories.

Many years would pass before he would even speak of her to his family. So strong would be the judgment of his relationship with Teresita that he kept his love a secret from his family. It was only after the death of his sister Mary in 1851 that he began to reveal his true feelings to his brother, George. Author George Hammond described Mary Barclay as "staid, decorous, and protected, . . . whose love and respect" Barclay cherished.[16]

These are not the adjectives one would use to describe Sandoval! How could he share his feelings for her with his family when he knew the extent of their differences? Barclay moved in a culture far removed from his own upbringing. After many years as a frontiersman, he had made Sandoval's culture and life his own. In December of 1844, Sandoval left Kinkead and moved with Barclay to Hardscrabble, located in a higher valley west of El Pueblo, on the Mexican side of the river.

Removed again from "social restrictions," Barclay found himself not only the leader in this struggling settlement, but also the head of an extended family. He describes the residents in one of his letters:

> Indeed, the men who have located here are all those whom the wreck of the mountain trade and hunting parties have left on the surface, unfitted to return to former haunts or avocations, with minds alienated by new convictions from home and early friends, and habits transformed by constant excitement and daring adventure from the dull plodding of the sober citizen to the reckless activity and thrilling interest of a border life, open to the aggression of the savage and the pursuit of free will, free trade and free thinking.[17]

The move away from El Pueblo and Sandoval's former relationship lessened the judgments. Constant work, building, farming, hunting, and trade soon occupied their lives in Hardscrabble.

Nevertheless, they were unlawful squatters on land belonging to the Mexican government, and their activities included the smuggling of liquor manufactured at Taos and traded to the Indians. They were, by some interpretations, outlaws on the fringes of society, far enough removed from laws that were loosely enforced to begin with.

Barclay had farmed in Canada and worked on the frontiers of the United States and Mexico, always in pursuit of his goal of becoming a wealthy landowner. He saw opportunity after the end of the Mexican-American War. Barclay was a leading trader in the region and had become familiar with territorial agents. He learned that the U.S. government was hoping to build a fort in northern New Mexico. His plan was to build it and sell it to the military.

In 1848, the family took on the construction of Fort Barclay at the junction of the Mora and Sapello rivers:

> The structure covered an acre of ground, with walls sixteen feet high, thirty-three inches thick. At opposite corners were two great portholed bastions, each containing a six-pound howitzer and other armaments. Inside the walls were forty rooms and offices, a well, bake-ovens and stables. Outside were two hundred acres of cultivated land irrigated by two main ditches, and an acre-and-a-half vegetable garden entirely fenced.[18]

The fort was an immense undertaking, requiring substantial resources in the financing and maintenance of buildings, land, and workers.

This was now Sandoval's domain, a far cry from the primitive dwellings she had occupied before. She had returned to the Mora area with much more than she had left with, but hope and enthusiasm would soon die and her relationship with Alexander would deteriorate when it became obvious that the fort was a failure.

Winters were harsh and the cold winds relentless. Though the fort itself was a durable and imposing sight on the open plains, the family, the crops, and the animals could not thrive in the harsh environment. The final blow came when the military declined to buy Barclay's fort, opting to build Fort Union only seven miles away on part of Barclay's land.

This proved an incredible setback to the Barclays' morale. They faced growing tensions within the family, and by 1851 Joseph Doyle, Teresita's son-in-law, was ready to return to the Arkansas due to "financial stringencies" and "family troubles."[19] It was a desperate time, when the very walls of the Barclays' home must have been a constant reminder of failure.

In an ironic twist, Barclay found that only by sharing the feelings he had kept from his family could he free himself of his burden. "Barclay laid bare his soul to his brother and confessed his relationship with Teresita, he complained how badly their affairs had worked out in spite of the support he had provided for her and her family."[20] In today's terminology, the family had become "dysfunctional," and after ten years together the two parted.

Barclay recorded the failing relationship in his diary. Sandoval's personality as a strong-willed woman—whom he refers to as "T.S."—comes through in bits and pieces. The husband of a niece further reveals this personality in his own correspondence: When Barclay ordered men to husk corn instead of hauling sand to the women making adobe, the women appealed to Teresita to intervene; because of his inequitable decision, the man states, "I had to receive a little of Mrs. Barclay's temper."[21] Sandoval also took her son-in-law George Simpson to court (the *alcalde* in New Mexico) for beating his wife and children.

At a time when assertiveness was unacceptable behavior for white women, Sandoval was a woman to reckon with. She was commanding when the situation called for it, but, according to Barclay, it was her jealous tirades that he could no longer tolerate.

With the dissolution of the family imminent, Barclay described the inevitable separation to his brother, George. In a rambling yet eloquent style, and with a pervasive sadness, he details his perspective of the situation. He laments at length that his generosity and consideration of her well-being went unappreciated, and that Sandoval was at the core of his decision to move to New Mexico:

> Yet, after rearing half her family from infancy without increasing her maternal toils, ameliorated her condition of life and given her what would appear competence compared to her former position, the demon of unfounded jelousy has taken possession of her mind and blasts increasing every endeavor of my life by unjust rage and rancorous vituperation. It is a mania no reason can appease, no proofs satisfy. Force might subdue her, but out upon the thought. A thousand times better separation unde every sacrifice, for who whould suffer for my faults but me (and it must eventually came to that) than ever raise my hand to strike the woman with whom I have shared so many of lifes cares and pleasures. . . .
>
> I came to New Mexico chiefly influenced with the design of procuring her a permanent home in case of casualties of my wandering life might deprive her of that support . . . . Howsoever the intent, man's hopes are built on sand and his transgressions never fail of retribution, for even his best endeavors . . . seldom are awarded aught but disappointment.[22]

The self-pity and loneliness that run through Barclay's words do not take into account Sandoval's contributions to the relationship. His alliance with her family gave him the partnerships he needed for the Fort Barclay endeavor. Barclay derived resources and labor from her sons-in-law, and he admits that it was Sandoval's "industry and economy" that he so admired that first day he saw her walking from the river.

She carried his dream with her as well, but, because this was long before a woman's work was considered a contribution, her efforts into the enterprise were left understated. In the end, Sandoval was blamed for the failure and was simply asked to leave. Regardless of his failure to sell the fort, Barclay was not a destitute man. The legal partnerships that resulted from the enterprise were divided among the men of the family. After Sandoval's departure, she was forced to rely on Doyle's support for the rest of her life, which was another forty-one years.

We can only guess at Sandoval's feelings regarding the failures. Were her tirades a subconscious, or even conscious, result of the fort's failure? Were her past indiscretions haunting her? Did she blame Barclay for everything? We can only wonder what her emotions and thoughts were as she rode away from the fort, never to see Barclay again.

We do have a clearer indication of Barclay's thinking:

> Doyle is married to my good wife's daughter, and as the breach between us had been extending between us, I proposed that she should accompany them having long evinced disatisfaction under my deportment and protection. Having all her family with her, son and daughters and grand children, no opportunity could possibly present itself for dissolution. Piqued, I believe, that I treated the affair so dispassionatly, she determined to follow the suggestion and went off with them . . . .To say that I am happy under the changes (however advisable or prudent) were to belie my feelings and a spirit of lonliness and desolation pervaids my home.[23]

In his writings, Barclay hints that it was more than jealousy that drove the wedge between them. He demonstrates an ongoing respect for "T.S." and continues to long for her. Did she feel the same way? From beginning to end, she always had her family. With every move she made, her family went with her, and in the final years of her life they were there for her.

We know little about Sandoval after her departure from Barclay at age forty-two. As the era changed, society had little tolerance for, or understanding of, women such as her. With the discovery of gold and the rush of American settlers, Pueblo became an industrial center in need of more agriculture and fuel to supply the growth. Before her death, Sandoval would see the arrival of not only the railroads, but the steel mill and smelters that would bring many European immigrants as well.

She would also see her daughters' status rise far beyond her visions. The two young girls who first married at El Pueblo were by then wives of respected men. Joseph Doyle went on to become a leading merchant and state legislator, and his wife resided in "La Casa Blanca," the first wooden house in the area. Doyle's plaza was located about twenty miles south of Pueblo, adjacent to other early Pueblo settlers.

The bad days of their marriage behind them, Juana and George Simpson became well-known and respected residents of Trinidad. He was a writer and poet, and she was a teacher. Much of their respectability derived from Juana, who sought her own education after he abandoned her and the children for some time.

"T.S." had experienced the earliest beginnings of Pueblo. She had lost her brother Benito Sandoval at El Pueblo as the result of an attack by the Mouache Utes, who rose up against the American government in 1842. Her two nephews and another woman, Chepita Miera, had been taken captive. Her uncle "El Viejito" Barela became a hero when, at the age of ninety-four, he warned everyone in the nearby plazas of the attack.

El Viejito and Sandoval's sons-in-law, along with Kit Carson, would negotiate for the release of her nephews at Abiquiu, New Mexico. Though Chepita did not survive her captivity, one of the boys was returned. The other had already been traded to the Navajos. He was released a few years later, but only after a trader gave rifles and blankets in exchange. Theirs was a dangerous existence. Yet, the women ventured to the borderlands with their children for the same opportunities the men sought: fortune, adventure, freedom, land, and love.

We know a little more about one woman, Teresita Sandoval, because of her contact with white men, because she made strong decisions for herself, and because she was a founder of Pueblo, Colorado. Her final days, though comfortable, would not be without sadness. She survived both Joseph and Cruz Doyle, who both died in their forties. Thomas remained in the area, and married Clara Gutierrez. Juan Andres Kinkead accompanied his father, Mathew, to California. Rafaela became the wife of Joseph Kronig, who purchased Fort Barclay from Doyle, but she died there soon after the birth of her second child. No documents have been found that give more information about the child, Rufina.

María Teresa "Teresita" Barela-Sandoval-Suaso-Kinkead-Barclay lived out her life in security and comfort, though far removed from the Victorian society of the "New Pueblo." Whatever social power she may have once held had diminished. We know nothing of her friendships with other women at any of the early settlements. She never married again.

American laws usurped many of the rights that Mexican and Native women had held prior to the war with the United States. Under Mexican laws, women could inherit and purchase land and livestock, or share in ownership with their husbands. (Barclay notes in his diary that he tended Sandoval's livestock.[24]) They could pursue their own business interests, and a woman could initiate divorce. The *alcalde,* or Mexican courts, upheld those rights for most women. Sandoval lived a life based on these rights, and it would be years before Anglo-American women would gain what had been lost to other women of another time.

Sandoval died in 1894 at the age of eighty-three and was buried on her daughter's land. Her grave—eroded by time—is lost. The prominent Doyle-Sandoval graves lie on a hill overlooking Casa Blanca, but they cannot speak of the Mexican women who settled Pueblo. Though overlooked or forgotten by history, these women's ever-elusive spirits have left their own indelible marks in the form of their descendants and the culture they nurtured as "women in between."

Notes

1
Elizabeth Jameson and Susan Armitage, eds., *Writing the Range: Race, Class, and Culture in the Women's West* (Norman: University of Oklahoma Press, 1997), 5.

2
John Brown, *The Mediumistic Experiences of John Brown, the Medium of the Rockies* (Des Moines: Moses Hull & Co., 1887), 87.

3
Janet Lecompte, *Pueblo, Hardscrabble, Greenhorn: Society on the High Plains, 1832–1856* (Norman and London: University of Oklahoma Press, 1978).

4
Marian Meyer, *Mary Donoho: New First Lady of the Santa Fe Trail* (Santa Fe: Ancient City Press, 1991).

5
Judy Romero-Oak, "Padre Martinez," *Spirit: Rocky Mountain Southwest* 8 (Spring 1995), 5-11.

6
Marc Simmons, *Coronado's Land: Essays on Daily Life in Colonial New Mexico* (Albuquerque: University of New Mexico Press, 1991), 76.

7
John C. Ewers, *Plains Indian History and Culture: Essays on Continuity and Change* (Norman and London: University of Oklahoma Press, 1997), 195.

8
Harriet Sigerman, *Land of Many Hands: Women in the American West* (London and New York: Oxford University Press, 1997), 201.

9
Ibid.

10
Lecompte, *Pueblo, Hardscrabble, Greenhorn*, 72.

11
Albert L. Hurtado, "When Strangers Met: Sex and Gender on Three Frontiers," Jameson and Armitage, *Writing the Range*, 122-37.

12
Ibid., 122.

13
Lecompte, *Pueblo, Hardscrabble, Greenhorn*.

14
George P. Hammond, *The Adventures of Alexander Barclay* (Denver: Old West Publishing Co., 1976).

15
Ibid.

16
Hammond, *Adventures of Alexander Barclay*.

17
Ibid., 42.

18
Lecompte, *Pueblo, Hardscrabble, Greenhorn*, 210.

19
Hammond, *Adventures of Alexander*

Barclay.

20
Ibid.

21
Ibid., 63.

22
Ibid., 58.

23
Ibid., 63.

24
Ibid.

Some Memories from My Life, as Written by Elfido Lopez, Sr.

Richard Louden, editor and annotator

ABOUT THE ANNOTATOR

An associate of the Lopez family, Richard Louden is a rancher, writer, and historian. He is a lifelong resident of southeastern Colorado and has published many articles on the history and archaeology of the area. Louden has served on the National Advisory Council of the Santa Fe Trail Association and is a past president of the Colorado Archaeological Society, as well as an officer and member of various other organizations involved with the history and archaeology of the Southwest.

THE ELFIDO LOPEZ STORY speaks to a different era, a different culture, and a long-lost set of values. While much has been said in early journals and accounts of American travelers in the Southwest of the alleged indolence and sometimes perceived moral laxity of the rank and file of the area's Hispanic population, the Lopez narrative gives a new and different perspective. It speaks to the applied energies of the people utilizing the limited resources available to them. It also says something of communal interests sometimes foreign to these visiting Yankee commentators. It speaks of a sense of sharing and concern for others, a sense of family and community.

In many respects Lopez was a self-made man, and his training began early. As the seven-year-old cowherd for the town of Las Animas and as a fourteen-year-old cowboy for one of the greatest ranching empires of all time, he early developed a work ethic grounded in initiative and reliability.

Certainly he was self-educated, limited though it was. Never afforded the opportunity of any formal schooling, he managed to master the rudiments of reading and writing with the help of his wife, before and after their marriage, and some of his probably not-too-literate cowboy friends. His recollections would almost make it sound as though he never became literate until after marriage, but such was not completely the case.[1]

The Lopez narrative was compiled from seven different documents given to the Colorado Historical Society by the family. Most were varying versions of the same memoirs. Some touched on items and incidents not included in the more complete versions. An attempt was made to select the best version from all the accounts, combine them into a single narrative leaving nothing out, and tell the story in Lopez's own words with a minimum of editing. Occasionally a word had to be supplied or deleted in the interest of continuity or understanding.

In 1937, during the time Elfido Lopez was setting down some of his memoirs, it was my privilege to live as his neighbor in the little town of Branson, Colorado, where I was attending high school. My teenage memory of him is as a burly, jovial fellow with a moustache who interspersed his free-flowing conversation with numerous interjected "By gollies."

My grandmother, with whom I stayed, was interested in Lopez's family history and encouraged him to record it. She interviewed him at length, taking notes, and that year published a portion of these same memoirs in the *Trinidad Chronicle-News*. In addition to my grandmother's story, the Lopez story has been covered in much greater detail in the little booklet, *Pioneers of the Picketwire* by Morris F. Taylor, well-known local historian and author. Anyone interested in further pursuit of the Lopez story will find this account worthwhile reading.

Some of Lopez's boyhood memories seem to border on childhood fantasies but are so fixed in his adult memory that we can only speculate as to what actually transpired to form such a vivid, exaggerated picture. In his adult memoirs, Lopez sometimes resorts to exaggeration for descriptive purposes, but he has never been accused of inventing facts.

As one with an especial interest in early ranch and cowboy history, I have found this little set of memoirs most intriguing. It refreshes the knowledge of some old customs and offers some insights into cowboy lore not often found in other recollections. It invokes memories of some not-too-well remembered greats of local cow country history.

It is unfortunate that his recall does not touch a bit more on the later years when the family moved out of the canyons to what they always referred to as "out on top." It was here they homesteaded and lived a major portion of their lives in a picturesque setting with a home poised on the rim of a small canyon. Here they laboriously erected their improvements, ranched and raised a family, and educated the children despite obstacles. The adversities they overcame and the things they achieved far outweighed the setback of having to undergo a foreclosure, which is dealt with at some length in the manuscript.

It was perhaps a consciousness of his own lack of formal schooling—but more likely a prompting by the insistence of his wife—that led Elfido Lopez to great lengths to make certain that his children received an education. In the early years his wife, Rebecca, subscribed to magazines, and these, together with what books she managed to accumulate, served as teaching aids in the home. At times they were able to have some of the children in school at Higbee, Colorado, staying with family members who lived in the area.

When they moved to the homestead they utilized their home as a classroom, and later Elfido built a small stone building to serve as a schoolhouse. Repeated efforts by Elfido and Rebecca to secure a school district for their area eventually paid off, but for three years they paid the teacher out of their own resources. In addition, they boarded the teacher, who at first held classes in the home. They were eventually reimbursed for the salaries.

Rebecca Lopez bore eleven children, three of them dying in infancy, and was a truly remarkable woman in her own right. Her father, William G. Richards, settled near Higbee in the Purgatory Valley just a few years earlier than Damacio Lopez, Elfido's father, and was married to Manuelita

Lujan of another pioneering family of the area. Rebecca's mixed heritage fitted her ideally to straddle the two cultures present in the valley, combining the best and most applicable from the early Hispanic and Anglo ways.

In this rugged canyon area, remote from doctors and medical care, she filled a niche as a midwife and nurse. She assisted in the birth of sixty-four babies, and throughout the community she was called upon to minister to a host of common ailments and such epidemics as smallpox and diphtheria. She treated these and an assortment of injuries with a few basic medicines, folk remedies, and common sense. Possessed with an innate sense of courtesy and gentility, her Good Samaritan image, coupled with her gentle nature and a strength of character, endeared her to the community and her family. She somehow fit comfortably into the role of a great and true lady, whether she was living in a cave house in the canyon or in a homestead "out on top."

Many of the Lopez family grew to adulthood and still live in the area, and it has been my privilege to become acquainted with some of four generations of them. Down through these generations they have maintained a certain consistency of character that is easily picked out. They are an open, friendly, closely knit clan with a carryover of a deeply ingrained sense of courtesy, politeness, and manners, some of which is undoubtedly traceable to their Hispanic heritage. There is, among them, a discernible sense of honor and integrity that seems to relate to their pioneer ancestry and some of the values indicated in these Lopez memoirs.

Elfido would, perhaps, be proud.

The Elfido Lopez Memoirs
Branson, Colorado
February 15, 1937

I am giving a true story of my lifetime. I was born in Trinidad, Colorado, January 11, 1869. My father's name was Damacio Lopez and he came from New Mexico. He was born in Santa Cruz where Española is now. I don't know what year he came to Trinidad but it must have been 1866 or 1867.[2]

My father's father was Spanish. His mother I'm not sure but I think she had some Indian blood. I knew both of them and both of them were good people. My mother's father came from Spain, also her mother. I did not know either one of them, only what my mother told me about them.

She used to tell us that her father was a school teacher. His name was

Juan DeArce but mother used to say his name was Juan De Arcia. We have found out since that his name was Juan DeArce and also that he was the first secretary under Governor Perry.[3] We also found this is in history. I have not seen it myself but got it pretty straight from the ones that have seen it. I am going to get a copy as soon as I can.

My mother's name was Loreta De Arcia. That is what she called herself but she could not read or write and I found out since her right name was Loreta DeArce. In those days among the Spanish people they did not think it was necessary to teach the girls to read or write, only to teach them to keep house. It was funny but it was that way. I never saw my mother's people. All I know is what my mother told us kids about her mother and father. I think my mother said she was born in Bernalillo, New Mexico, near Albuquerque. I don't know where she was married but somewhere in Sapello, New Mexico.

I remember some things my mother used to tell us kids about the people of her time. Most of the people were poor but they never let anyone go without something to eat. She said the people used to tell the neighbors to come and get food when they needed it and they would go to the neighbors and get food when they needed to. In those days a man that had a wagon and team was considered a rich man but there were quite a few that had 6 or 7 wagons and 8 or 10 ox teams. In the fall of the year the ones with wagons would ask the others to go with them to about where Colorado is now to kill buffalo. They killed buffalo with a spear on horseback. They would run into the herd and stick the spear in behind the buffalo's shoulder. Each man would try to kill 3 or 4. Other men would be on hand to do the skinning and cut up the meat and take it to camp to make *sesinar*, or jerked meat. They dried the meat on ropes strung between posts. The next day they would kill more buffalo. Sometimes the men would get killed themselves. A horse had to be a good one to catch a buffalo.[4]

Well, when they got enough meat they would start for home in New Mexico. Now, the poor men that came with the wagons they would get so much dried meat for their work, probably 2 or 3 sacks, whatever they was supposed to get. These same poor men would take the big bone from the hind leg. Maybe 2 or 3 bones. Well, it is funny but they would take that bone home and they would call it *el hueso gisandero*—the bone to season your food.[5] Well, the woman that owned the bone she would cook beans today. The next day another woman would borrow the same bone to put in her beans. It would take 8 or 10 days to get back to the owner again. Then it would go again around the neighborhood. My mother says she knew one bone to go around the neighborhood for 2 years straight. Nothing in the bone, only the name of the bone. So I guess that was sure enough hard times but my mother says she never seen anyone starve to death.

The way they used to do about their shoes, they wore moccasins. About their clothes, they just had to put patches sometimes 3 or 4 times on the same place. They sometimes didn't have money to buy thread. Well, they would tear up a flour sack or some other kind of goods and they would pull out the threads. They would put 2 or 3 threads together and they would twist them up to make one thread. In that way they would sew their clothes.

The people would make their children work more than they would let them play and above all they would make them respect the older people. I know my father would send me on an errand for himself but he would tell me if an old man told me to do something for him for me to go and do what the old man told me to do. So I could not come back with whatever my father sent me after. When I got back my father would say why didn't you come quick and I would tell him about the old man and he would be pleased. I think it is good for children to work and keep busy. It keeps them out of devilment. The children today do not keep busy and do a lot of mischief. Also if they had more to do they would learn how to work.

When my folks came to Trinidad the first baby was born. It was a boy. His name was Miguel Lopez and he lived about two years. They named him after my father's father.

Well when I was two years old my father and 11 more men went to Red Rocks[6] to file on their homesteads. They had ox teams. There was 12 men altogether. Six men could afford to buy spades. The other 6 made them of wood. So they decided to make a ditch. They had no way to survey the ditch so they started at the head of the ditch. It was 9 or ten feet deep. The men that had good spades spaded the ground up and the ones that had wood shovels they throwed the loose dirt out. Their ditch was about 3 feet wide and it sure was a crooked one.[7] They would let the water run behind them, would bank it up until they worked on the front and then would let the water run. If they needed any more digging they would dig more and that way they made their ditch. It took them about 4 months to finish their work.

Then they had to plow up. They had no plows but they made plows out of the forks from trees. One fork was the handle and they made points out of pieces of iron they sharpened on a rock and nailed to the wood. They said it was hard to plow. The plow would go every way excepting straight. Well they managed to farm that way. They raised everything they put in. Of course they put in wheat, melons, corn, beans, pumpkins, sorghum, chile, garbanzos and most anything they had.

I don't think each man put in more than 3 to 4 acres of wheat as they had no way to cut it, only by hand. They had hand scythes. When the wheat got ripe the men got together and they would cut one man's first, all together. The women would get together and cook for the men. They had *metates*, a flat rock, to grind blue corn on to make tortillas when they had no wheat flour.[8] They had to do their cooking on the fireplace. They had no stoves then. Tables was buffalo hide. They would spread the hides on the floor. They didn't have many dishes. About all they had was saucers and teaspoons. Sometimes they made spoons out of wood. But after you were through eating there weren't many dishes to wash.

I remember the women were very happy. They would sing songs, talk and they would be very jolly.

Well they would finish one man's [field] in one day, go on to the next and the next until they had finished the last one, all working together. They never thought they were doing too much for the other. They seemed to be glad to help each other.

When a child went to anyone's house the women always gave them something to eat. It was the way with all of them. They had not much of anything but they always had something. You would never hear any of them complain about anything but what it was all right with them.

They had dances the same as they do now. Some of the women had no shoes. Some of them had moccasins. They danced just as happy as they do today but one thing they did—the girls were not to talk to the boys. I remember going to dances. I never talked to the girls and they never talked to me. The parents of the girl would tell the girls not to talk to the boys before they left home. Another thing was not to refuse any boy a dance. We got along very well with it as it was their custom.

Kind of like this custom women used to not go to the roundup wagons but today they don't think anything about it. They will mix up with the men everywhere and the men don't mind it. It seems to me everything has changed.

Well about thrashing their wheat. Some of them had goats. Some had sheep and there were plenty of children. They would make a stack just like they do now but only at each place. They would all get around the stack and make the goats go around the stack. One man would get on the stack to pitch the wheat on the ground and make the goats go around and around on it. After they had all that wheat thrashed they would put some more on the ground. They would wait for wind to clean it out. Where ever they thrashed they would fix a place called the *era*.[9] They would get a hoe and level a place off and put water on it and get it good and wet and trample it down with the goats. It would get almost as hard as a rock. It would be hard as long as it was dry. They would sweep it clean with brooms and some branches from cedar. It would be close to the stack and a man would get on the stack and pitch the wheat on this hard place. All the children made the goats go around and around the stack. The goats would tramp the wheat until it was thrashed. They would throw the straw away and put some more wheat down until it was finished. Then they would wait for the wind to blow. That was the way they thrashed.

Then in the Fall they would take their wheat to Trinidad. There used to be a flour mill about where Marty has his feed store now. There was a big ditch with lots of water in it and it would turn a big wooden wheel and the wheel done the work.[10] The mill man took so much wheat for grinding. I don't know how much he took but I know that he took wheat for the men didn't have no money at that time.

We camped the wagons somewhere near where the Nicols hide house is now—close to the river.[11] I remember the first night we turned our ox team loose there. There was good grass right there, lots of trees and bushes. After night came there were lots of buggies going from Trinidad to El Moro and back.[12] They had lights on the corners of the buggies and the horses were trotting. I thought it was the prettiest sight I had ever seen. I don't think I slept hardly any. It sure looked good to me. After that I went lots of times with my father to sell watermelons. We had good sized melons and some small ones. The big ones sold for 25¢ and the small ones as low as 5¢ apiece. We could not sell all of them in town. We would go on up the river and would trade melons for wheat. They had a measure they called *almur*.[13] It was about a foot square and 4 inches high. My father traded so many melons for so many measures of wheat. Sometimes they would say level full, sometimes heaped full. We would come by the mill and grind the wheat on our way home.

There are a few other things from my boyhood days I would like to tell. When my father moved to Red Rock he said he would turn his ox team out to graze and if they would lay down he had a time to find them as the blue stem grass was so high. My father would cut hay in the summer with the scythe. Of course he did not cut too much, only to feed the ox in the wintertime. I remember our meadow. It was a good sized one. In order to clean it out: my father would set it on fire. There was a lot of hay burned out where the timber was. It was thick when one went into it. It would

The Lopez family at their homestead "out on top." Left to right: Albert, Elfido, Alice, Joe, Anna, Rebecca, and Elfido, Jr. An older son, Billie, was away at work and an older daughter, Lottie, was at school. A baby daughter, Wanda, was asleep inside the house. Photograph courtesy Joseph T. Darde.

look dark inside. The kind of timber that we had was cottonwood, box elder and willows.

There was some old cottonwoods that I heard the men talk about. Some of them would take 7 men with their arms straight out to reach around. They had nothing to measure with and that was the only way they could measure.

Our house was close to the timber and there was a whole lot of different kinds of birds. There was red and yellow canary birds. Some had a ring around their neck. Mocking birds they would begin to chatter right early in the morning. We could not sleep for the noise. There were lots of mocking birds and lots of other kinds of birds.

The box elder trees were very thick all over the river but in those days they had no wire to fence with so they had to cut box elders. They would cut them down and then out of one they would make 4 rails to fence their land. Today they are all gone. No timber. No birds and no grass and no people there.

When I was a rather small boy, I don't know how old I was, there was the first eclipse I had ever seen. Well it got almost dark. We could see the stars. The chickens ran in the chicken house. The women they were sure scared. Some thought it was the end of the world. After it got dark there was a lot of big bugs that fell on the ground. They had horns and after they hit the ground they would pull out and walk fast but after the sun came out the people went to look for the bugs and they could not find any. That has been a mystery to me that I have never seen any more bugs like them. There was a lot of them fell.

I would like to tell about what I heard as a boy. I know the place all right, where the house used to be. In those days people came from Texas with cattle and they would just settle where they thought that it would make a good ranch. Well this time there was a man came from Texas with a herd of cattle. I don't know how many men he had working for him but he had a faithful negro working for him. This man came some time in the summer with his cattle. So late in the Fall one very cloudy day he told this Negro man that it might come a snow and for him to hitch up the team and haul lots of wood. So the man hauled wood all day and that night it began to snow hard. After supper this Negro pulled a rock out of his pocket and asked the boss what he thought of it. The Negro had broke it with the back of his ax so this boss knew what it was and he said it was gold. He told the Negro man that he would put up all the expenses and go halves with him. The Negro told him all right but to let him go to Texas and bring his family and then he would show him the place. So it happened it was one of those snows. It lasted all winter but next Spring this man let the Negro man take a wagon with a mule team and the Negro pulled out for Texas to bring his family. So he got to his home and loaded his household goods ready to come back and while he was going in and out he fell dead. So the boss never did know where the Negro got the rock. There was a lot of looking but they never found anything.

Anyone that wants to look I will go and show where the house used to be. If we find the mine I will want just half the income. If we find nothing I just lose my time.

I must have been 6 or 7 years old when my father moved to what they used to call West Las Animas, called Las Animas now.[14] He went there to work on the railroad grade. My father had a few milk cows and we sold some milk. When we got there I herded the town cows for $1.00 a head a month. There must have been 15 or 20 of them. I herded them on foot.

The end of the railroad was right there. I then could not figure out how I could see the train come from the east and go right back quick. I could not see how the engine could turn on that narrow track. So I wanted to find out how it turned back. I followed the road up and they would run the engine into that place where they had a round track and they would push the track by hand. It sure looked easy the way they done it.[15]

At that time there was lots of wagons and ox teams came there to haul freight to take to New Mexico.[16] Some wagons had as many as six teams, twelve to one wagon. The people in Las Animas were making the town jail there. Some freighters hauled the rock from a place they called Tarbox Arroyo.[17] The jail is still there but they don't use it for a jail anymore.[18] I was back there about a year ago. The town is not anything like it used to be. I couldn't find a house I used to know. It is a whole lot bigger and there are lots of big buildings.

We lived there for 2 years then we came back to Red Rock to our old home. My father had begun to have more cows and he had a little store.[19] I herded my father's cows. I had to herd them on foot. I was 8 or 9 years old then.

There was a queer thing happened to me one day. I had a long stick I carried to kill rattlesnakes. I killed lots of them I wasn't afraid to kill them. Well one day I was walking along and I seen a big snake. I took it to be a rattler. She was coiled up and she had lots of feet just like little chickens. The feet were bright red. Well I started to kill it with my stick. To my surprise she made for me. She sure was quick. I ran from her and while I was running I looked back. She was right on my heels so I just went faster. After I ran awhile, I say 100 yards, I looked again and she was right at my heels. I was 2 or 300 yards from where I used to cross the river. I never looked back anymore. I ran across the water and going up the hill I was played out and the sand was loose and I couldn't run anymore. I looked back and the snake was not there. I never knew where she quit me. I went home and told my father but he did not believe me. He said that I was scared but I know I wasn't scared. I had killed so many of them before but my father never believed me.

While I was pretty small my mother sent me to pick plums. Across the river from our house there were a lot of plums. She gave me 2 buckets. I had to cross the river and I took off my clothes and went in swimming. I did not put my clothes on and thought I would swim again when I came back. The trees were loaded with plums. I went to eating and filling my buckets. I ate so many I lost all taste. I started to go away and my limbs began to get stiff. Even my eyelids got stiff. Finally I stumbled and fell down. I could not move. I had no feelings but I fell on an ant bed. I could see them in bunches all over me but I could not move away. I know that they were stinging me but I could not feel them. After a while I saw my flesh getting red. Pretty soon I began to have feelings. They made my blood circulate. I am sure they saved my life. I am sure I tried to be good to ants from then on. The stings sure burned me after I got over my spell.

At another time when I was a full grown man I had something like a colic cramp. I was out riding by myself. I got pretty sick. I had with me a big piece of tobacco. I swallowed all of it in little chunks. It done me no good at all. So I got so sick I didn't know what to do so I took off my clothes and laid down in an ant bed. They sure went after me. I sure felt them that time but in five minutes I was all right only the ant stings hurt me for a while longer.

When I was either 11 or 12 years old I went to work for the Prairie Cattle Co. Dick Head he was the manager. He had his office in Trinidad.[20] William Withers was superintendent at the JJ Ranch.[21] Withers needed lots of men to work. He had 3 roundup wagons and a dogie wagon, 4 altogether.[22] They would bring steers from Texas and turn them loose on the range. Next spring they would gather them up and send them up north. They would take them part of the way and the buyers would take them the rest of the way.

Withers hired me to go with one of the bosses named Frank Furst, the crankiest man I ever seen but when he was good he sure was good.[23] I was sure afraid of him until I got used to him. Then I sure liked him.

Well my first night on night guard was the longest night I had ever seen. I was so sleepy I could hardly keep my eyes open. The boss sent me with a man by the name of Leonardo Garcia. He was from Old Mexico. He sure was a good man and a good bronco rider. I don't think I ever saw him cutting up or fooling with anyone. It was strictly business with him. He told me how to ride so far from the herd and be careful not to scare them. He rode in one direction and I rode the other way. I was so sleepy I put my elbows on the saddle horn and my hands on my chin. When he came around he told me to keep a riding all the time. So finally I got over my sleepiness. I done all right. I stood guard with him pretty near all summer. The guard was 2 hours long and after about 2 weeks I was all right.

After I was there a month he asked me what strange things I had seen with the cattle in the night. I told him the only strange thing I had seen was that they would get up and sometimes go to grazing or get up and stay up awhile and then lay down on the other side. "No," he said. "You look good from now on and I will give you another month and then you tell me what strange thing you see." I kept looking but I never seen anything new. When the month was up he asked me what I had seen. I told him I hadn't seen anything strange. Well he said I'll give you another month. So at the end of another month I told him there was nothing queer that I had seen about them. He said there was and for me to watch good and I would see the majority of the white cattle would be on the north side of the herd. It might be just one but the majority would be on the north side of the herd. I kept a good look out and it was sure that way.

That was my first year out and I sure did like to work out. I worked pretty near all summer but in the fall my father came after me. I worked there until they finished the summer work. Those days we did not have lanterns. We ate breakfast by the campfire and we worked almost 16 hours a day. I, a kid, got $25.00 per month and the rest got $30.00 except the boss. He got $75.00. We all tried to hold our jobs. Very seldom a man got fired.

Well the next year they sent for me again and gave me $30.00. I then thought I was a big man getting a big man's wages. In the fall the company would pay us off and only kept the top hands or what they called top hands. The men that they kept they would put in winter camps. They were supposed to brand up what the roundup wagons missed and also pull the bogs in the spring. The cattle would run to where there was water to get away from the heel flies.[24] Then they would bog down and had to be pulled out on a horse.

This same man was supposed to keep the ears of the calves that he branded. The JJ earmark was crop the left ear.[25] In the spring when they called the boys in to start out with the wagon they would bring in the ears. That was the way they kept tally. The boys done all right for a long time but after while they got to branding some calves for themselves. They would start some little brand and they would tell only their best friends about what they were doing. Finally they found them out and all the company could do was fire them.[26]

There were a lot of stray brands in those days. At one time some 1 or 2 or 3 someone started a brand *X - T* and they would burn out another brand so much you could not make out what it was. They would put on a plain *X - T*. They tried to find out who was doing it but never did find out. Finally the Cattle association had the JJ to gather them and ship them for the Association.[27] Of course I was working for the JJ at the time and we gathered over 700 head of that one brand. No one ever knew who branded that brand.

We would leave the JJ Ranch the first day of April to go down to the Point of Rocks way down on the Cimarron.[28] It would take 10 days to get there. Our horses would be shed off and there was good beef on the range. Sometimes we would have to stop for 2 or 3 days at a time on account of so much rain but the rain would be warm. Down on the Cimarron there was no wood and very little drift wood. About all we had was cow chips. The cook sometimes would take a box of wagon grease and dip chips with grease to start a fire.

I don't remember for sure how many wagons there were but there were as high as 10 to 15 wagons in one body working up the Cimarron River. There was cattle, cattle and more cattle everywhere. Horses and more horses. It sure was a pretty sight. Horses bucking every where. Some would get throwed. Some would stay. Most all would ride with a buck strap on one side. There weren't many who could ride slick.[29] I don't think I ever saw but one man that rode slick. His name was Bill Woods. He was raised in Higbee, Colorado.

In those days the saddles we rode were good saddles but straight. Not like what they have now. I am 68 years old now and I think I could get on a saddle that they use now and I could still ride good.

We sure did work hard. We would go to bed after dark and get up and have breakfast by firelight and be on our horses by daylight. I think we put in 15 to 16 hours a day as we had to get up and stand two hours at night. We used to brand all the way from 150 to 400 calves every day. The Company branded on the average 1500 calves a year. They ran around 50,000 cattle.[30]

All the men tried to hold their jobs. They were satisfied but lots of them could never get ahead because they would like to go to town and drink whiskey. It was a wild life when we got to town. They had hitch racks in the middle of the street. Long ones. I never counted the horses tied up there but I think sometimes there were 150 head at one time and maybe more. When the boys got drunk they would get on their horses and go out of town shooting and hollering.

The cattle would be fat and I think there was 2000 head to where there is only one today. We didn't know what it was to feed salt but cattle were fat. In those days people never fed their cattle any kind of feed. They would feed only the horses they rode out in camp. They fed two horses for each man and that was just corn, no hay at all.

One thing we didn't have was ear ticks. I remember the first ear ticks I ever saw. We rounded up 3 or 400 to brand, fine calves and there was a yearling steer the only poor one in the bunch. The boss said that steer must have bad teeth. I'm going to rope him and find out so he roped him and opened his mouth. His teeth were all right. He said I don't see anything wrong with him. There was a man from Texas said to look in his ears. He looks like some of those steers in Texas that have ear ticks. So the boss looked in his ears and sure enough his ears were full. That was the first one I had ever seen with ticks and from then on I kept seeing some more. I really think the tick is what keeps cattle poor these days. I, myself, have tried every thing but they will keep coming back.

Now the little fly that bites cattle they've only been here about 40 years. I remember the first time I saw them. We were taking a herd of steers to Syracuse, Kansas. When we got to the Arkansas River I went ahead of the herd to run a bunch of cattle out of the way and before I got to them they were fighting flys with their tails. That was the first time I ever saw them. It took them 2 years to get to Red Rock. Now they are all over the country.

The JJ had put me with another boss. His name was John Headington. I believe that man was the best roper that I've ever seen. I do really believe that out of 100 throws he wouldn't miss 5 and he was so quick to make another loop. I must have been 13 or 14 years old. I was a pretty husky boy, pretty stout and a pretty good calf flanker.[31] The boys all wanted me for a partner whenever we had to flank calves and that was every day. One day there was just one roundup wagon but there was about 20 men with the wagon. When we rounded up and cut out what was called the strays, that was other brands besides the straight *JJ*, the stray count was 75 head and the *JJ*'s was 200 even. After dinner the boss told a fellow to take half the men and go and brand the stray bunch. Well, I happened to go with the boss. There was 2 men to flank, 2 men to brand, 1 man to earmark and the others to hold up the bunch of cows and calves. Well, I was one of the flankers with another man. He was a very stout man but he could not hold his calf down after he got him down. He was supposed to flank one calf and I was supposed to flank the next.

The boss hung up his vest on a tree and he looked at his watch. He had a horse he called Logan Boy, not a very big horse. He never used him for anything but roping calves. The horse knew his business just like a man so John pulled the bridle off Logan.

This man with me could not hold his calf down after he flanked him so I told him to just hold the calves' legs and I would flank them all. I don't remember John missing a throw that day. When he got through roping he went to his watch. He came to the branding fire and asked the ear marker how many ears there were. The ear marker counted the ears. There was 200. Then John asked if we had any idea how long it had taken us to brand that many calves. We could not tell him. Well, John said it took us just 80 minutes.

I tell that now but no one believes me. But I can say one thing. In those days ropers had more practice. The man a roping he would come up to where the man was waiting for a calf. The roper would not stop but keep right on a going. The man to throw the calf would go right down the rope until he met the calf. The man on the horse kept right on going until the flanker got his hand over the calf and in the flank. The man throwing the calf had to be quick and after he had his calf down be sure and keep him down. In those days there were lots of calves and we had lots of practice. Today a roper will bring his calf up to the man flanking and he will stop his horse. He don't go on like they used to. Another thing, the man when he is going to throw his calf won't go down the rope but he will get hold of the rope and try to pull the calf up to him. This is too much work and will play a man out quick.

Another thing we used to do, the boss would tell his men that went with the herd to take the herd on water and leave them there and hold them there for 2 hours. Now I see they will take them to water, let them drink awhile and then they will take them out right away. They won't let them stay long enough. They won't be satisfied if you put them on the bed ground that night. They will give a lot of trouble. They will be restless and want to keep traveling.

The second year I worked for the JJ I got acquainted with a man named Jack Johnes. He was running a wagon for W. J. Wilson from Denver.[32] Wilson had a lot of steers and lots of horses. He branded WJ, W on the left side and J on the left hip. Jack Johnes asked me what I was getting a month. I told him I was getting $30.00. He told me he would give me $35.00 so I quit the JJ and went to work for Johnes. At that time I did not know W. J. Wilson until afterwards. Wilson was sure a good man to work for. I was well satisfied with him.

While I was working for him we shipped 3000 head of steers to Chicago. There was 4 train loads for us. I went with the cattle. It was my first long trip. We stayed in Chicago 3 days but I could not see anything much. It was too foggy. We also stopped in Kansas City for 2 days. It sure done me a lot of good.

I worked for Wilson for about 2 years. He finally sold all of his steers but he bought the _22 Ranch near the Kansas line. He also rented the RRR Ranch. 3R is what they called it. It is near Greenhorn Mountain and he sent me up there to work.

I will tell you a funny thing that happened up there. The next day after

I got there they sent me to work with an outfit by the name of Watson's if I remember right. They branded *13* or *13*.[33] They had lots of horses. A fellow by the name of Tom Watson was wagon boss. The day after I got there he told another man and me to drive the area close to Canon City. I had never been there before so I went with this man. I don't remember his name. We rode along slow on a long flat. All at once this man said yonder is a chicken-eater. I looked up and I could not see anything. I said what do you call a chicken-eater. He said a coyote. I said I can't see anything. He said I don't either now but I did a while ago. All at once we could see something moving along the ground very slow. I had on my six

shooter. I told him I am going to take a shot at that fellow. He said no use. It was too far away. I said I'd scare him to death anyway. I got off my horse and turned the reins loose. I raised my gun above his back for what I thought was 300 yards. I saw the earth fly up a little more than half way and pretty soon I saw the coyote jump up and fall down. The man said by gosh you sure killed him. He pulled out on a run and my horse pulled out also.

The man never saw that my horse had gone away. It took me some little while to catch him but I caught him all right and caught up with the fellow. I said where is the coyote. He said up on the next hill. We went there and found him plumb dead. I took the scalp and gave it to the cook. This man I was with told the other fellows that I had killed him 2 1/2 or 3 miles away. They begged me to shoot. I told them I didn't like to shoot for fun. So after that they wanted to see a jack rabbit jump up but I didn't. It was just an accidental shot but a good one at that. I suppose it was better than a mile and a half. Anyway it was a long way off.

Mr. Wilson got killed by an old crank we used to call Buttermilk Bill. He killed Wilson and then turned the gun on himself and he died before Wilson. That was done in a hotel in Denver after I quit there.

When I was 21 years old I married Miss Rebecca Richards at Higbee, Colorado. She then was 18 years old. Her father's name was W. G. Richards.[34] He came to Higbee about the same time that my father came to Red Rock. He was one of the oldtimers. He had a big family. He had 7 boys and 4 girls—very good people. My father had 6 boys and 5 girls.

A while after I got married I took down with pneumonia. After I got well I could not work for over a year. I lived on credit. After I could work the doctor bill and all came to $500 and at $30.00 it took me 3 years to come clear. I could get work only in the summer, about seven months out of the year. I was making just about enough to live on the rest of the winter. So it happened that H. B. Brown from Trinidad who used to have a hardware store there also had a cow ranch in Plum Canyon. He gave me $30.00 the year around. I was to board myself and he gave me 50 cents for 3 meals while he was at the ranch. After about a year he sold out to William Green from Ludlow. Old man Green was the father of ex–county commissioner W. H. Green.

I worked for Green—about 5 years at $30.00 a month. I boarded myself. Out of the $30.00 I had to support my wife and the 2 oldest children and we kept having more children. We raised 8 children altogether. We also always had comers and goers but we managed to save $15.00 a month. We did not live high but we lived pretty good on $15.00 a month. I would go to town with $75 in the spring and would buy enough supplies for all summer. Then I would go again in the fall and buy enough for the winter. In the spring I would buy 12 or 15 yearling heifers. That way I got up to 250 head of cattle. I had $800.00 in the bank. Then the bank advised me to buy more cattle. That was the worst mistake I ever made. I just worked for the bank all the time after that until they closed me out.

I will tell any man to keep out of debt. If you've got a cow don't put her against another cow because as long as you have anything the bank will let you have money but as soon as you go down they will say we can't see how we can loan you any more money. I would have been very well fixed if I had stayed with my 250 head that I had clear that I got making $1.00 a day. I let them talk me into it and then I went down they just let me go down farther.

Now I am 68 years old and my health is not good just like any other old man. I said I raised 8 children. Well only 7 are living today. The oldest died when he was 20 years old.[35]

I always tried to raise my children right, to always be trustful. I always advised them never to lie or steal. I will tell any man or woman to be careful who they let their children run with. I was a boy once and I know by experience when I was with a good boy I was just as good as he was but when I was with a bad one I was a little worse than he was. I never did anything so awful bad that I couldn't tell it but still I know I did wrong.

I see that the wealthiest men today are those that had the toughest times in the world. I know what I want to say but I can't put my words together. I never went to school three months in my lifetime. About all I know is what my wife taught me after we were married.

I will tell a little joke on myself. When I was about 9 or 10 years old my wife came to visit some friends that she knew close to our house. There was where I first met her. I had sisters and some little brothers. Well one day I lost my handkerchief and she found it so she wrapped it up in a piece of paper and a little piece of red ribbon and she pinned it pretty nice and wrote a little note saying she found it and was returning it. I could not read at all so I just copied the same note and I sent it back to her. I thought I was doing something pretty good. That was the beginning of our corresponding so from then on I tried my best to learn how to write. I can't spell much but I make people understand me all right.

Well I've had good times and bad times in this world but I would not trade my reputation for the First National Bank of Trinidad and Rocco DiPaolo throwed in to boot.[36]

I could write a whole lot more that I've not told but I will quit for now.

Notes

1

While Elfido Lopez did acquire some of the basics of literacy, he did not master grammar and punctuation. It was necessary for me to break his writing down into sentences and paragraphs and to correct the spelling by guessing what word was intended by an assemblage of letters. Nevertheless, I tried to intrude as little as possible into his use of language. I corrected his grammar to some extent, but left some of the redundancies, improper verbs, and double negatives in order to retain the flavor of his speech. In a like vein, I inserted a minimal amount of punctuation.

2

Damacio Lopez was in Trinidad at least as early as November 26, 1866, on which date he filed a claim on 160 acres astraddle Raton Creek, apparently a mile or so southwest of the village. Las Animas County records, Office of the County Clerk, Book 1, 32.

3

No Governor Perry appears on the roster of territorial governors. The person referred to here seems most likely to have been Albino Perez, who served as Mexico-appointed governor of New Mexico from 1835 to July 1837, at which time he was assassinated by insurrectionists. Warren A. Beck, *New Mexico: A History of Four Centuries* (Norman: University of Oklahoma Press, 1962), 121.

4

The kill techniques and the meat handling described here are patterned very closely after the Plains Indians buffalo hunt.

5

The correct spelling here should undoubtedly be *hueso*, the Spanish word for bone, and while *gisandero* probably refers to flavoring or seasoning, no Spanish equivalent could be found.

6

While Lopez consistently refers to this area as Red Rock, it was, and is, generally referred to as the plural, Red Rocks. These twelve settlers actually located at the mouth of Minnie Canyon, a northern tributary of the Purgatory and an integral part of Red Rocks area. Plat Book, Office of Las Animas County Treasurer.

7

The ditch was crooked enough that when the Prairie Cattle Company acquired the land, it straightened the ditch, which immediately began to erode and wash out until it had to be abandoned. Emma J. Bradley, "Narrative of Elfido Lopez," *Trinidad Chronicle News*, June 19, 1937.

8

The use of the stone *metate* and *mano* (unmentioned but required) to grind their "blue corn" again relates to their Indian association and heritage.

9

Era is a Spanish word specifically describing a thrashing floor.

10

Marty Feeds is still in operation as a feed processing plant after more than one hundred years at this location. Street repair work in 1992 revealed the ditch that once supplied water power for the mill, somewhat lower than current street levels. The mill was apparently one established by Charles M. Farrand in 1869 or 1870 and known as the Quick Step. "Reminiscences of E. J. Hubbard," DeBusk Collection, Trinidad State Junior College.

11
Lopez refers here to the no-longer-present Krille-Nichols Hide House. The location was just across the Commercial Street Bridge of the Purgatory, east along the river with their camping site probably in the area now occupied by the Atchison, Topeka & Santa Fe railroad tracks.

12
If the buggy traffic was indeed traveling between Trinidad and El Moro, it must have been in the year 1877 or later, after Damacio had returned to Red Rocks from his stay in Las Animas. The settlement of El Moro, across the river from Gray Creek and about three miles east of Trinidad, did not take on the name and begin to flourish until 1876. In that year the Denver & Rio Grande Railroad laid track into El Moro, ignoring the larger settlement of Trinidad.

13
This unit of measure is the *almud*, one-twelfth of a *fanega*, a fanega being approximately equivalent to a bushel.

14
West Las Animas was established in 1873 when promoters brought the Kansas Pacific Railroad there, bypassing by several miles the infant town of Las Animas. The original settlement soon moved to the new location, and the "West" was eventually dropped.

Morris F. Taylor, *Pioneers of the Picketwire* (Pueblo, Colo.: O'Brien Printing & Stationery Co., 1964), 26.

15
Ibid., 27. The Atchison, Topeka & Santa Fe Railroad reached Las Animas in 1875. This was the road bed on which Damacio was working. A roundhouse was located at the end of the track.

16
As the railroads crept westward each new end-of-the-track station became a shipping point for Santa Fe Trail freighting. During this period, from 1872 to 1878, a series of roads leaving the Mountain Branch of the trail at Granada, Las Animas, and Fort Lyon snaked their way southwestward over the newly created military freight cutoff route between the two older branches of the trail. Richard Louden, "The Military Freight Route," *Wagon Tracks: Santa Fe Trail Association Quarterly* 7, no. 3 (May 1993), 8-9.

17
Tarbox Arroyo is a few miles south of Las Animas near old Boggsville. The stone outcrop is on the banks where it empties into the Purgatory. Personal communication with Phil Peterson of La Junta, February 19, 1994.

18
Ibid. The Las Animas Jail is still intact, part of it an adjunct to the Las Animas Kit Carson Museum, the rest utilized as a county garage.

19
Damacio Lopez, in addition to operating a small general store and being fluent in both Spanish and English, assisted in the post office serving the

neighboring Bent Canyon area.
Taylor, *Pioneers of the Picketwire*, 30.

20
Young Elfido was apparently a bit
older than he remembered at the
time he was employed. The Prairie
Cattle Company did not come into
being until January of 1882, and Dick
Head did not assume his position as
manager until 1883, suggesting that
Lopez was probably fourteen years old
at the time. "Foreign Cattle Empire
Was in Higbee Area," *Arkansas Valley
Journal*, January 4, 1973 (reprinted
from *Texas Livestock Weekly*).

21
Ibid., 2. William Withers was superintendent of the JJ Division of the Prairie
Cattle Company with headquarters
at Higbee, fifteen miles south of La
Junta. It also had the Cross L Division
on the Dry Cimarron, east of Folsom,
New Mexico, and the LIT Division at
Tascosa, Texas, controlling some five
or six million acres and claiming to
run about 100,000 head of cattle.

22
The "dogie wagon" was an extra
wagon used to haul newborn calves
too weak and wobbly to keep up with
a driven herd at night, and, perhaps at
noon, they were unloaded and reunited
with their mothers for nursing. They
were loaded up again when movement
of the herd was resumed and continued
to be hauled until they were able to
keep up with the herd on their own.

23
While Lopez spells this name "Furst,"
it undoubtedly refers to Frank Forrest,
at one time designated "outside range
boss" for the Prairie Cattle Company
and well-recorded JJ employee.

Personal communication from R.
D. Louden, the annotator's father
and one-time JJ employee; C. W.
Hurd, *Boggsville: Cradle of the
Cattle Industry* (Las Animas, Colo.:
Boggsville Committee; printed by the
Bent County Democrat, 1957), 81.

24
In the spring the heel fly attempts to
lay its eggs in the heels of cattle, pen-
etrating the skin. The besieged animals
seek any available water or mudhole in
which they can submerge their lower
limbs, hiding their heels from the flies.
At that time in history, before supple-
mental winter feeding had become
accepted, the cattle were often in a
weakened condition and bogged down
easily when they ventured too deep
into the mud.

25
The "crop" simply meant squarely cutting off about one-fourth of the end
of the ear and was used, in addition
to a tally for the branding count, as
a method of identifying ownership at
a distance, from the unbranded side,
or when winter hair length made the
brand hard to read.

26
These big cattle companies and
livestock associations often took
measures more drastic than mere dismissal. Bylaws of the Colorado Cattle
Growers Association in its first brand
book, issued in 1884, specify that any
employee caught branding a maverick
(an unbranded animal whose ownership cannot be established) or otherwise illegally appropriating livestock
must be turned over to the association
by members to be "blacklisted" and
such other action as may be needed to
bring him to justice. This black-balling

tactic resulted in many cowboys, some guilty and some only suspected, being unable to find ranch jobs, sometimes turning them toward criminal pursuits. Richard Goff, Robert H. McCaffree, and Doris Sterbenz, *Centennial Brand Book of the Colorado Cattlemen's Association* (Denver: Colorado Cattlemen's Centennial Commission, 1967), v.

27
The Colorado Stock Growers Association, organized in 1867, under provisions of its bylaws, claimed all animals classified as strays whose ownership could not be established within a six-month holding period. Richard Goff and Robert H. McCaffree, *Century in the Saddle* (Denver: Colorado Cattlemen's Centennial Commission, 1967), 79.

28
Point of Rocks on the Cimarron River in the extreme southwestern corner of Kansas was a well-known landmark on the cutoff route of the Santa Fe Trail and the location of an early ranch headquarters.

29
"Riding slick" refers to staying astride an unruly horse without the use of the rein-free hand to grasp the saddle horn or the bucking strap—a long leather strap fastened to a favored side of the saddle for grabbing when the ride gets too rough. The A-fork saddles of the period had no "swells," protuberances on the front of the saddle, which made them much more difficult to stay in than most modern-day western saddles.

30
Lopez must have intended to write

"15,000." In their last year of operation before selling their cattle to the Prairie Cattle Company, the Jones brothers branded 11,000 JJ calves. With the expansion by the Scottish syndicate, 15,000 seems a reasonable figure. Hurd, *Boggsville*, 80.

31
A flanker is one of a team of two whose job it is to throw the calf on his side and hold him there while he is being branded. In this particular operation the flanker goes hand-over-hand down the rope to meet the calf being dragged from the herd by the roper, and when he contacts the calf he reaches over its back, placing one hand on the underside of the neck and the other in the flank. He lifts the calf off his feet and lays him down on his side, grasping his upper front leg, and his partner grasps the hind legs. Ideally, this flipping of the calf can be done when he bounces at the end of the rope and can be easily rotated while his feet are off the ground. Timing is as important as strength. Ordinarily team members alternate, flanking every other calf.

32
W. J. Wilson is listed in the first Colorado Cattle Growers Association Brand Book, 1884, as having range on the Republican and Arkansas rivers. His brand was recorded as an "O" on the left shoulder, but, like many other big operators of the time, may have used other brands such as the "WJ" mentioned by Lopez. The RRR outfit rented by Wilson was registered in the same brand book as the Colorado Ranch Company with range on the Arkansas and St. Charles to the Huerfano. Goff et al., *Centennial Brand Book*, 18, 19.

33
The "13" brand was founded by Tom Watson, patriarch of a large family of Watsons headquartered on Hardscrabble Creek, between Pueblo and Canon City. The brand is still in the family, held by William Watson of Trinidad. Personal communication with William Watson, March 3, 1994.

34
William G. Richards came to the Nine Mile Bottom area in 1865 and settled on the north side of the Purgatory near what soon became known as the pioneer settlement of Higbee. Paul D. Friedman, "Final Report of History and Oral History Investigation at the Proposed Pinyon Canyon Maneuver Area," 88, on file with the U.S. Department of the Interior, National Park Service, Denver, Colorado.

35
A son, Billie, died at twenty from a horse accident while working on a ranch near Pueblo. Three other children, two sons and a twin daughter, died in infancy.

36
The First National Bank of Trinidad was the bank that had foreclosed on him, and Rocco DiPaolo was a businessman and entrepreneur in Trinidad at the time who was noted for his ability to earn a fast buck.

Pastimes in the Life
of Pablo Cabeza de Baca

Translated and edited by Vincent C. de Baca

ABOUT THE TRANSLATOR

The great-grandson of Pablo Cabeza de Baca, Vincent C. de Baca received his doctorate in Latin American history from the University of California at San Diego. He has published articles and critical reviews on the Mexican Revolution, Chicano history, and New Mexico history. Dr. C. de Baca has presented papers to the American Historical Association on the subject of Tijuana vice activity, and, recently, he spoke about his family history at the Cuarto Centennial New Mexico Genealogical Conference. He is a tenured assistant professor of history at Metropolitan State College of Denver.

This translation of Part I of Pablo Cabeza de Baca's memoirs is followed by the original Spanish-language text. Vincent C. de Baca wishes to thank Sr. Antonio Cabeza de Baca, his great uncle, for giving him a copy of his father's memoir. Dr. George L. Archuleta, adjunct professor at Metropolitan State College, proofread the Spanish version. Also at Metro State, Dr. Joan Foster and Dr. Stephen Leonard supported his efforts to complete this work.

PASTIMES IN LIFE: A BRIEF HISTORY

Economic edition from a Man of few letters
Pablo C. de Baca

First, Only and Last Existing Edition
Mora, New Mexico
January 2d, in the year of our Lord, 1935

REFLECTIONS

Dedicated to my Children, dear creatures, whom God has deigned to place under my care.

INTRODUCTION

This little history has been written for you, my children. And beyond my mischiefs, you will probably find something of profit that could guide you later, when you have entered to the use of reason. I present you the experience of life around you, how to treat your neighbor, and how to respect and remain loyal to your Holy Religion.

Pablo C. de Baca

PRELUDE

This book that I present you was composed only as a simple history of a humble man who reflected on the times during his life. Have you ever seen a blacksmith who would fix his own clock? It would be absurd to believe it, yet just such an absurdity confronts you as I try to edit a History without the least knowledge of a historian. Therefore, I advise you to not read what I write here only to criticize it, because I did not dedicate my time to only call your attention to the world. I simply want to note the course of my simple life, not so that you only learn about the world, but to draw the attention of my children who did not have to the pleasure of growing before realizing or keeping some memory of your father who, upon writing this, felt his strength disappearing. Perhaps, you will see that the Lord, in his unknowable wisdom, has marked my departure from this precocious and fleeting life. More importantly, who could distrust of the divine mercy of God who not just makes the sick healthy but he gives life to the dead. And now, beloved creatures, what I have written awaits your forgiving acceptance for the countless errors that you will find in this.

P. Cabeza de Baca y Delgado

THERE WAS ONCE an isolated ranch previously well-known by the name of SANTA CLARA, where only about three or four families lived as local merchants. The above-mentioned locale is now known by the name of Wagon Mound and is located in northeastern New Mexico about forty-five miles from the plaza of Mora, the seat of Mora County. One of the original families residing at this place were my parents: Don Francisco C. de Baca and Mrs. Martina Delgado, who moved there [circa 1866] from the Villa of Santa Fé, one year after their marriage. My father was a cattle rancher who increased the size of his ranch and his cattle herd considerably. At this place, an immense meadow belonged to the inhabitants where they cut hay under U.S. government contract for the troops stationed a short distance from there at Fort Union; and by these means, they earned a good income.

Another resident named Don Fernando Nolan, my father's uncle, claimed the greatest part of the Santa Clara Grant. Don Fernando, a lawyer by profession, was considered to be and, in fact, was very wealthy in property and cash. An intrepid man, he was addicted to alcoholic drinks; and when drunk, he was invested with enough false courage to fight an army. With the passage of time, everything changes. In old age, his strength weakened, his property and wealth were drained, and he died poor, almost in misery, in the plaza of Santa Fé.

After some years living at Santa Clara, Papá changed residence moving from there to Las Vegas where he established a commissary store. It was during a time of scarcity, and the price of provisions increased at alarming proportions: a sack of flour became worth eight dollars. Later, the Romero Brothers hired Papá as the manager of their hacienda at Romeroville, which was once called Puertecito. When the Santa Fé railroad line was being built, they sent Papá to the town of La Cuesta, located on the Pecos River, to manage a store that the Romeros had just established there. It was at the time when the Santa Fé line between Las Vegas and Santa Fé was built in the year of 1880. La Cuesta was a prosperous place while the railroad line was being constructed and many people worked cutting rail ties at San Miguel, Rivera, San José, and La Cuesta. After construction of the line ended, Papá bought the store from the Romero Brothers and there we lived for more than fourteen years where I spent the best years of my life.

As mentioned earlier, in 1865, Francisco C. de Baca from Peña Blanca was united in Holy Matrimony with Martina Delgado y Nolan from the Villa of Santa Fé. In this state, they had thirteen children: María [b. 1865,

Santa Fé]; Gregorita [b. 1867, Santa Fé]; Juana Refugio [b. 1869, Peña Blanca]; Fulgencio [b. 1871, Peña Blanca]; Miguel [b. 1872, Las Vegas]; Pablo [b. 1874, Santa Clara]; Juan [b. ?, Las Vegas]; Aurelio [b. 1878, Puertecito]; Francisco, Jr. [b. 1880, La Cuesta]; Hipólito [b. 1882, La Cuesta]; Dolores [b. 1884, La Cuesta]; Erenea [b. 1886, La Cuesta]; and Arsenio [b. 1891].

Gregorita: The Innocent Angel

One summer day, Gregorita, a little two- to three-year-old girl, was playing on the porch, when our mother was busy washing clothes. As the noon hour was approaching, mother thought the little girl would be safe there and went carelessly into the kitchen to prepare the meal. Not more than a half hour had passed, when mother went to look for her, she screamed, "Oh, what horror!" The child had vanished from sight; at first, she looked throughout the house and the surrounding area without finding her. Soon, everyone at home and neighbors quickly went looking for her, but nobody could imagine where she was. Suddenly, while everybody was running here and there, mother glanced toward one of the irrigation ditches where she washed laundry. A sharp pain pierced her heart and she cried, "My Jesús, what is this!" Headlong, she rushed to the place and with anguish, desperation, and screams of pain, she took the girl in her arms; DEAD, she was dead! She had drowned. Mother tried to walk forward with the child in her arms, but she felt her strength leave, and all her energy fail. The violence of her pain at that instant ran through her veins, she felt unleashed like a lighting bolt, then all her senses fell faint into a profound delirium, and she remained unconscious for a long time without realizing what passed before her eyes in those terrible moments. When she regained consciousness, she found herself in bed and opened her eyes. She looked around the room, and focused on a small table surrounded with flowers and lit candles. She saw the pale cadaver of her Innocent Angel, who seemed to be smiling with the Angels in Heaven.

Miguel: The Little Thief from Heaven

This boy was only a few years old. God wanted to augment the choir of Angels with such a beautiful and kind boy. With so singular a name, he barely lived long enough to leave us vivid memories of his tender infancy.

Pablo

I, Pablo, was born on February 2, 1874, at Santa Clara. I was baptized by Reverend Father Guerín, in Mora, with the assistance of my godparents:

Don Atilano Abeyta and Mrs. Dolores Lalande, residents of La Cueva. When I was born, my uncle Don Fernando Nolan, who claimed to be a fortune teller (which he did only as a pastime) foretold that I would become a sailor. I do not understand the meaning of such a prediction; the truth is that nothing scares me more than the water, I hardly use it to wash myself. I tremble at the thought of being caught in rain outside my house, crossing a rising river, or even being near a lake. And, until recently, I was fortunate, so to speak, to visit Lakes Michigan and Erie, and cross the Hudson River to the great city of New York which I will speak about later.

Perhaps, Don Fernando meant to say that I would be a sailor who would have to navigate the storms and demands of life on earth, fighting the danger of drowning in the evil temptations and betrayals offered us by this fleeting world. Undoubtedly, this is the sea that I must sail while constantly avoiding the shipwreck of my little boat so that, one day, I will awaken happily able to steer my boat to the port of salvation where my Captain awaits me.

In 1878, when I was four years old, the construction of the Santa Fé railroad crossed part of Papá's land. Together, he and the other owners of the Santa Clara land grant had to sell their property. From there, we moved to Las Vegas, where Papá established residence and started a dry goods store. Due to a wheat shortage or maybe the "boom" caused by the railroad construction, the price of flour had gone up and it was sold for eight dollars a sack.

The Romero Brothers, in those times, were extremely wealthy and were considered the most powerful merchants and political bosses in San Miguel County. They seemed to control the main axis of all traffic to Las Vegas and the adjacent towns. As mentioned previously, the Romero Brothers Company hired Papá to manage their Romeroville store and he was in charge of the whole Romeroville ranch where he was the *mayordomo*. Even today, you can see a stone wall along the entire summit of the mountain beginning at the canyon's mouth, following the summit in the direction of Santa Rosa, extending a distance of sixty miles; it was Papá who directed this gigantic work more than fifty years ago.

Meanwhile, as Papá worked and toiled in these jobs, my older siblings attended a private school conducted by a teacher who was a Spanish outsider. Don Trinidad Romero brought the teacher expressly to educate the Romero children, yet my siblings and some other children were allowed to attend this school. I was still too young to attend school and so me and the other little ones in my brood spent our days entertaining ourselves. Because of my young age then, I recall very well that our favorite game was taking off our socks, rolling up our pants, and getting into a mud hole or a pond by the lake near our home. During school vacations, the other boys joined us and we passed the day at the lake fishing for frogs and *tepocates* [tadpoles]; we pretended to sell them at the market. My older brother and another neighbor played the traders of "Rare Animal Meats" from the above-mentioned species: frogs, toads, and *tepocates*. When we arrived with a load of these, we quickly sold them and we got our payment in play paper money, buttons, or pebbles. Then, the "merchants" immediately began to quarter those poor little animals, and hung their legs and ribs in their butcher shop, just as meats are hung in the real butcher shops.

When work on the rail line passed Romeroville, businesses closer to the railhead began to improve. Since the Romeros had another store at La Cuesta in the Pecos River Valley, it was decided to send Papá there to manage that business. Because the post office changed names, La Cuesta has had various names; it has been called: Concho, Aragón, and, at present, it is named Villanueva.

Here in this place, I passed most of the days of my youth. Of course, the best days of my life were spent in the loving care of my good mother, who sacrificed in life for the love of her children. A mother is the affectionate teacher in the home, where you learn good character, and you are infused with Christian faith, hope, and charity. It is the foundation and perennial pedestal on which the future of Christian youth is based; she teaches the faith, and then she goes on to educate about the skills that will be useful to you later in life. Mamá took great pains to teach us how to do our house chores well, and to do it neatly, as when cleaning a room, fixing the beds, cooking in the kitchen, and washing dishes. Later, she told us this about work, and she made us understand, that work was never an insult regardless of how humiliating or unpleasant it may be. And she told us, "When you become men, and if you become rich, you will not be bothered for having learned [to work], since you will be better able to command, and if poor, it will also be useful." Therefore, we did whatever she told us to do with pleasure. My siblings and I learned how to sweep, cook, make beds, cut firewood, gather it from the mountain, and carry water.

Since we lived on a summit, it was necessary to carry two to three barrels of water in a cart. The road uphill was rough and stony, so sometimes the wheel got stuck. And then, "Oh, how hard we worked," many times we had to empty out the barrels. During summer we attended to our work of weeding and watering, sometimes we tried to water the corn *milpa* [field] barefooted. Therefore, then and now, it does not embarrass me to do any type of work that fate provides. I say this because I remember that my older brother hated it when he was picked to do some of the housework like cooking, making a bed, or having to sweep. He said, "This makes me feel very ashamed. The people will think that I am a woman. Mommy, sending me to cut firewood all day is better than all this." However, she would not let him stop doing it. Upon finishing the chores inside or outside the house, we were then free to play our games, or make what mischief we wanted, but always under the surveillance of Mamá, who watched so that our games were good.

The house where we lived was a spacious residence constructed in the form of a *placuela* [a four-sided adobe structure with connecting rooms lining the inside walls enclosing an open patio]. There were two rooms on the northeast side: one served as the store and the other was the *trastienda*, or what the *bolios* [white people] call a "warehouse." That is where Papá tended store, and sometimes everyone in the family helped Papá at the store. There, I learned the occupation of cashier at a very early age. At ten years old, I could stay alone in the store on occasions when Papá and the family traveled to Las Vegas.

The town of La Cuesta lacked good schools in those times. And, in general, they hired teachers from this same locale: old timers who had a little bit of knowledge of letters. Our books were note cards from which we all recited aloud, in a singing rhythm, the: "Ba-ba, Be-be, Bi-bi, Bo-bo, Bu-bu." Then: "Ca-ca, Ce-ce, Ci-ci, Co-co, Cu-cu," and so on. And then beginning in three syllables: "Ban-ban, Ben-ben, Bin-bin, Bon-bon, Bun-bun." And our school room was nothing less than a gloomy and dark shack. Our consolation was to scrape dirt with our feet for the purpose of raising enough dust to choke the teacher, Matias, who was always too busy writing or hiding behind any book or almanac that he was reading. One certain day, the teacher was in a bad mood and I did not know my lesson. He caught me and gave me a licking; then, he made me go to the "Donkey" corner where there was a cabinet, I climbed up and he put a cap with donkey ears on me. The cap consisted of a piece of paper rolled up like a cornucopia about twenty inches high. At the end of class, he told me, "You must take me to your house!" As I, in fact, did. And there, he said to my father, "Don Francisco, it is best that you no longer send this boy to school on a donkey, he will never learn anything." My parents greatly resented that, and I never returned to his school.

At that point, Papá decided to reform the educational system and he made sure that we were provided with good teachers. So, I have the great pleasure of saying that my teacher, during the next school term, was Don Ezequiel C. de Baca, who later was governor of New Mexico. Since

Pablo (right) at age sixteen with his cousin Hilario Delgado, ca. 1890.

Pablo and his first wife, Emilia Rudolph (a later spelling of "Rudulph"), on their honeymoon near Las Vegas, New Mexico, in 1897. The boy in the tree on the left is Arsenio, Pablo's baby brother.

Maestro Baca frequented our house, I had the opportunity to use my time to full advantage because he helped me during the evenings. So the Donkey finally finished the term ahead of all students.

The following year, we also had the good luck to have another good teacher who was sent there with the best recommendations; this was Don Milnor Rudulph, Jr., who came from Rociada, New Mexico. Oh and who would have thought that this honorable man would later become my brother-in-law, when I married his younger sister, years later, after I met the family.

In these two school terms, I made good progress in my studies, learning under the good direction of such expert and worthy teachers. After my last term, Papá decided to send me to the Jesuits' College in Las Vegas enrolled as a "Day Scholar." I lived and worked at the home of my Aunt Erinea, Mamá's sister. At first, I found the discipline of the College very rigid, but with time and after meeting the boys and my many Romero cousins, everything went well. Naturally, the guys got into plenty of mischief and some of it cost us plenty, when we discovered how to play

"Hookey." Like the old adage says: "Wickedness is like corn, it sprouts by itself." In general, we always got caught in these anyway.

I will now tell you about one such mischief. While walking to school, we were joined by two, three, four, then more cousins and friends during one hard winter morning. Along the road to school, we entertained ourselves with some of our usual games like spinning the top, playing *bolita* [little ball], or Hop Scotch. Once all of us were together, one comrade got the bright idea to play "Hookey" that day. And he told us, "Hey boys, let's go skating at the Brewery lake, the ice is great, I saw it this morning while coming here. What do you say, Hilario?" And he said, "Fine for me, I'll go if you go. And you, Felipe, will you come with us?" Then Felipe replied, "Well certainly, I'm a loyal soldier, and where my Captain goes, it is my duty to follow." That is how we all decided to go: Pablo, Hilario, Felipe, Eugenio, and Federico. Then, Eugenio said, "And what can we do without skates? There's no way around it, what does the Captain say we should do?" So the Captain said, "Well boys, we each have to go home and, with the excuse that we forgot a book like catechism, geography, or arithmetic, we'll take the skates out secretly. Later, we'll all meet back at the lake." In turn, we each yelled, "Fine, fine, long live the Captain!" And, immediately, we each went running to our own house.

In a while, we were all there with our skates. Reymundo Lopez was the champion skater, he made circles, squares, or figures in the ice and he even wrote his name on the ice. We tried to follow his daring feats. By the lake's edge, there was a hole cut to check the thickness of the ice. The hole was twelve inches in diameter; on one side, a stick systematically marked the increase or decrease of thickness. And over there, a large sign hung that was very easy to notice, so that nobody got near: "DANGER." Reymundo got an idea, so he told us, "We'll make turns by the hole's edge to see who can get closest." One after another, we followed him turn after turn. I (Pablo) noticed that they stayed back and were afraid to get close. I wanted to win the championship, so I took flight, I tried to make the turn, but . . . *zas*! [boom] ****** I saw ****** little stars. I was drenched up to my armpits. As the hole got bigger, I sank under the ice. Realizing this was not some great joke, my comrades pulled me out of there freezing cold, all wet, dripping water, with my teeth chattering. I could not go home because they would discover the plot. The companions decided to collect wood, build a fire on the bank, and dry my clothes there. After they had a good blaze going, I warmed one side while the other froze again. I burned on one side, and froze on the other. In the end, when I thought I was dry, "*caramba*," my clothes were all burnt; if you touched them, they fell to pieces.

Now, what to do! Together, we realized our disobedience: we had ditched school, and we had deceived our parents, the teacher, and everybody. I could not go home alone because I was trembling from head to feet and my body felt roasted over coals like a rack of ribs cooked on a brazier. It was necessary to go home and report my guilt, some of the guys accompanied me to the house. And once there, my aunt already knew the whole story by some unknown means, but another roasting from the lashes of a whip or halter bent in two awaited me. Later, when my Uncle Margarito [Romero] arrived from working at the store, he was told what happened. After devilish misbehavior, I got a beating, and a good scolding which I have never forgotten.

After I finished school and stopped mixing in mischief, Papá left me in the care of the very good Father Ferrari, editor of *La Revista Católica*. There, I was occupied setting type and printing novena prayer booklets. I trembled on the days that the *Revista* was printed because thousands of copies were passed through the printing press by me and a companion. The press had a large, heavy wheel and we tossed the sheet of paper on the plate, and we had enough time to exchange one page for another. Then, we took the sheets of paper, folded them into book form, and bound them together. The mailed magazines had to be rolled, addressed on glued labels, packed in baskets, and carried to the post office, a quarter-mile away. Then, we still had copies for local distribution which we delivered door to door on Saturdays. I learned so much and I appreciated the good and holy Father Ferrari. He was nothing less than a saint, so humble and generous, living a life of penance and prayer. He never left the printing office unless it was a great necessity. When going to the plaza on important business, we never saw him leave without his old and faded cassock that seemed to grow on him. I could say a lot about him, but I will provide this short description of he who needs no eulogy, because like I said before he was a saint. His great skill and admirable effort editing the *Revista* did not replace his virtues and burning zeal to infuse the human race, through his writings, for the salvation of souls. Anyone who knew him saw his simplicity, humility, and kindness; they saw a religious model and an edifying observer of obedience to his superiors and religious companions.

After another term at the Jesuits' College, I went home. About three or four years earlier, Francisco Crestino was born, this boy had a disposition of kind, innocent simplicity. He left us many memories about his brief life. He barely completed six years of age [circa 1886], when he was taken by

Pablo's daughter Martina and his nephew Frank Trambley at Hot Springs, New Mexico, ca. 1908.

Pablo and his second wife, Candelaria Trambley, with their son Carlos in Mora, New Mexico, ca. 1925.

a terrible smallpox epidemic. At his tender age, this boy won the community's appreciation by his graciousness to everyone, his greatest pleasure was giving coins to the old men and poor children of the village. As soon as he saw a poor person approaching our house, he ran to Mamá and he asked her for something to give the beggars, he got great satisfaction by doing this. He shared his candies with the neighborhood children, or whatever he brought, even a piece of bread. One day, he met a boy without a hat. It seemed to hurt him, so he took off his hat and gave it to the poor child. Mamá cried at the sight of this act.

He was just as loving with little animals. His favorites were two cats who had followed him since they were kittens. At his play table, they always sat on the arms of an immense chair made by a native carpenter, it was so rustic and strong that it could support the weight of a baby elephant. He fed them there and talked with them and they were very attentive, but they were not able to serve themselves. It was curious how these animals always knew their place since each one sat on their customary side. As time passed, this affable boy enchanted everyone he met, but a bitter cloud darkened his future until it stopped his very existence.

It was a dry summer of almost unbearable heat; the dawn sky was a magnificent blue, without the smallest cloud or any indication of rain. The sun shone brilliantly amid a most silent calm; the only movement was a slow, soft breeze withering the crops and all other vegetation. By mid-summer, the heat was most intense. Little by little, the terrible pestilence of smallpox reached a point that the cries of dying victims could be heard everywhere. There was no recourse to doctors, no drugstores, the people knew very little about patent medicines. But fortunately, Mamá was known as a charitable lady who never refused the needy poor asking for help during their illnesses and appealing to their liberal charity. God endowed her with enough knowledge about illnesses that she generally guessed right in prescribing them medications which, in general, consisted of native herbs or roots.

It was during this smallpox epidemic that, despite the great danger of the infection, she offered God her service to relieve the poor and needy. She never lost a chance to visit as many sick persons as she could, and thanks to Divine Providence, she was able to heal many of the people she assisted. The plague wrecked so much havoc and it made giant strides taking one, two, three, and even four victims from each house. Until then, Mamá had avoided infection in the family by using disinfectants and other necessary precautions. But, God's will did not permit us to escape everything; in his higher designs, there was already one selected from our house.

One day, the child Francisco awoke with a strong fever. Hours later, he was covered with so many pustules that his face and entire body had a complete layer. He stayed in this condition for some days, the fever got worse and his strength drained away day by day. Finally, the boy became grave, and he looked pale. But he silently and gently opened his defeated eyes, he gave one glance around, and he fixed on Mamá with a pleading stare. And he soon closed them never to reopen them, he died like blowing out a candle. After he was dead and already set in his coffin, Mamá allowed us to see that little, heavenly Angel from the doorway for some moments. As we looked, all broke into grievous screams because we were moved that his faithful friends, the cats, seemed to understand his misfortune. They circled the table sadly scratching the legs of the table where the coffin lay and crying in a gesture of true feeling.

This boy was buried inside the chapel at La Cuesta on the left side of the cross-vault and immediately alongside our grandfather, Don Jesús C. de Baca, who died in 1890 at the age of eighty-one years old, after becoming paralyzed for a year. By his own admission, grandfather had never suffered a previous illness in his life, and he had never spent a day in bed.

In the College of Las Vegas

Due to changes or deals occurring in the Santa Fé Diocese, the reverend Jesuit priests were ordered to leave the state, and close their college in Las Vegas. And, in 1890, they opened a new school in the city of Denver named Sacred Heart College. It was a majestic gray-stone building constructed with magnificent living rooms, general study areas, chemistry labs, classrooms, an elegant refectory [dining room], and a kitchen. The top floor held a spacious dormitory divided in two sections accommodating 250 students in four housing units. In one section, six- to fifteen-year-olds lived, and the other section accommodated youths from sixteen to twenty years of age. On the second floor, the reverend Jesuit priests had their private rooms and a beautiful chapel where Holy Mass was celebrated every day. It was here that I had the happy luck to witness the ordination of two priests who received the Jesuit habit; one of them was my chum, Father José Garde, a *mejicano* from Mexico City.

I attended the first year that the college opened up. The term spent there was very happy, I took full advantage of my time, and I still have pleasing memories, even now. While there, I won the seat of honor as the Captain, or first, of my class. And, in recognition of the honor, I sat beside the professor on a separate bench labeled "LEADER" in golden letters indicating the position. All the students, anxiously and forcefully, tried to replace me in that position, but I did not lose it because I stayed clever and was always prepared in class.

Mischiefs and exploits are never lacking in school. On a certain vacation day, we planned an escape to the city some three miles from the college. Nine of us boys fled, one after another, along a concealed, alfalfa-covered fence. When we got to the road, we considered ourselves out of danger of being seen by our superiors. We continued walking until we arrived at the station of "Motor Cars" (small trains) that traveled from Berkely Lake to Elitch Gardens where the famous Sells-Floto Circus floats spent the winter season. From there, we used "transfer tickets" to ride the cable cars that carried us to the city. Arriving at Denver, we divided into groups of two or three so we would not look like an army or a band of hunters.

We agreed to reunite at a certain place, at a certain hour, and we agreed to wait there until everyone appeared. During our return, we were cheerful and satisfied about our good time. We did not think about the stiff consequences or feel remorse for the deception of our daring and shameless little trip. Approaching school, our anguish began, then we trembled as we got closer, finally, we had no remedy to excuse the crime. Oh, how that afternoon cost us dearly in penance exercises suffered in payment for that little walk! After all, it seemed to us that the excursion was too short considering the high price that we were sentenced to pay.

We cautiously approached the college thinking we could arrive without being discovered. But "*Camotes*" [rascals], the priests already knew and the whole school had already been told of our silly *diplomacia*. We were taken to the Prefect of the College, without the slightest courtesy, where we were received with words that felt like steel tips. Later, Father Superior interrogated us about our actions; then, he sent us back to the Prefect who swiftly imposed the punishment that we received. First, we were deprived of dinner that afternoon (I believe that, perhaps, we had already eaten well in the city). Second, we could not speak to anyone for three days and we were separated from other students and slept in the infirmary. Third, we only ate bread and water for the three days of isolation. Fourth, during the fifteen-minute recess, we marched while the other boys played; we watched them from a distance and our punishment served as a warning to them. Fifth, another punishment had us once line up from youngest to oldest at the door of Father Mandalari, the Prefect of the College. Then, he called us one by one, locked the door with a key from the inside, and he applied about fifteen lashes with a Black Snake [whip]. Four comrades had received this punishment, the rest of us agreed to resist it completely. So we left there, we reported to Father Superior Persone, and we complained about this punishment. At last, he took our just complaint into consideration and he suspended the whipping punishment.

Upon finishing school, my brother Fulgencio came to get me in Denver, and we spent a few days in the city. And then, we returned to my parents' side at La Cuesta. After a season there, I decided to start a business. I communicated with Eugenio "Güero" Baca, my cousin in Las Vegas, so we could become the two "Wayfarers." I got a horse and cart from Papá and my companion got another horse for our trip. We then bought a selection of goods and we went out to trade. After visiting some nearby villages, we went to Puerto de Luna where Eugenio's brother lived and we stayed there two days. Then, we traveled to the town of Salado, in January [1892], and we were caught in a snowstorm of twelve to fifteen inches. We spent four days there in poor accommodations and the snow had not decreased at all. My companion and I impatiently determined that we had to leave so we went in the direction of his brother-in-law's ranch located about ten miles away. It was late and impossible to walk faster than the slow step of the horses. The more we walked, the higher the snow got. The road was nowhere to be seen so we walked in the direction of a narrow canyon. In normal conditions, it might have taken us perhaps two hours to get there, but then, the sun had set long before, and the stars began to shine.

The cold seemed to get colder with each step. We thought that walking would warm us from the exercise; indeed, we sweated. But fatigue forced us to get back on the cart. Since our feet were already very wet, we took off the shoes and wrapped our feet in a blanket. But, a little later, the cold was so intense that we could not move. We no longer paid attention to the direction that the horses took; we simply double-tied the rein to the cart. It was impossible to move an arm or even fingers, we wanted to speak though we were hardly able, so we only looked at each other.

With great difficulty, we could laugh; however, it is known that laughing is a sure sign of a person freezing to death. We were already expecting death since nothing thereabouts indicated any recourse to avoid our sad situation. In a little while, we would soon be victims of the plains where we would later serve as food to the country beasts; in two or three more days, the coyotes would be there fighting over our flesh. Thinking about all this failed to improve our situation, but what else could we do since we had no strength. Moving an arm was impossible, our hands were cold stiff; talking was impossible, the jaws were stiff. We could hardly move our eyes to see one another and this only caused us further anguish. However, looking at each other caused involuntary laughter that made us suffer even more due to the effort we used in moving the jaws. So we slowly went onward, no longer hoping to find someone who would help us, but rather awaiting the moment of dying frozen.

Maybe it was after midnight when we seemed to hear the distant howl of some dogs; and, at the same time, we noticed that our faithful horses had continued walking throughout the snowstorm. We also saw them raise their ears to the barking dogs and it seemed that they picked up the pace; for a good while, we no longer heard the dogs bark. And again, the deathly, deep silence of the night continued and the livid light of distant stars adorned the sky as they seemed to stand out of fright upon feeling the intense night cold. So we continued silently at a slow pace on the road; again, I heard the dogs barking more clearly and we knew people nearby would help us.

Oh, what joy, what great consolation, what sublime encouragement we felt upon seeing a weak, intermittent, little light appearing in the distant brush, that seemed to disappear between a large mountain and the persistent, whipping night wind. Briefly, we lost sight of it and we were anxiously waiting to see it again. Once we were fully alert, a mysterious, inner impulse assured us that we approached rescue.

With all the truth in our hearts, we lifted our eyes to heaven to give infinite thanks to God, who liberated us from that seemingly inevitable, icy death that we were already expecting at any moment. But, the mercy of God was greater than the weak faith that we could not resist, the Lord must have heard the prayers of our good and holy mothers who prayed for us, their absent children, who were separated from their paternal home for the first time.

Again, I saw it shining and the little light appeared more brilliant, it undoubtedly came from the large mountain. We fixed our view on the light's source and soon we followed it to a small house distinguished in the dark night, we no longer lost sight of it. As we approached, we saw it more clearly. The dogs already had heard the noise of the cart and they were barking in an annoying, continuous tone. We rather liked and encouraged their continuous bragging which indicated our arrival, giving us new strength and new enthusiasm. With desperate anxiety, we wanted to arrive sooner to get up and leave the cart. Oh, but this was impossible, everything in our being seemed to handicap movement, everything in our body was paralyzed, even the blood in our veins seemed frozen stiff like a stick. Without the help of any human being, undoubtedly we would have been lost during that night of anguish. The little house emitting the light was, in fact, an improvised hut built temporarily on the ranch owned by Don Jesús Casados, a rich farmer and powerful cattleman in that area. He was precisely the brother-in-law of my companion. There were three or four men in that house who were building a house of residence for Don Jesús. For us, God permitted these unknown gentlemen to be the proper cause of and the path for our salvation from premature death. God worked this, and it was not mere chance as those of so little faith think, but we who saw things clearest had no doubt that it was God's work and that chance had nothing to do with it.

When we were near the house, it was necessary to leave the road and drive down some distance in order to arrive there. We wanted to direct movement and change direction toward the house, but, *caramba*, it was impossible for us to move! We could not even speak, we had stiff jaws and our tongues did not articulate at all. But the beasts' instinct did not need us in the slightest to direct them toward the house's door. And upon arriving, they stopped in front of the door. The noise of the carriage and the desperate barks of the dogs caused the three or four alarmed men to come out and see who had arrived there at that late hour of the night.

And they asked, "Who lives? Who is it? What is there? What do you want?" Nobody responded. We could hear, but we could not speak, we could not even control ourselves. At last, they determined to approach the cart and see what it contained. And there they found us, already more dead than alive. Lifting our dead weight, they took us inside the house. They spread us over a bed on the floor, then quickly stoked the fire and heated water. They washed our face and hands, then they gave us hot coffee to drink. Little by little, we thawed without getting too close to the fire. By means of rubbing us with hot water and violent exercise of our arms, we recovered a normal state and complete health again.

After being there a short time, everything changed, everything was joyful and pleasant and we celebrated the "Nerrow Scape [sic]." Meanwhile, we waited for the bad time to pass, we were lucky to get work there constructing the house for about six or eight days. And when the time finally permitted, we left in the direction of Las Vegas. After Don Jesús had taken such good care of us at his ranch, he paid us very well for the work that we had done by filling our wagon with salted meat; and upon arriving at Las Vegas, we sold them at the house of Gross, Kelly & Co.

At St. Michael's College

The college was directed by the La Salle Christian Brothers. It was the first teaching institution established in New Mexico by the arduous, painful efforts and costing a thousand sacrifices of our worthy and illustrious Most Excellent Archbishop Lamy. It was in this institution where I had the happy luck to continue my studies, thanks to the sacrifices that my father made for the education of me and my siblings. We never lost that inheritance and, at the same time, we were taught the best Christian education under the guidance and careful efforts of good religious clergy.

In the time that I attended this school, I witnessed an unpleasant spectacle five blocks away from the front of the College. The State Capitol gave a very beautiful dimension to the city of Santa Fé. As seen from the College's second floor balcony, this grandiose building, that had cupolas adorned with elegant bronze statues, was the pride of the city.

One day, the fire alarm sounded about eight or nine in the morning. The entire city went into motion upon hearing the news that the fire was in the Capitol. The brothers could not stop the noisy boys and they finally gave them permission to go to the upper floors of the dormitory. From the windows, we could see the terrible fire that quickly destroyed the beautiful building. The fire began on two exterior sides or in the cupolas that were at each edge of the building. These margins were lined with enormous bronze statues which melted in the flames and dripped distinctively colored, molten balls that we saw falling suddenly from these. Later, it was said that the building had been set on fire for political reasons because someone wanted to change the capital to Albuquerque; however, I do not know this myself. A new building now occupies the same place although it is not as elegant but very roomy.

I left before finishing the school term because Papá had been elected to the San Miguel County Commission and he had to change residence to Las Vegas. And it became necessary that I stay at La Cuesta to take care of the family goods and property until they made other business arrangements. After Papá finished his term as commissioner, I worked at E. G. Murphey's Pharmacy for ten years at the Old Town Plaza in Las Vegas. Before and after I got married, the working hours were very long; for example, my companion and I arrived at seven o'clock in the morning and stayed all day until ten at night. And we only had half a day on Sunday to rest—this discouraged me from continued employment as a druggist.

PASA TIEMPOS DE LA VIDA:
HISTORITA EDICIÓN ECONÓMICA POR EL HOMBRE
DE POCAS LETRAS
Pablo Cabeza de Baca y Delgado

Primera, Unica y Ultima Edición Existente.
Mora, Nuevo México
Enero, 2 del Año del Señor 1935

REFLEJOS

Dedicada a mis Hijos, seres queridos, que Dios se ha dignado poner bajo mi cargo.

INTRODUCCIÓN

Esta historita ha sido escrita para ustedes mis hijos y fuera de las travesuras, probablemente encontrareis algo de provecho que os pueda dirigiros mas tarde, cuando hallan entrado al use de razón.   Presentándoles las actividades de la vida a su alrededor, su comportamiento con su prójimo, y el respecto y lealtad a su Santa Religión.

Pablo C. de Baca

PRELUDIO

Este libro que os presento con la simple historia de un iliterato compositor con el único ideal de pasar reflejos de la vida de el autor de sus días. Habeis visto que un herrero sea el propio mecánico para componer un reloj? Sería cosa absurda creerlo, pues tal caso se presenta aquí al querer yo redactar una Historia no teniendo el menor conocimiento de historiador, por lo tanto os advierto no tomeis lo que aquí escribo para criticarlo unicamente he dedicado mi tiempo a escribir no para llamar atención al mundo, simplemente pretendo hacer algunas notaciones del trascurso de mi simple vida no para que lo sepa el mundo, sino y unicamenta para llamarles atención a mis hijos que tal vez no tendrán la dicha de crecer antes de realizar o guardar alguna memoria de su padre y al escribir esto siente desvanecerse sus fuerzas y tal vez el Señor en sus insolvables misterios tiene marcado mi desenlace de esta vida precoz y pasajera.   Más, quién puede desconfiar de la divina Misericordia de Dios que no tan solo sana al enfermo sino da la vida a los muertos.   Y ahora estimados seres lo que escribo espero lo acepten dispensandome la infinidad de errores que en ello encontrareis.

P. Cabeza de Baca y Delgado

EN UN SOLITARIO rancho anteriormente conocido bajo el nombre de SANTA CLARA donde unicamente residían unas tres o cuatro familias a quienes pertenecía como mercenarios dicho lugar hoy lo conocemos por el nombre de Wagon Mound; dicho lugar está situado al noroeste del estado de Nuevo México y a una distancia de cuarenta y cinco millas de la plaza de Mora cabezera de dicho condado de Mora. Una de estas familias de los originales pobladores de este sitio eran mis padres don Francisco C. de Baca y la señora Martina Delgado que un año después de su matrimonio se habían trasladado allí, procedentes de la Villa de Santa Fé. Allí, mi padre se había dedicado al criadero de ganado mayor y llegó a aumentar su hacienda de reces a considerable número. Uno de estos residentes, (el hijo de don Gervasio Nolan), don Fernando Nolan, tío de mi padre, reclamaba la mayor parte de dicha Merced da Santa Clara. Hay en este lugar una inmensa vega que pertenecía a los habitantes y la corta de zacate que allí hacian la entregaban bajo contrato a las tropas del gobierno, que por aquellos entonces estaban estacionadas a corta distancia de allí, en el Fuerte Union y por este medio se hicieron buenas ganancias.

Don Fernando Nolan, abogado por profesión, se consideraba y efectivamente poseia bastantes bienes y dinero efectivo. Hombre intrépido y adicto a bebidas alcohólicas, que al tomarlas se revistía de valor insuperable para combatir un ejército. Con el trascurso del tiempo todo cambia. En su vejez debilitaron sus fuerzas, sus bienes y recursos se agotaron, murió pobre, y casi en la miseria, en la plaza de Santa Fé.

Después de algunos años de vivir en Santa Clara, mi padre cambió de residencia; trasladose de allí para Las Vegas donde estableció una comisaria; era durante un tiempo de carestia, y los viveres habían alcanzado alarmantes proporciones. El saco de harina llegó a valer ocho pesos. Más tarde los Romeros emplearon a papá como mayordomo en su hacienda de Romeroville, ó el Puertecito, como anteriormente se llamaba. Cuando la linea del Santa Fé se estaba construyendo, mandaron a papá para la Cuesta en el río de Pecos para que tomase cargo del comercio que acababan de establecer allí. Era el tiempo que se construia la línea del Santa Fé de Las Vegas a Santa Fé el año de 1880. La Cuesta fue lugar de prosperidad durante este tiempo de construcción en esta línea ferrea donde se ocupaba tanta gente en la producción de tallas que se cortaban en San Miguel, Rivera, San José y la Cuesta. Después que hubo terminado el trabajo de esta línea, papá les compró el comercio y se quedó allí donde vivimos por más de 14 años donde pasé yo los mejores años de mi vida.

En 1865, Francisco C. de Baca de Peña Blanca se uñió en Santo Matrimonio con Martina Delgado y Nolan de la Villa de Santa Fé, de cuyo estado tuvieron trece hijos: Maria (1), Refugio (2), Gregorita (3), Fulgencio (4), Miguel (5), Pablo (6), Juan (7), Aurelio (8), Francisco Jr. (9), Hipólito (10), Dolores (11), Erinea (12), and Arsenio (13).

Gregorita: La Inocente Angel

Gregorita, niña de 2 a 3 años, en un día de verano, se devertía en el portal de la casa, donde su mamá se ocupada en lavar ropa, a esto que se llegada la hora del medio día, la mamá creendo que la niña se estaría bien allí, se fue descuidadamente a la cocina para preparar la comida, no había trascurrido quizá una media hora, cuando salió mamá para dar vuelta a la niña, cuando: "O, que horror!" La niña había desaparecido del sitio aquel, de pronto la busca por toda la casa y los alrededores sin encontrarla, pronto de parte a todos los de la casa y vecinos, y todos se dan prisa en buscarla. Había muchos quien la buscaban, mas nadie podía imaginarse donde estaría; de repente que corren para acá o allá, la madre da una mirada hacía uno de los cajetes que estaban allí donde lavaba, y un lance de dolor traspasa su corazón y exclamando: "Jesús Mío, qué es esto!" Precipitadamente se lanza aquel sitio y con angustia y desesperación, dando gritos de dolor, toma a la niña en sus brazos, muerta, muerta estaba! Se había ahogada; quizo abansar con ella en sus brazos, pero siente que se le corta el aliento, desfallecen todas sus fuerzas, la violencia del dolor en aquellos instantes, penetra por todas sus venas; siente deslizarse como el rayo veloz, todos sus sentidos hasta caer desmayada en profundo delirio, y así permanece por largo espacio sin darse cuenta de lo que pasaba en aquellos momentos terribles. Cuando ya vuelve en sí, se halla en cama, abre sus ojos, extiende su vista al rededor del aposento, y sobre una mecita rodiada de flores y velas encendidas, ve el palido cadaver de su inocente angel, que parece sonreirse con los angeles del cielo.

Miguel: El Ladroncito del Cielo

Niño de pocos años de edad, quizo Dios aumentar el coro de sus angeles con tan hermoso y amable niño, con nombre tan singular, que apenas vivía suficiente para dejarnos lividos recuerdos de su tierna infancia.

Pablo

Nació Pablo el 2 de Febrero de 1874 en Santa Clara. Fuí bautizado en Mora, por el Rev. Padre Guerín asistiendo de padrinos Don Atilano Abeyta y Señora Dolores Lalande, residentes de La Cueva. Cuando yo nací, mi tío Don Fernando Nolan, que la tiraba por adivinó (mas, lo hacía por pasa tiempo) pronosticó que yo llegaría a ser un Marinero. No sé yo en que significado tomar tal pronostico; lo cierto es que no hay cosa que yo tema más extremadamente que el agua, apenas el uso para lavarme. Tiemblo me coja una lluvia fuera de casa, encontrar un río crecido o acercarme a una laguna. Y hasta pocos años ya, tuve la dicha por decirlo así de conocer los lagos Michigan, Erie, y atravesar el Río Hudson y pasar a la grán ciudad de Nueva York de que más tarde los hablaré.

Tal vez Don Fernando quería decir que yo sería un Marinero que tenía que navegar por las tormentas y las interperies de la vida mundana, combatiendo peligros de hundirse en las malas tentaciones y engaños que nos ofrece el mundo pasajero. Este sin duda será el mar que tendré que navegar y constantemente vigilar mi barquia para que no naufrague, para que un día amanesca tan dichoso que pueda conducir mi barca al puerto de salvación donde me espera mí Capitán.

En 1878 que cumplía yo 4 años de edad se construía la línea ferrea del Santa Fé, la cual atrevesaba por parte del terreno de papá y que tuvo que vender juntamente con los demás dueños de la Merced de Santa Clara. De allí nos trasportamos para Las Vegas, donde papá estableció residencia y una comisaria de abarrotes. No sé si por razón de carestia de escases de grano, o a causa del "Boom" que causaba la construcción de la línea, la harina había subido de precio y se vendía el saco por ocho pesos.

Los Señores Romeros, que en esos tiempos gozaban de gran fortuna y se consideraban ser los mas fuertes comerciantes y cabezias políticos del Condado de San Miguel, parecían ser el eje principal de todo el tráfico de Las Vegas y sitios adyacentes. Poco despúes la Compañía de los Romeros ocupó a papá para que tomase cargo de una de sus comisarias que tenían en Romeroville y cargo general de todo el rancho de Romeroville donde hacía las veces de Mayordomo.

Hoy día aun se ve por toda la cumbre de la montaña un cerco de piedra que comienza a la boca del cañoncito, sube por la cima de la montaña en dirección a Santa Rosa, ocupando un trecho de 60 millas. Fue papá quien condujó este gigantesco trabajo hace más de cincuenta años.

Mientras tanto que papá trabajaba y afanaba en estas ocupaciones, mis hermanos mayores atendían a la escuela privada que conducía un maestro afuereño Español que había hecho venir Don Trinidad Romero espresamente para la educación de sus hijos, mis hermanos y algunos otros les permetían atender esta escuela. Yo que todavía estaba muy chico para atender a la escuela y algunos otros pequeñuelos de mi camada, nos pasábamos el tiempo en divertirnos. A pezar de mi corta edad entonces, recuerdo muy bien nuestro juego favorito que era el descalzarnos, remangar el pantalón y meternos a un poso o estanque forma de lagunita cerca de la casa. En días de vacación, nos acompañaban los otros muchachos y pasábamos el día en la lagunita pescando ranas, y tepocates, los que pretendíamos venderlos en el mercado. Mi hermano mayor y otro vecino figuraban comerciar en carnes raras de animales de las especies mencionadas: ranas, sapos y tepocates. Al llegar nosotros allí con una carga de estos, pronto los vendíamos y recebíamos nuestro dinero, en efectivo papel, botones o guijarros, los comerciantes en seguida se ponían a descuartizar aquellos pobres animalitos, y colgaban patas y costillares en su carnicería, tal como se ve en las carnicerías grandes.

Cuando el trabajo de la línea ferrea había pasado de Romeroville, los negocios se mejoraban mas adelante, y los Romeros que tenían un comercio en La Cuesta, en el valle del Río de Pecos, determinaron mandar a papá allí que tomará cargo del comercio. (La Cuesta a causa de cambios de estafeta se le han cambiado diversos nombres; se ha llamado: Concho, Aragón, y a la presente se le nombra Villa Nueva.)

Aquí en este lugar pasé la mayor parte de mi juventud, y por su puesto los mejores días de mi vida bajo el cuidado de mi cariciosa y buena madre, que sacrificaba su vida por el amor de sus hijos, la madre que es la Maestra Cariñosa del hogar, donde se aprende la buena crianza, se infunde la Fé, Esperanza, y la Caridad del Cristiano. Es el fundamento y pedestal perene en que se basé el porvenir de la juventud cristiana, y al paso que se instruye en la Fé, se va educado en el trabajo que más tarde le será útil en la vida. Mamá se esmeraba en enseñarnos a hacer bien los quehaceres de la casa, y hacerlo con aseo, tal como limpiar un cuarto, poner las camas en regla, en la cocina cocinar, y fregar trastos. Luego en los trabajos de afuera, y así nos decía y nos hacía comprender que el trabajo no era ninguna afrenta por humilde o desagradable que sea, y nos decía, "Cuando ya sean hombres, y si le hacen a ser ricos, no les estorbará haber aprendido, por que más bien podran mandar, y si fuesen pobres les será también de utilidad." Así pues que con gusto hacíamos lo que se nos mandaba, yo y mis hermanos aprendimos a barrer, a cocinar, alsar las camas, partir leña, traerla del monte, y acarrear agua.

Por vivir nosotros en la cima de una loma, era necesario traer el agua en un carro en dos o tres barriles. Como el camino era pesado y pedregoso, a veces el tiro se machaba. Y entonces, "O, que trabajo," que de mucho había que trabajar, tantas veces tuvimos que vaciar los barriles. Los Veranos atendíamos a la labor escardando y regando, a veces descalzos cuando se trataba de regar una milpa de maíz. Así pues que entonces y ahora, no me da verguenza hacer toda clase de trabajo por funesto que sea. Refiero esto, por que me recuerdo que mi hermano mayor le repugnaba mucho cuando le tocaba tener que hacer algo de los negocios de la cama, o tener que barrer. Decía, "Esto me da mucha verguenza pensará la gente que soy mujer. Mamacita, mandeme partir leña todo el día mejor que todo esto." Sin embargo, no dejaba de hacerlo. Al acabar los quehaceres de la casa o fuera de ella, ya estábamos libres para nuestros juegos, o trabasuras que quisieramos, pero siempre bajo la vigilancia de mamá, que veia que nuestros juegos fueran buenos.

En la misma casa de residencia donde vivíamos, que era una habitación espaciosa y construida en forma de plazuela, había en uno de los costados al lado noreste, dos salas, la una servía para tienda y lo que llaman los bolios, "warehouse." Así es que papá, y a veces todos los de la familia atendíamos y ayudábamos a papá en la tienda. Allí aprendí desde muy chico el oficio de cayero, a los diez años de edad, yo podía quedarme solo en el comercio en ocasiones que papá y la familia hacían un viaje a Las Vegas.

En esta población de La Cuesta, en aquellos tiempos, carecíamos de buenas escuelas. Y por lo general, se ocupaban maestros del mismo lugar, viejitos que tenían un poquito de conocimiento de las letras. Nuestros libros eran la cartilla donde se nos hacía recitar a todos en voz alta, y con un sonsonete cantante el: Ba-ba, Be-be, Bi-bi, Bo-bo, Bu-bu. Luego: Ca-ca, Ce-ce, Ci-ci, Co-co, Cu-cu, y así. Y luego empezando en tres sílabas: Ban-ban, Ben-ben, Bin-bin, Bon-bon, Bun-bun. Y nuestro salon de escuela era nada menos que un jacal lobrego y oscuro consuelo de tierra que a propósito escarbábamos con los pies para levantar todo el polvo para ahogar al maestro Matias, que siempre estaba enbavucado debajo sus antiparras escribiendo o leyendo algún libro o en un almanaque. Cierto día que el maestro se hallaba de mal humor, y yo no sabía mi lección, me coje, me da una pela, luego me hace ir al rincón del "Burro" donde está un cajon, me para arriba y me pone la gorra con orejas de Burro. La gorra consistía en una tira de papel enrollado en forma de cornocopia y como viente pulgadas de alto. Al terminar la escuela, me dice, "Tendrás que ir conmigo a tu casa," como en efecto lo hizo. Y allí, le dice a mi padre, "Don Francisco, mejor es que no mande más este muchacho a la escuela. Es un burro, nunca aprenderá nada." Mis padres resientieron mucho aquello, y no volví jamás a su escuela.

Desde entonces, papá determinó poner remedio al sistema de educación y logró conseguirse nos proporcionaran buenos maestros. Así el siguiente término de escuela tengo el gran placer de decir que mi maestro fue don

Ezequiel C. de Baca (primo hermano de papá), quien más tarde fue Gobernador de Nuevo Mexico. Como el maestro Baca se asestía en nuestra casa, tuve la ventaja de aprovechar bien mi tiempo, puesto que el me ayudaba en las noches, así que el Burro al fin del término se hallaba a la cabeza de todos.

Al año siguiente también tuvimos la feliz suerte de tocarnos otro buen maestro quien iba dirijido allí con las mejores recomendaciones, era este don Milnor Rudulph Jr. procedente de Rociada, Nuevo Mexico. O, y quién había de pensar, que este Señor mas tarde llegaría a ser mi cuñado, al casarme yo con su hermana menor después que muchos años mas tarde, conocí la familia.

En estos dos términos de escuela había yo hecho buen progreso en mis estudios, bajo el buen principio que había logrado aprender de tan expertos y dignos maestros. Al terminar este último término, papá pensó mandarme al Colegio de los Jesuitas en Las Vegas, donde entré de "Days Scholar" y me asistía en casa de mi tía Erinea (Delgado de Romero), hermana de mamá. Al principio me pareció muy rígido la disciplina del Colegio, más con el tiempo y la introducción con los muchachos y muchos primos que tenía entre los familias de los Romeros, todo pasaba bien. Y naturalmente, no faltaban las trabasuras entre la plebe, y algunas de estas nos llegaron a costar buen precio como cuando se nos descrubría de haber jugado "Hookey." Es como dice el antiguo dicho: "La maldad es como el maiz, solita sale." Por lo general siempre se nos cojia en estas.

Era una de estas trabasuras la que ahora les contaré. Sería a mediados de un riguroso invierno, al salir para la escuela nos íbamos juntando dos, tres, cuatro, y más, los primos o amigos para ir de paso en el camino hacia la escuela divirtiendonos en alguna de nuestras acostumbradas diversiones, ya jugando al Trompo, jugando a la Bolita, o Hop Scotch. Cuando ya nos habíamos juntado todos, a uno de los compañeros se le ocurré la idea de jugar "Hookey" ese día. Y nos dice, "Hola, muchachos, vamos a patinar a la Laguna de la Cervezería, que fine está el hielo, lo vi esta mañana que venía, que dices, Hilario?" "Fine for me, yo sí boy si bas tú. Y tú Felipe, nos acompañas?" "Pues, seguro que sí, soy soldado razo, y donde quiera que ba el Capitán, mi obligación es seguirle." Así es que vamos todos: Pablo, Hilario, Felipe, Eugenio, y Federico. Eugenio dice, "Y qué hacemos sin patines? Así no costea ir, que diga el Capitán, que hacemos?" El Capitán dice, "Well boys, tenemos que ir cada uno a su casa y con achaque que olvidamos algun libro, el catecismo, la geografía, o la aritmetica, sacamos los patines a las escondidas, luego nos juntaremos todos allá en la laguna." Todos a la vez gritamos, "Fine, fine. Viva el Capitán!" Y al momento partimos todos corriendo cada quien a su casa.

Al rato, todos estábamos allí con nuestros patines. Reymundo Lopez era el "Champion" patinador, formaba circulos, cuadros, o figuras en el hielo y aun escrebía su nombre sobre el hielo, todos queríamos seguirle en sus hazanas. Por allá en una orilla del lago, había un agujero hecho a propósito con el fin de observar el grueso del hielo; era este un agujero de doce pulgadas de diámetro, un palo al lado marcaba sistematicamente el grueso según crecía o desmunuia y de allí pendía un letroro muy facil de notar, para que nadie se asercase allí, "DANGER." Se le ocurre a Reymundo y nos dice: "Vamos dando vueltas allí al rededor de este, haber quien llega mas cerca."

Uno tras otro, le seguimos vuelta y vuelta. Yo (Pablo) viendo que todos se quedaban bastante atrás temiendo acercarse, quiero sacarme el Championship, armo vuelo quiero dar la vuelta, pero . . . Zas! ******Vi ****** estrellitas, me sampé hasta los sobacos. Que al haber sido más grande el agujero, me hubiera hundido debajo del hielo, y no estubiera contandoles este gran chasco. De allí me sacaron los compañeros, helandome de frío todo mojado escurriendome el agua a dando diente con diente. No podía irme a casa porque descubrirían el complot. Determinan los compañeros juntar lena y hacer una lumbrada allí al borde de la laguna, y secarme allí la ropa. Luego que formaron una buena lumbrada, yo me calentaba de un lado mientras el otro se me volvía a helar; de un lado me quemaba, del otro me helaba. Por fin cuando ya creía estar seco, caramba, mi ropa estaba toda quemada, al tocarla se caiva en pedazos.

Ahora si, que hacer? Toditos nos acordamos de la desobediencia, habíamos faltado a la escuela, habíamos enganado a nuestros padres, al maestro, y a todos. Yo no podía ir solo a casa porque temblaba de pies a cabeza y sentía mi cuerpo asado el las brazas como cuando se asa un costillar de carne sobre un brazero. Era preciso ir a la casa y reportarme culpable. Algunos de los compañeros me acompañan hasta la casa. Y al llegar allí, ya mi tía sabía toda la historia, no sé de que manera, pero ya me esperaba otro brazero de azotes con un latigo a cabestro doblado en dos. Más tarde cuando llega mi tío Margarito (Romero y Delgado) de su trabajo en la tienda, se informa de la ocurrencia y tras de cuernos palos, una buena represión de el que nunca la he olvidado.

Después que terminó la escuela y con ella todas las travesuras que mesclamos en sus entremedios, papá me dejo a cargo del muy buen Padre Ferrari, redactor de *La Revista Catolica*. Allí, me ocupaba en poner tipo y imprimir Novenas. Temblaba los días que teníamos que imprimir *La Revista*, miles de ejemplares tenían que pasar por aquella imprenta, la cual tenía yo y otro compañero que correrla por medio de siguena, que consistía en una gran rueda pesada a la cual teníamos que tirar dándonos un rato de remuda el uno al otro. Luego tomar las tiras de papel, doblarlos en forma de libro encuadernarlas, las que tenían que salir por correo, que enrollarlas, y ponerles un papelito engomado con la dirección, ponerlas en unas canastas y llevarlas a la estafeta una distancia de cosa de un cuarto de milla. Después nos quedaban las que había que distribuir en la plaza, estas teníamos que distribuir casa por casa los sabados. Mucho aprendí y aprecie del bueno y santo Padre Ferrari, era nada menos que un Santo, tan humilde y bondadosoviviendo una vida de penitencia y oración. Nunca se veia salir de la imprenta a no ser una gran necesidad y al salir a la plaza con algun negocio de importancia, nunca le vimos salir sin su vieja y descolorida sotana que parecía crecer con él. Mucho podría yo contar de él, pero me limito a dar esta corta descripción de él, que no necesita de elojios, pues como antes dije, era un Santo. Su gran ciencia y admirable actividad que mostraba en la redacción de *La Revista* no superaba a sus virtudes y ardiente celo que deseaba infundir al genero humano por medio de sus escritos para la salvación de las almas. Y todos los que se ponían en contacto con él, veian en el su sencillez, humildad, y bondad; veian un religioso modelo y edificación en la observancia de obedencia hacia sus superiores y compañeros religiosos.

Después de otro término que pasé en el Colegio de los Jesuitas allí, me fui a casa. Tal vez unos tres o cuatro años antes había nacido Francisco Crestino, niño que era de indole, amable, inocente, sencillez. Nos dejo muchos recuerdos de su corta vida; apenas cumplía seis años de edad cuando fue acojido por la terrible plaga de la viruela. A su tierna edad, este niño supo grangiarse el aprecio de la vecindad, por su afabilidad con todos, su mayor placer era el dar limosnas a los ancianos y niños pobres de la aldea. En cuanto veia acercarse un pobre a su casa, corría hacia donde estaba mamá, y le rogaba le diese algo que llevarle a su limosnero. Era una gran satisfación para el hacer esto. Con los niños del varrio, compartía con sus dulces, o lo que solía traer con sigo, aun un pedazo de pan.

Un día que se encuentra con un niño sin sombrero parese darle lástima, se quitá su sombrero y lo da al pobrecito. Este acto hizo vertir lágrimas a mamá que lo veia en el acto. Lo mismo era de carinoso con los animalitos. Sus favoritos fueron unos dos gatos acostumbrados desde chiquitos a seguirle. En su mesa, nunca faltaron uno de cada lado sobre los brazos de un inmenzo cilleton que le había hecho un carpintero del país, tan rústico y balumoso que bien podía soportar el peso de un "Baby Elephant." Allí los alimentaba y conversaba con ellos y los gatos muy atentos, pero no eran capaces de servirse solos, curioso que estos animalitos siempre sabían su lugar cada uno su lado acostumbrado.

En tanto trascurría el tiempo este niño tan afable encantaba a cuantos le conocían, mas una nube de amargura vino a oscureser su porvenir hasta poner fin a su existencia. Era un verano seco, de calores casi insoportables. El firmamento amanecía de azul magnífico, pero sin ninguna nubecilla o la menor indicación de llubia. El sol lucía esplendoroso en medio de la más silenciosa calmo, solo corría un lento y suave vientesillo bochornoso que marchitava las plantas y toda la vegetación. Sería a mediados del verano, cuando los calores se hacían más intensos y persistentes, cuando poco a poco comienza a culminar la terrible peste de la viruela hasta el punto de desarrollarse en tal grado que por de quiera se oyen lamentos de las victimas que se va llevando.

Allí no había recursos de doctores, ni boticas, bien poco se conocían las medicinas de patente. Pero afortunadamente, mamá la conocían como una Señora caritativa y que nunca se negaba ni ponía obstáculo alguno cuando se trataba en auxiliar al pobre menesteroso prestándoles auxilio en sus enfermedades. Y aun obsequiándolos con sus liberales limosnas Dios la había dotado del bastante conocimiento el las enfermedades, y por lo general era muy acertada en prescribir sus medicamentos, que por lo general consistían en yerbas o raizes del país.

Fue en esta ocasión de esta plaga de Viruela que ella a pesar del gran peligro del contagio ofrecía a Dios sus servicios en alivio de los pobres y necesitados. No perdiendo ocasión para visitar cuantos enfermos podía, y gracias a la Divina Providencia, pudo por medio de sus desvelos y esfuerzos sanar muchos de los casos que pudo atender. Durante esta plaga, que tantos estragos hacía y caminaba a pasos gigantescos, llevandose uno, dos, tres, y hasta cuatro victimas de cada casa. Hasta entonces había podido mamá evitar la familia del contagio de la peste por medios de desinfectantes y otras precauciones que sean necesarias. Mas la Voluntad de Dios no permite nos libremos todos, en sus altos designios. Había ya escojido tan siquiera uno de nuestra casa.

Un día, pues, amanece este niño Francisco vencido de calentura, y a pocas horas, se halla cubierto de viruela con tal fuerza que su cara y todo su cuerpo se vuelve una capa completa. Permanese así por algunos días, arrecía la calentura y sus fuerzas se van agotando de día en día. Por fin, el niño se agravía. Se ve palidecer pero silencioso y apacible abre sus vencidos ojos, da una mirada al rededor y con suplicante mirada los fija hacia mamá. Y ya los cierra para no volverlos abrir más, había muerto como el soplo de una vela. Despúes que había muerto y ya estaba tendido en su ataud, mamá nos permite asomarnos al marco de la puerta por unos momentos para ver aquel Angelito del Cielo. Al mirarle, todos consternados de verle prorrumpimos en llanto, pero más nos conmueve al ver que sus fieles amiguitos, los gatos, parecen entender su desventura y tristemente redean la mesa refregandose en las patas de la mesa donde está el ataud y llorando en ademán de sentimiento.

Este niño está sepultado dentro de la Capilla de La Cuesta en el cruzero al lado izquierdo y también al lado o en seguida de nuestro abuelo, don Jesús C. de Baca (hijo de Juan Antonio Cabeza de Baca y María Josefa Gallegos), quien había muerto en 1890 a la edad de 81 años, después de haber padecido de paraliz por el espacio de un año, según el mismo contaba decía que durante su vida nunca había sufrido ninguna enfermedad, nunca había pasado un día en cama.

En el Colegio de Las Vegas

Debido a cambios or transaciones que ocurrían en la Diocesis de Santa Fe, se les pasó orden a los reverendos Padres Jesuitas salir del estado, y cerrar su colegio en Las Vegas. Y en 1890 se abría un nuevo colegio en la ciudad de Denver bajo el nombre de Sacred Heart College, edificio majestuoso construido de piedra labrada de color gris con suntuosos salones dedicados los unos para el estudio general, quimica, etcetera, elegante refectorio, cocina, y un espacioso dormitorio dividido en dos secciones para acomodar 250 alumnos de 6 a 15 años y otro tanto en la otra parte para la acomodación de jovenes de 26 a 20 años. Dicho dormitorio es el último piso del edificio que consiste de cuatro viviendas. En el segundo piso, se encuentran los cuartos privados de los reverendos Padres Jesuitas y una hermosísima capilla donde se celebra la Santa Misa todos los días.

Fue aquí donde me cupo la feliz suerte de presenciar la ordenación de dos sacerdotes que recebían el hábito de Jesuitas, uno de ellos que era mi condiscípulo; era el Padre José Garde, mejicano de la Ciudad de Méjico. Yo fui allí el primer año que se abría este colegio; el término que pasé allí fue muy feliz. Aproveche mi tiempo y ahora todavía guardo muy gratas memorias y mientras estuve allí alcance a ganarme el puesto de Honor y el primero o Capitán de mi clase. Y para significarlo, había un banco separado al lado del profesor y un letrero dibujado con letras de oro que indicaba el puesto: "LEADER." Todos anhelaban y se esforzaban en derribarme de aquel puesto, pero yo me mantuve siempre listo y preparado para no perderlo.

Como las travesuras o hazanas no faltan nunca en la escuela, se nos ocurrió cierto día de vacación escaparnos para la ciudad que distaba 3 millas del colegio. Eramos unos nueve muchachos que nos fugamos uno tras otro agasapándonos toda la orilla de un cerco cubierto de alfalfa hasta salir al camino. Una vez allí consideramos estar fuera de peligro de ser vistos de nuestros superiores. Luego, seguimos hasta llegar donde había una estación de los "Motor Cars" (un tren pequeñito) que conducía a Berkeley Lake y de allí a Elitch's Garden donde el famoso Circo Sells Floto pasá la temporada del invierno. De allí había que tomar "Transfer Tickets" para los Cable Cars que conducían a la ciudad. Al llegar a Denver pensamos dividirnos de dos o tres compañeros y no parecer un ejército o pandilla de cazadores, quedando de acuerdo en reunirnos en cierto lugar a cierta hora, y no salir de allí hasta no estar todos juntos.

En nuestra vuelta, veníamos alegres y satisfechos del buen tiempo que habíamos tenido sin acordarnos ni sentir remordimiento de las diplomáticas y rígidas consecuencias de tan atrevido y descarado paseito. Al acercarnos al colegio, ya empezaron nuestras congojas. Entonces si que temblavamos acercearnos. No había remedio tendríamos que acusar el delito. Ah, cuanto nos costría aquella tarde de sin sabores y que ejercicios de penitencia no tendríamos que sufrir en abono de aquel paseito! Que al fin y al cabo, no pareció tan corto al jusgar el alto precio que teníamos que pagar por él.

Muy cautelososamente nos fuimos acercando al colegio, pensando poder llegar sin ser advertidos. Pero "Camotes," que ya lo sabían no solo los Padres sino todo el colegio se había enterado ya de tan simple diplomacia. Fuimos recibidos por el Prefecto del Colegio y no con ninguna cortesía, pero con palabras como puntas de acero. Luego, fuimos interrogados en el acto por el Superior del Colegio y quien nos devolvió al Prefecto que con brevedad nos impuso el castigo que debíamos recibir. Lo primero fue privarnos la seña aquella tarde (tal vez creo vendríamos bien comidos de la ciudad). De allí, quedamos incomunicables por tres días y separados de los demás alumnos teniendo hasta que dormir en la enfermería, durante los tres días de castigo solo nos mantubimos a pan y agua. Durante las horas de recreo, mientras los demás jugaban nosotros teníamos que marchar durante los quince minutos que duraba el recreo y a una distancia donde nos podían ver los demás muchachos para servirles de escarmiento.

Otro castigo fue de ponernos en línea de menor a mayor a la puerta del Padre Mandalari, que era el Prefecto del Colegio. Y este fue llamando uno por uno, cerrar la puerta por dentro con llave y aplicarle unos quince chicotasos con un "Black Snake." Habían pasado cuatro de los compañeros este castigo, los demás que quedábamos convenimos en hacer toda resistencia y de allí nos fuimos, nos reportamos al Padre Persone Superior, y quejamos de tal castigo. Por fin, tomó el en consideración nuestra justa queja y suspendió el castigo de los azotes.

Al terminar la escuela, fue mi hermano Fulgencio a Denver por mi. Pasamos unos dos días en la ciudad y volvimos a La Cuesta al lado de mis padres. Después de una temporada allí, quize emprender algún negocio. Comuniqué con Eugenio "El Guero" Baca, un primo mío de Las Vegas, para salir los dos de "Viandantes." Consiguiendo un carro y un caballo de papá y el compañero otro caballo para nuestro viaje, luego compramos un surtido de efectos y salimos a comerciar. Después de visitar algunas aldeas cercanas, nos dirijimos hacia el Puerto de Luna donde vivía una hermana de Eugenio.

Después de dos días allí, nos dirijimos al Salado y al llegar allí nos cojio una nevada de 12 a 15 pulgadas. Era entonces el mes de Enero. Después de pasar cuatro días allí y malamente acomodados y aquella nieve que no se menoraba nada se impasiento mi compañero y se determinó que debíamos salir de allí y tomamos dirección hacia un rancho de su cuñado que distaba unas diez millas. Era de tarde y no era posible caminar más que el lento paso de los caballos.

La nieve era más alta cuanto más caminábamos. El camino no se veia ninguno. Solo caminábamos al rumbo siguiendo toda una canada. En tiempo regular, nos hubiera tomado tal vez dos horas llegar allí, pero ahora, caramba, el sol se había metido hacia largo rato comienzan a brillar las estrellitas. El frío cada paso nos parece mas frío. Pensando que al hecharnos a pie nos calentaríamos con el ejercicio como en efecto hasta sudamos, pero el cansancio nos obligó subir al carro. Como ya llevábamos los pies bien mojados, nos quitamos los zapatos y nos envolvimos una fresada en los pies. Mas a poco nos va consentrando tanto el frío hasta dejarnos sin movimiento. Ya no hacíamos caso que rumbo llevaban los caballos; la rienda la habíamos amarrado al dupel del carro. Querer mover un brazo o siquiera mover los dedos era ya imposible.

Sólo al mirarnos queríamos hablar y no podíamos; apenas nos podíamos reír, sabido es que reír es señal segura que hace la persona que muere heldada. Así que ya nosotros sólo esperábamos la muerte, pues nada por allí indicaba recurso alguno que nos librase de tan triste situación. Dentro poco, ya seríamos victimas del llano donde después serviríamos de alimento a las bestias del campo; en dos o tres días más los coyotes ya habrían ruido nuestra carne. Mas pensar en todo esto, no nos mejoraba nuestra situación pero, qué hacer pues? Ya faltaban las fuerzas, queríamos mover un brazo era imposible, las manos tiesas de frío. Querer hablar era imposible; las quijadas estaban tiesas. Apenas si podíamos mover los ojos para vernos el uno al otro y esto servía solamente para más acongojarnos. Y sin embargo, al mirarnos nos causaba una riza involuntaria que más bien nos hacía sufrir por el esfuerzo que teníamos que hacer en mover las quijadas. Así a paso lento seguíamos, ya no esperando llegar donde nos dieran auxilio, sino que se llegase el momento de morir helados.

Sería quizá después de la media noche, cuando nos pareció oír el lejano aullido de algunos perros. Y al mismo tiempo, notamos que nuestros fieles caballos que hasta entonces no habían dejado de seguir, caminando sobre aquella nevada. Pronto también, les vimos parar las orejas al ladrido de los perros y nos pareció que arreciaban el paso. Por buen rato, ya no volvimos a oír más los ladridos de los perros. Y de nuevo, continua el sordo y profundo silencio de la noche y la lívida luz de las lejanas estrellas que adornavan el firmamento y que parecían resaltar de sobresalto al sentir el intenso frío de la noche. Así seguíamos silenciosos y al paso lento de la carretera cuando de nuevo se dejo oír mas claramente los ladridos de los canjes y nos pareció que ya no estaríamos lejos de algún socorro humano que viniese en nuestro auxilio.

Oh, que gozo, que gran consolación, que ánimo tan sublime sentimos al ver aparecer por allá en el lejano espacio de la emboscada una débil y entermitente lucesita, que parecía salir de entre el espeso monte y azotada por persistente briza de la noche la hacía desaparecer y la perdíamos de vista por algunos momentos. Y que con ansiedad esperábamos volver a ver, y una vez que estubimos bien enterados y un interior impulso misterioso nos lo aseguraba ya que se acercaba nuestro rescate. Con todas las veras de nuestro corazón, levantamos los ojos al cielo para dar infinitas gracias a Dios que nos libraba de aquella tan helada muerte que ya nos parecía inevitable y la esperábamos de un momento a otro. Pero, mayor fue la Misericordia de Dios que la débil Fe que nosotros ya no pudíamos resistir; El Señor debe haber oído las oraciones de nuestras buenas y santas madres que rogaban por nosotros sus ausentes hijos que por primera vez nos separábamos del hogar paterno.

De nuevo, se vio brillar y mas reluciente aparecer la lucesita que salía indudablemente de entre el espeso monte. Fijamos la vista allí donde salía la luz y pronto alcansamos a distinguir en la oscuridad de la noche el bulto de una casita que ya no perdimos de vista. Entre más nos acercábamos, mas claramente la veiamos. Los perros que ya hacia mucho tiempo habían sentido el ruido del carro, ya no cesaban de ladrar y en voz de fastidiarnos su continuo ladrar. Más bien, nos agradaba y alentaba su continuo alarde que indicaba nuestra llegada allí, revistiendonos de nuevas fuerzas y un nuevo ánimo, quisimos con la desesperada ancia de llegar más pronto levantarnos y salir del carro. Oh, esto era imposible, todo nuestro ser parecía estar impedido de movimiento alguno, todo nuestro cuerpo estaba paralizado, aun la sangre de nuestras venas parecía estan congelada. Estábamos tiesos como un palo, sin el auzilio de algun ser humano que con prestara ayuda, indudablemente hubiesemos perecido aquella noche de angustias.

La casita de donde salía la luz, era precisamente una chosa improvisada que habían construido temporariamente en un rancho que acababa de tomar posesión don Jesús Casados, rico hacendado y fuerte ganadero de aquellos contornos. Era precisamente hermano político de mi compañero. Allí en esta casita, estaban tres o cuatro hombres que habían ido para levantar una casa de residencia para don Jesús. Fueron estos señores desconcidos para nosotros. Pero, que Dios permitió que fuesen la causa de y la senda por donde devíamos de librarnos de tan prematura muerte, Dios obraba allí y no la mera casualidad como lo piensan tantos de poca fe, mas nosotros que veiamos las cosas más claras, no dudamos que Dios obraba allí y que la casualidad nada tenía que ver allí.

Cuando ya estuvimos cerca de la casita era preciso dejar el camino y ladearse alguna distancia para llegar hacia allí. Quisimos hacer movimiento para dirijir el tiro y cambiarlo en dirección a la casita, pero que caramba, imposible movernos! Ni siquiera podíamos hablar; teníamos las quijadas tiesas y la lengua no articulaba nada. Mas, el instinto de las bestias no necesito de nosotros solitas se dirijieron hacia la puerta de la casita y al llegar allí se detubieron al frente de la puerta.

Al ruido del carro y los desesperados ladridos de los perros, salieron tres o cuatro hombres alarmados a ver quien llegaba allí aquellas horas de la avansada noche. Y ellos preguntan: "Quién vive? Quién es? Qué hay? Qué se ofrece?" Nadie responde, nosotros sí podíamos oír, pero no podíamos hablar nada, ni siquiera reguirnos. Por fin, ellos se determinan acercarse al carro y ver que contenía aquello. Allí nos encuentran ya más muertos que vivos; levantándonos en peso, nos llevan para dentro de la casita. Nos tienden sobre una cama en el suelo, se dan prisa en atisar la lumbre y calentando agua nos lavan cara y manos, luego nos dan a beber café caliente. Poco a poco, nos van deselando pero sin dejarnos arrimar al fuego. A fuerza de frotarnos con agua caliente y ejercicios violentos de los brazos hasta volver a recobrar el estado normal y completa salud.

Corto tiempo después de estar allí, todo había cambiado, todo era gozo y gustosos celebrábamos el "Nerrow Scape." Mientras tanto que esperábamos se acabara de pasar el mal tiempo, tubimos la suerte de conseguir trabajo allí en la construcción de la casa, trabajamos por unos seis o ocho días. Y cuando ya el tiempo lo permitió, salimos de allí en dirección a Las Vegas; pues don Jesús después de habernos dado tan buena acojida en su rancho, nos había hecho muy buen pago por el trabajo que le habíamos hecho pagándonos con llenarnos el carro de saleas. Y al llegar a Las Vegas, las vendimos en la casa de Gross, Kelly, & Co.

En el Colegio de San Miguel

El colegio de San Miguel, dirigido por los Hermanos de la compañía de La Salle, fue la primera institución de enseñanza que se estableció en Nuevo Méjico por los arduos y penosos esfuerzos y a costa de mil sacrificios de nuestro digno e ilustre Señor Arzobispo, Excelentísimo Sr. Arzobispo Lamy. Fue en esta institución que tuve la feliz suerte de poder seguir mis estudios, gracias a los sacrificios que hizo mi padre para la educación mía y mis hermanos, herencia que jamás la perderemos y que a la par que nos instruíamos en la ciencia, la mejor educación Cristiana bajo la dirección y esmerados esfuerzos de los buenos religiosos.

En este tiempo que atendía yo a la escuela, presencié un espectáculo desagradable. El Capitolio del estado que daba frente al Colegio, y a una distancia de cinco cuadras, daba un aspecto hermosísimo a la ciudad de Santa Fe. Desde el balcón del segundo piso del Colegio, este grandioso edificio adornado sus cupulas con elegantísimas estatuas de bronce y diversos metales; era el orgullo de la ciudad.

Un día a esto de las ocho o nueve de la mañana, dan la alarma de quemazon! Y toda la ciudad se pone en movimiento al oír la noticia que el incendio era en el Capitolio. Los hermanos no pueden contener el alboroto de los muchachos y, por fin, dan permiso de subir a los pisos de arriba y el dormitorio. Y por allí por las ventanas, podíamos ver el terrible fuego que destruia rapidamente aquel hermosísimo edificio. El fuego comenzó en los dos lados exteriores o sea en las cupulas que había a cada orilla del edificio. Las cuales estaban rodiadas de enormes estatuas de bronce las que fueron derritiendose y por entre las llamas se miraban distintamente gotear bolas de diversos colores que se arrancaban de estas. Después, se divulgo que tal había sido incendiado politicamente debido a que se intentaba cambiar la Capital a Albuquerque. Lo que no se consiguió y un nuevo edificio ocupa el mismo sitio a la presente, aunque no tan elegante pero sí espacioso.

Antes de acabarse el término de la escuela, tuve que salir por causa que papá había salido electo de Comisionado por el Condado de San Miguel y tenía que cambiar su residencia para Las Vegas. Y era preciso que yo me quedase al cuidado de la propiedad y bienes en La Cuesta por alguna temporada mientras se arreglaban los negocios de otra manera. Después que papá terminó su oficio de Comisionado, me quedé yo trabajando en la farmacía de E. G. Murphey en la Plaza Vieja de Las Vegas donde permanecí por dies años. Antes y después de casado, las horas de trabajo eran larguísimas, pues mi compañero y yo habríamos el despacho a las siete en la mañana y todo el día hasta las dies de la noche. Y solamente teníamos medio día los Domingos para descanzar. Esto me desanimó para no seguir el empleo de boticario.

DISPLACEMENT AND ADAPTATION, 1900–1945

Recollections of the Colorado Coal Strike, 1913–1914

M. Edmund Vallejo

ABOUT THE AUTHOR

M. Edmund Vallejo, who received his Ph.D. in education from Kansas State University, is the retired Pueblo School District 60 superintendent of schools. He has published several articles in educational journals and is the author of *Colorado Landscapes*, a book of color landscapes and original poetry. He serves as second vice-president on the Colorado Historical Society Board of Directors.

I T HAS BEEN over eighty years since the Colorado coal strike of 1913–14. Although historians have concentrated on the Ludlow Massacre, the citizens of Walsenburg and Trinidad, the largest communities in the strike area, also faced the violence and hardship that the strike brought. The following story is about a few people, who once lived in Walsenburg and many of whom still live there: people who were caught up in the tides of labor unrest. It is the story of the divided loyalties that characterized these turbulent times and of the arrangements that family members and our neighbors and friends had to make in their lives. The ambiguities that developed in these circumstances—the difficulty of judging right from wrong and even of telling scab from striker—stand as testimony to the unpredictable human element that is at the core of all social history.

My father's family had little involvement in the strike. But my father's sister, Gertrude, married Jim D. Farr, now ninety-two years old, who was nephew to Jefferson Farr, the infamous sheriff of Huerfano County during those trying days. My mother, Frances Nelson Atencio Vallejo, and her sister, Ana Atencio Lucero, recall vividly the events of those days. My mother's surname of Atencio was given to her by her father and mother, Antonio and Elisa Atencio, but she was "adopted" by her uncle and aunt, John and Maria Nelson. It was the custom to adopt in those days when one sibling had a large family and the other did not. Maria Nelson and Antonio Atencio were sister and brother, and since Maria had no children, she "adopted" my mother and my mother's adopted brother, Moses Nelson.

I am particularly indebted to Tom Trew, neighbor, pioneer coal miner, and close family friend, who contributed greatly to the recollections recorded in this account. I also owe special recognition to professor Robert Zieger of the Kansas State University History Department for his aid and encouragement in completing this account. Appreciation is also due Mr. Robert Roehr, director of the Pueblo Regional Library, and his staff for their assistance. Greatest thanks go to my mother, Frances Nelson Vallejo, and my aunt, Ana Lucero, for having the patience to relate many of the personal family incidents.

The strike that occurred in the coal fields of southern Colorado in 1913–14 was unusually violent. The record shows that the United Mine Workers of America (UMW) lost the strike, and its viciousness aroused unprecedented public reaction.[1] There had been other major strikes in 1892 and 1903 in the same coal fields, and the 1903 strike was particularly significant because of the methods used to break the strike. The strategies used included the importing of foreign strikebreakers, the quartering of state militia troops at the mines, and the hiring of armed guards through professional detective agencies. In addition, the state administration went to the courts to justify its moves to terminate the strike at all costs. The men who suppressed the 1903 strike had been conditioned to dealing with unionism by their previous clashes with the Western Federation of Miners in earlier confrontations throughout Colorado.[2]

Three major coal companies mined most of the coal in the region, but the John D. Rockefeller family–owned Colorado Fuel and Iron Company (CF&I) was the largest. Most of the difficulties centered around the CF&I. The coal companies owned and operated the towns that housed the miners, holding title to the homes, the stores, the saloons, and even the churches.[3] There were four larger coal mines within the immediate vicinity of Walsenburg, all of them owned by the CF&I. These were the McNally Mine, the Cameron Mine, the Robinson Mine, and the major coal camp located at the end of West Seventh Street in Walsenburg, the Walsen Mine. The southern Colorado coal operators hired men from many countries. Fifty-four languages and dialects were spoken in the counties of Huerfano and Las Animas, and many of the miners were first brought into the area as strikebreakers during the 1903 strike.[4]

The Nelson, Atencio, and Valdez Families

During the 1913 strike, John Nelson, who was born in Scotland and immigrated to the coal fields of Pennsylvania, was employed as a fire boss at the Walsen Mine. Although not considered as part of management, his position was a very important one because it was the fire boss's responsibility to inspect the mine for gas before the workers went down into the mine, and Nelson took this task seriously. In 1910, he had built a two-story brick house six blocks east of the mine property on West Seventh Street where he and his wife, Maria, boarded bachelor miners who worked at the Walsen Mine. The CF&I had a boarding house for bachelors at the Walsen Mining Camp, as it did at all its camps, but when there was room, many preferred Maria's cooking, and the Nelson Boarding House was prosperous.

Maria Nelson's brother, Antonio Atencio, lived on the same side of the street a few doors west of the Nelson Boarding House, and Atencio worked at the Walsen Mine as a mule driver. His wife, Elisa, bore him thirteen children, including Miguel, who was also a young miner at the Walsen

Mine. Two of Elisa's brothers, Tircio Valdez and Eutimio Valdez, were employed there as mine guards.[5]

Union Organizing and the United Mine Workers of America

Many of the same poor conditions that prevailed in the southern Colorado coal fields in the strike of 1903 were still apparent in 1913. The miners demanded an eight-hour day, semimonthly pay, abolition of pay in company scrip, a 2,000-pound ton instead of a 2,400-pound ton as formerly, and a better supply of pure air as "prescribed by State law."[6] Most of these demands were already law but went unenforced.[7] It was the presence of these conditions that had triggered the 1903 strike, which lasted four months before it was broken. At that time, the militia rounded up between four hundred and five hundred striking miners and loaded them on trains bound for New Mexico and Kansas. The men were unloaded on the prairie with warnings to stay away from Colorado; thus, the strike brought no improvement in the conditions of the coal fields.[8]

Prior to the 1913 strike call, the United Mine Workers sent John R. Lawson, citizen of Colorado and longtime UMW organizer, into the southern Colorado coal fields to recruit new members. It was part of a concerted effort to organize all the coal miners of Colorado. Lawson ran into trouble from the start. Not only did he have to contend with the various ethnic groups and their diverse languages, he had to deal with the coal operators' methods. Camp marshals, or mine guards as they were usually called, were recruited for their ability to recognize outside "agitators" and "malcontents" on the company payroll. Detectives and spies were also hired to keep an eye on union organizers, who eventually had to resort to meeting after dark on mountainside, secret rendezvous to sign up members. The not-so-cautious risked being railroaded out of town.

Lawson's recruiting efforts proved, in the long run, to be highly successful despite the handicaps. In 1907, he suffered arrest at the hands of sheriff Jefferson Farr of Huerfano County.[9] Within minutes after confronting Sheriff Farr about a complaint, Lawson was stopped by Silverio Martinez, the Walsenburg town marshal, and was arrested for carrying a concealed weapon that was placed there by Martinez.[10] Martinez, known as "Shorty" to his intimates, was a Farr man. He used to wear high-heeled boots and a tall Texas hat, which made him appear even taller than his six-foot frame. He was the son of Antonio Martinez and Frances Atencio, sister to Antonio Atencio. Frances Nelson Vallejo was his first cousin.[11]

In the summer of 1913, when the time was ripe for action, the UMW sent its vice-president, Frank Hayes, into Colorado to assist Lawson's state organizing effort, operating out of Denver. By this time, Lawson had succeeded in enrolling a large number of miners as regular dues-paying members. In September, the miners held a convention in Trinidad, and the delegates voted to call a strike on September 23 unless the operators met their demands. The miners sought union recognition, a 10 percent advance in wages on the tonnage rate, an eight-hour workday, pay for narrow work and dead work, a checkweighman elected by the miners, the right to trade in any store, and the right to choose any boarding place and doctor, as well as the enforcement of existing mining laws.[12] The primary demand of the miners, however, concerned the right of union membership and representation by the UMW—recognition of the union. The companies, on the other hand, persistently denied the union recognition and refused to discuss the other issues.[13]

Union Activity in the Nelson Household

One of the UMW members who had drawn up the strike resolution at Trinidad was John "Jack" Burke, a coal miner at the Walsen Mine who lived at the Nelson Boarding House.[14] Jack Burke was actively engaged in secret union organizing activities and worked directly under Adolph Germer, a fiery UMW organizer who was well known in Walsenburg for his rough language.[15] It was Germer, along with E. L. Neely of Walsenburg, who had gone to Pueblo very early in the strike in October to purchase guns and ammunition for the strikers.[16] Neely subsequently overthrew the Farr machine, and he became sheriff in 1916.[17] Burke trusted the Nelson family, and since there were no restaurants in Walsenburg other than drinking establishments, he would bring Frank Hayes, John Lawson, Adolph Germer, and Mother Jones to the Nelson Boarding House to eat and sometimes to sleep when they were in town.[18]

Frances Nelson Vallejo described Mother Jones as a "warm person with an Irish-looking face, very dynamic, loud, and boisterous." Every child in Walsenburg knew by heart the most popular song of the day, which Frances remembered Mother Jones singing:

The union forever, hurrah! boys, hurrah!
Up with the union and down with the law,
For we're coming, Colorado, we're coming all the way,
Shouting the battle cry of freedom.[19]

The Strike of 1913–14 Begins in a Blinding Snowstorm

Immediately after the publication of the union's demands following the Trinidad strike call, Colorado governor Elias Ammons and former U.S. senator Thomas M. Patterson tried to mediate, as did the U.S. Department of Labor. The operators, however, refused all offers of mediation, declaring that they knew of "no controversy between Colorado coal companies and their employees that rendered mediation the obvious way of settlement."[20] "All serious troubles," they insisted, "have been caused by labor organizations trying to force their regime on the businesses against the wishes of the workingmen and their employers."[21] John D. Rockefeller, Jr., who owned the controlling interest in the CF&I, expressed a similar view. Later, testifying before a U.S. Congressional committee, he stated: "We would rather that the unfortunate conditions should continue and that we should lose all the millions invested, than that American workingmen should be deprived of their right, under the Constitution, to work for whom they please. This is the great principle at stake. It is a national issue."[22]

On September 23, 1913, eight thousand miners and their families in the southern Colorado coal fields left their company-owned homes in the mining camps during a blinding snowstorm and moved into tents which the UMW had provided. These tents were grouped into colonies at the canyons in which the mines were located. The strikers were strategically placed so that nonstriking miners had to pass through the tent colonies to get to work. Governor Ammons, who subsequently proved to be sympathetic to the mine operators, considered the tent colonies "silent pickets," and some forms of picketing were a technical violation of Colorado law.[23]

In the early months of the strike, the U.S. Department of Labor sent officials to Colorado to confer with all the parties to the strike. Labor Department officials also attempted to reach Rockefeller in New York, but they could not persuade him to intercede. President Woodrow Wilson himself corresponded with officials of the CF&I in an attempt to get them to meet with the union and thus avert a crisis, but his intervention had no effect.[24]

Divided Loyalties in the Nelson Boarding House

When the strike started, division reigned in the Nelson household. John Nelson felt duty bound to remain at his post as fire boss at the Walsen Mine. He was a quiet, soft-spoken, hard worker, and he never expressed himself about strike issues. His adopted son, Moses, on the other hand, sided with boarder Jack Burke and was pro-union. Both Moses and Burke, of course, went on strike. Burke, meanwhile, could afford to stay on at the boarding house throughout the strike because he was still on the union payroll. Other boarders, however, had to seek housing elsewhere because they could no longer afford to live at the Nelson Boarding House.[25]

As the strike wore on, John Nelson found it dangerous to walk the six blocks to work each day because the route to the Walsen Mine went through the striking miners' residential areas on West Seventh Street. The miners and their families taunted those who worked at the mine as "scabs," even though many of them were neighbors and longtime friends. As a result, Nelson eventually took up residence at the mine, and his adopted daughter, Frances, was instructed to take an out-of-the-way route across the railroad bridge and west over the hills to take him homemade baked bread and other food. The company guards, two of whom were her first cousins on her real mother's side of the family, knew her and let her through without any difficulty.[26]

Although John Nelson was now out of the house and was boarding at the Walsen Mine, it was still common knowledge that the Nelson boarding establishment had harbored pro-company sympathies. Jack Burke kept things pretty calm, however, and at times even patrolled the house and grounds at night for fear that striking miners would harm Maria and her daughter, Frances, because John was working for the CF&I. Later, at the insistence of Moses and Burke, Nelson finally gave up his job at the Walsen Mine because of the danger to his family.[27]

The Seventh Street Massacre

From its very beginning, the strike followed the pattern of violence common to Colorado's earlier labor struggles. Armed men were brought in, and the CF&I hired the Baldwin-Felts Detective Agency, as it had in the 1903 strike, to guard the mines. The guards were sworn in as deputy sheriffs in both Huerfano and Las Animas counties. Gun duels were frequent, and the sheriffs of both Huerfano and Las Animas counties petitioned Governor Ammons to call out the state militia. At first, Governor Ammons was reluctant to comply; however, after a quick trip into the coal fields, he decided not to mobilize the militia.[28]

Events in Walsenburg, however, soon caused Governor Ammons to reconsider. The day after he took the train from Walsenburg to Denver, tragedy struck in the west part of town in what is now referred to as the "Seventh Street Massacre." The incident occurred, on October 24, 1913, at the Wahlmeier home, immediately east of the Antonio Atencio residence and a few doors away from the Nelson Boarding House.

Mrs. Wahlmeier was alone because her husband, like John Nelson, had boarded at the Walsen Mine to avoid the taunts of striking miners as he walked to work each day. On the morning of October 24, she found a note pinned to her door reading: "If you don't move out of this neighborhood within twenty-four hours, we will blow you out. Your husband is scabbing. We mean business."[29] After telephoning the mine superintendent, she was promised three wagons with an escort of deputized mine guards to collect her furniture so she could join her husband at the mine. When the wagons and the mounted guards arrived, the wagons were parked in the alley behind the Wahlmeier house.

Before the wagons could be loaded, however, a crowd of strikers and their wives and children, many of whom had just come onto the scene from the Seventh Street Primary School two doors away, harassed and jeered at Mrs. Wahlmeier and the guards. The guards moved onto West Seventh Street in front of the house and began to threaten and curse the crowd; however, the crowd started up with a new chant: "Scab Herders! Scab Herders!"[30] As the crowd thickened, several children scooped dirt from the unpaved street and threw it at the guards.[31]

From her vantage point in the house next to the scene, Ana Atencio, eldest daughter of Antonio and Elisa Atencio, observed a striker crouched behind the fence under the rear window with a rifle raised.[32] Up to that point, no shots had been fired by either side, but when the first wagon was being loaded, the gunman under the Atencio window took aim and fired, hitting a guard in the ear.

At that point, the guards opened fire into the crowd on the street, and the demonstrators scattered. In five minutes, it was over. Two miners were dead where they lay, one of them directly in the street in front of the Nelson Boarding House. Miner Kris Kokich lay draped over the fence in front of the Atencio home with a mortal neck wound. He was rushed into the Atencio home and laid on the bed until help could be summoned for him. Kokich died at midnight in a Walsenburg hospital.[33]

Meanwhile, Frances Nelson, who was coming home from St. Mary School, seven blocks from the scene, was shocked by the sight of a dead man in front of her home. She ran for the protection of her brick house, which had been riddled on the west side with stray bullets. Her sister, Ana, had taken refuge behind a table and didn't venture out until a group of men rushed in with the wounded Kokich. Tircio Valdez, who was a mine guard at the Walsen Mine and uncle to Frances and Ana, rushed out to the Atencio farm to notify Antonio and Elisa Atencio about the incident and to bring them back to care for their children at their home in Walsenburg.[34]

State Militia Mobilized

The Seventh Street Massacre was the first major bloodshed that Walsenburg had experienced since the strike began a month earlier. Angry strikers and other union sympathizers armed themselves. A crowd marched through the business district of Walsenburg calling for vengeance. Sheriff Farr and his deputies barricaded themselves in the courthouse. Guards stood in a line across the gateway of the Walsen Mine property. Baldwin-Felts deputies rushed up from Trinidad with a machine gun and stationed it at the courthouse, but no further fighting took place in Walsenburg that night or the next day; the strikers eventually returned to their homes.[35]

The Seventh Street Massacre precipitated quick action from the governor's office. On October 28, 1913, Governor Ammons signed an executive order mobilizing the Colorado National Guard. Upon its arrival in Walsenburg and the Trinidad vicinity, the state militia initially acted neutral as guardsmen disarmed strikers, guards, and deputy sheriffs. Indeed, a feeling of friendliness and comradeship developed between the striking miners and the soldiers.[36]

Within a few weeks, however, this feeling evaporated when the militia began recruiting mine guards into the National Guard and protecting strikebreakers hired outside of Colorado in direct violation of state law.[37] From that point on, the militia sided completely with the coal operators, and harassment of the strikers became commonplace.[38]

Management in the field determined labor policies of the CF&I, and the Rockefellers supported its conduct of the strike and its refusal to recognize the union. As absentee owners, they accepted without question the assessment of the situation made by their representatives on the scene and hesitated to interfere in an area usually regarded as the daily responsibility of local management.[39] Chief among the field managers was L. M. Bowers, chairman of the board of CF&I. Bowers opposed any measure of compromise with the union, even feeling that sitting down with its representatives in the same room would imply recognition.[40]

Strikebreakers Given Protection

The field managers, meanwhile, welcomed the calling out of the state militia, mainly to protect incoming strikebreakers; however, Governor Ammons forbade the use of state troops to escort imported strikebreakers because of state law. The operators, however, began a campaign to impel the governor to revise his original orders and to direct the troops to act as escorts. On November 18, 1913, Bowers sent a letter to Rockefeller outlining how he had secured the cooperation of all the Denver bankers. The bankers loaned the State of Colorado all the funds necessary to maintain the militia and afford ample protection "so that our miners could return to work, or give protection to men who are anxious to come up here from Texas, New Mexico, and Kansas."[41]

The operators were aided in their campaign because the state auditor refused to issue certificates of indebtedness to pay the salaries and expenses of the militia. Governor Ammons was finally convinced that preventing the troops from aiding strikebreakers constituted an interference with production. Although he did not formally declare martial law, he withdrew his initial orders and, in effect, placed the strike zone completely under the control of the militia commander, General John Chase.[42] Immediately, General Chase issued an order from his Trinidad headquarters putting Governor Ammons's decree into effect.

Former U.S. senator Thomas Patterson of Colorado subsequently testified before the Commission on Industrial Relations that from that time things went from bad to worse for the miners. He reported that many were arrested on suspicion without charge and were kept incommunicado, that they were refused visits by friends, and that they were denied the right to counsel.[43]

Mother Jones

Among those eventually arrested, denied civil rights, and held incommunicado for nine weeks in January of 1914 was Mother Jones. The eighty-three-year-old UMW organizer was sent into District 15 to join John Lawson in the southern Colorado coal fields. For several years, she had participated in America's labor wars, and her reputation preceded her into Colorado. As soon as she arrived in Trinidad, she was placed under arrest and deported back to Denver. A week later, however, she traveled back to Trinidad but was once more arrested without warrant and placed in Mt. San Rafael Hospital. Her detention precipitated a march by the women of Trinidad toward the hospital. General Chase's troops met them with drawn sabers and dispersed them. Six women were injured, and General Chase was knocked off his horse. Ultimately, the protest turned out to be a moral victory for the women.[44]

Mother Jones's continued incarceration without charge, without trial, and without bond angered the miners. They planned retaliation when word arrived from Washington, D.C., that the House of Representatives had authorized its Committee on Mines and Mining to investigate the Colorado coal strike. The committee began its sessions in Denver on

February 9, 1914, and, by the end of the month, Governor Ammons withdrew eight hundred to a thousand militia troops from the strike zone.[45] When the investigation moved to Trinidad on March 6, General Chase refused to testify.

Meanwhile, Mother Jones was released on March 16 and put on a train to Denver, but she was soon on her way back to Trinidad. She never got to Trinidad, however, because militia took her off the train in Walsenburg under Governor Ammons's orders and placed her in confinement in the Huerfano County Jail, one block from the train depot. She was ordered detained until she was ready to leave the strike zone. She remained for twenty-six days, after which she traveled to Washington, D.C., to take part in the Congressional hearings on the coal strike.[46]

The Calm Before the Storm

In the meantime, John D. Rockefeller, Jr., appeared before the House Committee on Mines and Mining in Washington, D.C., and reaffirmed for the committee his opposition to unionism. He pledged vast sums of money to retain the "open shop" while expressing boundless faith and confidence in the CF&I officers. A committee report, however, found no sympathy with his admission that he had not visited Colorado in ten years, nor did the committee look kindly upon his testimony that he had not even been to a CF&I board of directors meeting in the same number of years. When asked by the committee whether he had bothered to speak to any of the miners and investigate their conditions personally, he replied, "Oh, when I was investigating vice in New York, I never talked with a single prostitute. This is not the way I have been trained to investigate. I could not talk with 10,000 miners."[47]

On April 17, 1914, Governor Ammons removed the remainder of the troops from the southern Colorado coal fields except for two companies. These two, through attrition and connivance, had come to be composed of mine guards, pit bosses, adventurers, and professional soldiers who chose to remain on strike duty.[48] These men, within three days, were to be involved in one of the most controversial events in American labor history.

The Ludlow Massacre

On April 20, 1914, the day after the Eastern Orthodox Church's Easter Sunday, the Ludlow Massacre occurred and marked that day as one of the most infamous in Colorado's history. Ludlow had one of the largest tent colonies housing striking miners and their families and was located at the mouth of a canyon between Walsenburg and Trinidad. Hysteria and confusion have clouded the actual sequence of events. An undisputed fact, though, was that a militia company had taken positions on a hill overlooking the tent colony of Ludlow where the guardsmen had mounted a machine gun. Rumors were rampant that the colony was to be wiped out, for violence had already erupted at the Forbes Tent Colony near Trinidad only days before. Militiamen had disbanded that colony.

When two dynamite explosions alerted the Ludlow Tent Colony, the miners took up positions at the bottom of the hill. When the militia opened fire, hundreds of miners and their families ran for cover. Others took refuge in the ground, where pits had been dug underneath the tents to escape snipers' bullets. The militia fire killed two miners and one boy before the miners were routed. Then, acting under orders, the militia set fire to the tents and destroyed the entire colony. Eleven children and two women burned or suffocated to death in one of the tent pits. In addition, Louis Tikas, the leader of the Greek miners, was captured, shot, and killed, reflecting a "take no prisoners" mentality. The total death count was nineteen for the miners and their families; only one guardsman was fatally wounded.[49]

Reaction was instant. The press gave wide coverage in spite of the fact that war with Mexico was a possibility at the time. Rockefeller bore the brunt of the criticism heaped on the CF&I by the American public and the media for its conduct of the strike in general and for the Ludlow incident in particular. Upton Sinclair, popular speaker on the social issues of the day, led a picket line in front of Rockefeller's office in New York City and was arrested. In Colorado, George Creel, who later became America's chief propagandist in World War I, denounced the Rockefellers vigorously. "The martyred men, women, and children of Ludlow," Creel cried in revenge, "did not die in vain. They have written with their blood upon the wall of the world. Those like the Rockefellers, who profess Christ in public and crucify Him privately, have been awakened, and never again will the patter of prayers be permitted to excuse Judas's greed."[50]

The Ten Days War

Meanwhile, the killings at Ludlow had enraged the miners, and they went on a vengeful expedition throughout southern Colorado in what people in Walsenburg still call the "Ten Days War." During this time, incidents occurred between the striking miners and their adversaries that probably have not been equaled for their viciousness in any industrial conflict in American history.[51] Anarchy and open rebellion prevailed when guerilla groups of striking miners seized Trinidad and set fire to every coal company building they could find in the counties of Huerfano and Las Animas. With the militia pinned down around Ludlow, and with the lieutenant governor unwilling to act in the governor's out-of-state absence, wandering groups of guerilla miners sacked mines at Delagua, Aguilar, and Canon City.

Encouraged by a "call to arms" over the signatures of John Lawson and others, angry strikers were hard put to lay down their arms after appeals for peace by the lieutenant governor. Sixteen lives were eventually lost in the incidents that immediately followed the Ludlow Massacre. Conditions got so bad that Governor Ammons ordered out an additional six hundred militiamen to report for duty after he had arrived back from Washington, D.C. Only 25 percent of the men responded, however. At last, in desperation and under pressure brought by members of the Women's Peace League, who had encamped at the state capitol building until the governor acted, Ammons admitted that the situation was beyond his control, and he wired President Wilson for federal intervention.[52]

Walsenburg: The Final Battleground

Before the federal troops arrived, however, Walsenburg became the scene of one of the most deadly of all the Ten Days War encounters. The new fighting in Walsenburg began on April 27, 1914, one week after the Ludlow Massacre, when three hundred armed guerilla miners deployed along the "hogback"—a mile-long, tree-carpeted ridge stretching north of the city toward the west, adjacent to CF&I property at the besieged Walsen and McNally mines, both owned by CF&I.[53]

At the Walsen Mine, guards responded to the miners' fire with machine gun and cannon fire, which they sprayed sporadically down West Seventh Street into the city of Walsenburg itself. One miner and two noncombatants were fatally wounded by the fire before the end of the day. As the strikers entrenched themselves on the hogback and prepared for the coming of militia troops from Ludlow, Governor Ammons issued a manifesto calling on all peace officers of the state to arrest any man or woman found carrying arms. But in Walsenburg, Sheriff Farr barricaded himself in the courthouse and ignored the governor's mandate.[54]

Before the fighting had broken out, Antonio Atencio, his eldest son, Miguel, and his nephew, Avelino Valdez, were employed by the Fruth-Autry Ditch Company. At the time, they were making repairs to a ditch approximately halfway between CF&I's Walsen Mine and Robinson Mine properties and the hogback. When bullets started flying between the guerilla miners and the mine guards at the Walsen Mine, the three frightened workmen left their team of horses and crawled on their hands and knees along the ditch until they reached safety at North Veta, approximately six miles west of the scene of the shooting.[55]

Following the first day of action on the hogback, a military detachment from Ludlow arrived in Walsenburg during the night to find the Walsen Mine under siege. Before the end of the day, thirteen more were to die, including Major P. P. Lester, a militia physician, who was tending two wounded guardsmen when he was fatally wounded. Other fatalities that day included ten mine guards, one striker, and one noncombatant, who was shot off his motorcycle as he raced down the road from Pueblo to Walsenburg. Riding on the pillion with the ill-fated driver was Dora Endes, who was injured when the mortally wounded driver's vehicle somersaulted off the road.[56] Jack Burke, who lived in the Nelson Boarding House, along with two other striking miners, were later indicted for the murder of Major Lester, but the Supreme Court of Colorado subsequently threw out the charge.[57] The striking miners withdrew from the hogback when the federal troops arrived in Walsenburg on April 30, 1914.

Peace in Southern Colorado

With the arrival of federal troops in the southern Colorado coal fields, private mine guards and militia were withdrawn, and the strikers and deputy sheriffs were required to surrender their arms. Since importation of strikebreakers constituted a violation of state law, those who had come from other states were compelled to leave.[58] Peace had returned, but the strike dragged on into the summer of 1914. President Wilson attempted to conciliate, with the state government suggesting a three-year truce; rehiring of all miners not found guilty of lawbreaking; adherence to state mining laws; posting of wages, rules, and regulations; establishment of a grievance committee at each mine; and the naming of a three-man commission, appointed by the president of the United States, to serve as a court of appeals. The UMW agreed to the president's plan contingent upon approval by a miners' convention. Having spent some $3 million on the strike, national mine leaders saw President Wilson's plan as a chance to bring the strife to a conclusion. The coal operators, however, continued their stubborn policy of no dealings with the union and turned down the compromise truce plan. Meanwhile, the miners approved the plan in convention on December 7, 1914, and the strike officially and unilaterally ended on that date.[59]

W. L. MacKenzie King to the Rescue

A stalemate resulted because of the coal operators' stand; subsequently, it wasn't broken until Rockefeller took action to alleviate the problem. Rockefeller engaged W. L. MacKenzie King, a former Canadian labor minister and later prime minister of Canada, to help solve the dilemma. King came up with the "Rockefeller Plan," or the "Colorado Industrial Representation Plan," as it was officially called. The plan contained several features that addressed the problems that had precipitated the conflict. It proposed a management-worker committee to hear grievances; it granted several of the miners' demands, such as a checkweighman at each mine, the right to trade where one pleased, and the right to join a union without reprisals. The forerunner of the "company union," the plan was launched with fanfare in the fall of 1915, when Rockefeller and King traveled to Colorado. Rockefeller ate and danced with the miners and their wives and bounced miners' children on his knees.[60]

Although the union did not accept the Rockefeller Plan, it did serve as a stabilizing influence in the Colorado coal fields for several years. It wasn't until the Wagner Act and other "New Deal" legislation of the 1930s, however, that the miners finally gained union recognition. The Rockefeller Plan, meanwhile, did not prevent strife in the intervening years. A small strike occurred in 1918, and a larger one kept miners out in 1921–22 when the coal operators attempted to lower wages, a common practice at that time in all industries. Although militia troops were sent to Walsenburg, there was no violence, and at the end of the strike, the CF&I restored wages to their previous levels. The last significant strike developed in 1927 when the Industrial Workers of the World organized a sympathy strike over the deaths of Nicola Sacco and Bartolomeo Vanzetti, Italian immigrants who were executed for the murder of a shoe factory paymaster in Massachusetts. John Lawson, now a mine inspector, helped to settle that strike.[61]

The Big Names Are Gone, but the Family Names Still Live

After the strike, Jack Burke continued living at the Nelson Boarding House, and during Prohibition, he did some bootlegging. He was caught transporting liquor from Raton, New Mexico, however, and was tried, convicted, and served time in the Colorado State Penitentiary in Canon City. After leaving prison, Burke did not return to Walsenburg but worked in some independent mines and at other odd jobs. He corresponded with Frances Nelson and sent her a wristwatch as a gift, but she finally lost track of him. His trunk still remains at the Seventh Street Nelson Boarding

House location, now the private home of Frances Nelson Vallejo.[62]

Over the years, peace has reigned in the coal fields of Huerfano County. The advent of new fuels and new mine safety regulations, how-ever, has caused the demise of all major coal mines in the county. Walsenburg now serves as the home for many who work at the CF&I Allen Mine near Trinidad to the south. All the coal camps have long been abandoned, but the people still remember the bitter days of 1913–14. The big names long ago left the area, but the family names and the memories still survive.

Notes

1
Barron B. Beshoar, *Out of the Depths: The Story of John R. Lawson, a Labor Leader* (Denver: Golden Bell Press, 1942), ix.

2
George G. Suggs, Jr., *Colorado's War on Militant Unionism* (Detroit: Wayne State University Press, 1972), 11-13.

3
Stephen J. Scheinberg, "The Development of Corporation Labor Policy, 1900–1940" (Ph.D. diss., University of Wisconsin, 1966), 80.

4
Max Eastman, "Class War in Colorado," *Echoes of Revolt: The Masses, 1911–1917*, William L. O'Neill, ed. (Chicago: Quadrangle Books, 1966), 150.

5
Frances Nelson Atencio Vallejo Papers (undated typewritten and handwritten reports and correspondence in author's possession; hereinafter referred to as "Vallejo Papers").

6
U.S., Congress, Senate, *Industrial Relations: Final Report and Testimony Submitted to Congress by the Commission on Industrial Relations, Created by the Act of August 23, 1912*, 64th Cong., 1st sess., 1916, Doc. 415, VII-IX, 6424.

7
LeRoy R. Hafen, ed., *Colorado and Its People* (New York: Lewis Historical Publishing Company, Inc., 1948), 322.

8
Industrial Relations VII, 6477.

9
George S. McGovern and Leonard F. Guttridge, *The Great Coalfield War* (Boston: Houghton Mifflin Company, 1972), 81; George P. West, *Report on the Colorado Strike* (Washington, D.C.: United States Commission on Industrial Relations, 1915), 40.

10
Beshoar, *Out of the Depths*, 14. Beshoar identifies Marshal Martinez as "Severio," a misspelling of a common Spanish first name, "Silverio."

11
Vallejo Papers.

12
Eugene D. Porter, "The Colorado Coal Strike of 1913: An Interpretation," *The Historian* 12 (Autumn 1949), 4-5. A "checkweighman" is "a representative elected by coal miners to check the findings of the mine owner's weighman where miners are paid by the weight of coal mined"; *The Random House Dictionary of the English Language* (New York: Random House, 1971), 252.

13
Graham Adams, Jr., *Age of Industrial Violence, 1910–15: The Activities and Findings of the United States Commission on Industrial Relations* (New York: Columbia University Press, 1966), 152.

14
Beshoar, *Out of the Depths*, 59; Vallejo Papers.

15
Tom Trew, personal interview, March 12, 1974. Trew was a young coal miner during the 1913–14 coal strike in southern Colorado. His recollections contributed to the general theme of this account.

16
McGovern and Guttridge, *The Great Coalfield War*, 119.

17
Ibid., 339.

18
Vallejo Papers.

19
Ibid.

20
U.S. Department of Labor, *Second Annual Report of the Department of Labor* (Washington, D.C.: U.S. Government Printing Office, 1915), 40.

21
Quoted in the *Literary Digest* 49 (December 12, 1914), 1165.

22
U.S., Congressional Record, 63rd Cong., 2d sess., April 29, 1914, 7441.

23
Billie Barnes Jensen, "Woodrow Wilson's Intervention in the Coal Strike of 1914," *Labor History* 14 (Winter 1974), 67.

24
Vallejo Papers.

25
U.S., *Congressional Record*, 63rd

Cong., 2d sess., July 13, 1914, 42016.

26
Ibid.

27
Ibid.

28
McGovern and Guttridge, *The Great Coalfield War*, 125; Beshoar, *Out of the Depths*, 78-80.

29
McGovern and Guttridge, *The Great Coalfield War*, 125.

30
Ana Atencio Lucero, personal interview, March 14, 1974; Beshoar, *Out of the Depths*, 80.

31
Ibid.

32
Ana Atencio Lucero, personal interview. The name "Foster" was entered into the records of the Commission on Industrial Relations; see *Industrial Relations* VII, 6798.

33
Ana Atencio Lucero, personal interview; John Reed, "The Colorado Wars," *Metropolitan Magazine* 14 (July 1914), 11; McGovern and Guttridge, in *The Great Coalfield War*, 126, report the incident as occurring at Seventh and Main, six blocks east of the actual site.

34
Vallejo Papers.

35
McGovern and Guttridge, *The Great*

Coalfield War, 126.

36
Earl H. Findley, "Bitter War Bred under Wings of Strike," *New York Tribune*, May 10, 1914; *Industrial Relations* VII, 6799-808.

37
U.S., Congress, House, Committee on Mines and Mining, *Report on the Colorado Strike Investigation*, made under H. Res. 387, 63rd Cong., 1915, Doc. 1630, 7.

38
Scheinberg, "The Development of Corporation Labor Policy," 80.

39
Industrial Relations IX, 8593.

40
Jerome D. Green to W. L. MacKenzie King, June 12, 1914, W. L. MacKenzie King MSS, vol. 23, as cited in Scheinberg, "The Development of Corporation Labor Policy," 209.

41
West, *Report on the Colorado Strike*, 111-15.

42
Colorado Adjutant General, *The Military Occupation of the Coal Strike Zone of Colorado by the Colorado National Guard: Report of the Commanding General to the Governor for the Use of the Congressional Committee. Exhibiting an Account of the Military Occupation to the Time of the First Withdrawal of Troops in April, 1914* (Denver), 70-71; Adams, *Age of Industrial Violence*, 154; *Industrial Relations* VIII, 7170-71.

43
West, *Report on the Colorado Strike*, 116.

44
Mary Jones, *Autobiography of Mother Jones*, Mary Field Parton, ed. (Chicago: Charles H. Kerr and Company, 1925), 182-3; Beshoar, *Out of the Depths*, 127-41.

45
Dale Fetherling, *Mother Jones: The Miners' Angel* (Carbondale: Southern Illinois University Press, 1974), 184-5.

46
Ibid.

47
Report on the Colorado Strike Investigation II, 2865.

48
West, *Report on the Colorado Strike*, 123-4.

49
Ibid., 126-33; Beshoar, *Out of the Depths*, 166-79; McGovern and Guttridge, *The Great Coalfield War*, 210-31; Adams, *Age of Industrial Violence*, 156-60.

50
Beshoar, *Out of the Depths*, 209-10; Adams, *Age of Industrial Violence*, 146.

51
Walter H. Fink, "The Ludlow Massacre," *Massacre at Ludlow: Four Reports*, Leon Stein and Philip Taft, eds. (New York: Arno and the *New York Times*, 1971).

52
McGovern and Guttridge, *The Great*

Coalfield War, 240-58; Adams, *Age of Industrial Violence*, 160.

53
Ibid., 160-61.

54
Beshoar, *Out of the Depths*, 216; Reed, "The Colorado War," 11-15.

55
Vallejo Papers.

56
Ibid.; Beshoar, *Out of the Depths*, 216-21; McGovern and Guttridge, *The Great Coalfield War*, 260-67.

57
Beshoar, *Out of the Depths*, 317.

58
Coal Trade Journal 46, pt. 1 (May 13, 1914), 542.

59
Fetherling, *Mother Jones: The Miners' Angel*, 127-9; McGovern and Guttridge, *The Great Coalfield War*, 302-3.

60
Irving Bernstein, *The Lean Years: A History of the Worker, 1920–1933* (Boston: Houghton Mifflin Company, 1960), 160.

61
Beshoar, *Out of the Depths*, 363-4.

62
Vallejo Papers.

Los Betabeleros (The Beetworkers)

José Aguayo

ABOUT THE AUTHOR

José Aguayo graduated from the University of Denver with a Master of Arts degree in cultural anthropology. He is executive director of the Museo de las Americas in Denver. His research focuses on Mexican culture and history from the post-conquest period through the Revolution of 1910–20.

THE SAFEST INVESTMENT on earth *is* earth." "One-way colonist fares for homeseekers." Advertisements like these, following the completion of rail connections to eastern markets, spurred the settlement of the Colorado plains in the late 1880s and early 1900s. Settlers came to farm the arid prairie—until then described as useless and uninhabitable.

The channeling of winter snowmelt from the state's major river and tributaries added the missing element, allowing a dramatic increase in tillable acreage. Irrigation permitted farmers to experiment with crops other than grains watered only with natural rainfall. The sugar beet was one such crop, planted on land bordering the South Platte River, which sliced the state diagonally from south of Denver northeast to the Nebraska border. The cultivation of sugar beets eventually dominated farming in this South Platte Valley, growing at a rate that exceeded the pool of local labor available to tend the crop.

The Great Western Sugar Company contracted with farmers to grow a specified number of acres of sugar beets within designated factory districts. The company taught the farmers the latest techniques developed out of research conducted at its Longmont Experimental Station, established in 1910. Great Western fostered the development of better planting, cultivating, and harvesting equipment, even buying new equipment and lending it to the growers. University-trained Great Western fieldmen assisted farmers in the selection of suitable land for growing sugar beets and supervised the planting, fertilization, tending, and harvesting of the crop, the control of pests and diseases, and the transport of the crop to the factory for processing. The fieldman also oversaw relations between the grower and the laborers, who were recruited annually to do the seasonal handwork required to produce maximum tonnage from each acre.

Farm families and local labor tended the beet crop for only the first few years of production, when planted acreage was small. An article in the Great Western publication *Through the Leaves* proclaimed: "The youngster, when employed in bunches, enjoys the work, which is not really hard, and it gives them self-confidence." But other assessments of beet work described it as backbreaking, tedious labor that not many would choose to do voluntarily. Labor-saving innovations in machinery and "scientific" agricultural techniques came too slow to help the beleaguered farmer. It became necessary to import field hands from neighboring areas.

From the beginning, Great Western adopted the unprecedented policy of nurturing its product from field to market. The company brought in

German Russian families from Nebraska, who had experience working in that state's beet-producing areas. Japanese "solos"—single males—were also recruited starting in 1903. The company transported the laborers to beet-growing districts and arranged contracts with the farmers. German Russian laborers were preferred because they arrived in family groups that eventually settled permanently, eliminating the need to provide annual transportation from the Midwest to the Colorado beet fields. By 1909, sufficient numbers of German Russians lived in the South Platte Valley to satisfy labor requirements. But permanent residency created another problem: within ten years, the German Russian laborers were becoming tenant farmers and landowners themselves. Some of the earlier settlers resented the laborers' climb up the economic ladder. An excerpt from a Lafayette farmer's 1918 article in *Through the Leaves* titled "Does Beet Labor Respond to Good Treatment?" is typical of popular sentiment toward immigrants trying to better their lives: ". . . You simply can't treat them as you would treat people you have around the place, for if you tried that, it wouldn't be thirty days until you would be living in the shack and the Russian would be riding in your 'fliver'."

By about 1916, German Russians had left the fields of northern Colorado as laborers. The Japanese "solos," now married, also became permanent residents and farmers. Great Western ranged farther afield in its efforts to find reliable workers willing to do the seasonal drudgery necessary to bring in the required sugar beet tonnage to keep its chain of Platte Valley factories operating.

Great Western employed agents whose sole duty was the recruitment of field laborers. The company advertised in local newspapers, even calling door-to-door in southern Colorado, New Mexico, and Texas. Hispanos who had settled the region as of 1598 were experiencing economic difficulties, forcing them to seek employment away from their ancestral villages.

Magdalena Arellano recalls an agent's visit to her home in Antonito, Colorado, in 1922. She was fifteen at the time and employed by a wealthy family to care for their children at five dollars a week. "I was lucky," she says. "I was working, but the other members of my family could not find employment. When the agent for 'la compañía azucarera,' the sugar company, came, my mother, uncle, aunt, and I left Antonito for Fort Collins. The sugar company paid our rail fare and put us up overnight at the Linden Hotel when we arrived in Fort Collins. The next morning we were contracted out to a farmer, living in a shack 'en el rancho' while we worked in the beets."

Between 1912 and 1916, Spanish Americans satisfied the need for beet laborers. The start of World War I and the continued growth of the agricultural industry caused another surge in the demand for unskilled laborers. Mexican *peones*, driven by the violence of revolution (1910–20), population pressures, and general economic chaos scrambled north seeking rumored prosperity. Crossing the border was a simple matter in those days. The war and changes in immigration laws had stemmed the flood of immigrants from eastern and southern Europe. Agriculturists in the western states actively lobbied Congress to exempt Mexicans from restrictive immigration quotas, arguing that they would not become permanent residents. Instead, they would return to Mexico every year after the harvests. Before 1900, immigration from Mexico was negligible, averaging less than seven hundred a year. The numbers quickly escalated. Between 1900 and 1930, more than a million Mexicans came to the United States to work, mostly in Texas cotton fields and California vegetable and citrus industries. Forty-five thousand came to Colorado in search of rumored high wages in the tending of sugar beets. Initially, many of the migrants did return to their homeland, buying small parcels of land in Mexico or living during the off-season on their earnings in the United States. Upon returning to Mexico, they also described the opportunity for a better life north of the border. Some returned to Colorado, often bringing relatives or friends with them. Each new wave of migrant laborers was larger than the last and, as it receded back into Mexico, left increasing numbers of permanent residents in its wake.

The survivors of the Ortega family were some of the many who fled the terrible conflict between revolutionary and federal armies in Mexico. Seven-year-old Jovita remembers the family gathering only the possessions they could carry and jumping over corpses in the streets of Chihuahua as they hurried to the train station:

> My father, José Ortega, a soldier in Pancho Villa's Army of the North, died in 1912 during the siege of Chihuahua. Before he died, he told my mother that if she didn't survive the Revolution, I was to live with my *tía*, aunt, Severa Varela, and my two sisters should be sent to live with their *madrina*, their godmother. My mother died of diphtheria during the second battle for Chihuahua in 1915, so my grandmother and all of her family came to the United States, crossing the bridge at El Paso, Texas.
>
> When we arrived at the Chihuahua train station, there was already a huge mob of refugees pushing and shoving frantically to board the train. The coaches were full and we couldn't find space. Desperate

with fear, we boarded a freight train. I remember vividly the crowded cattle car, the floor matted with straw, and the wind blowing from side to side through the slatted wall as we sped to the border.

Jovita Ortega did not come directly to the Colorado beet fields. Her family lived in Texas for twelve years. In El Paso, they settled at 301 Spruce Street, only steps away from the Mexican border. They lived reasonably well with income from abuelo (grandfather) Matias Gonzales's junk selling and *abuela* (grandmother) Albina's enterprises. Every day, after school, Jovita's abuela sent her to sell eggs around the neighborhood.

Jovita loved school despite her aunt's constant maneuvering to keep her at home. Tía Severa inevitably pleaded illness, so Jovita had to do all of the housework. Every morning after cooking breakfast and packing lunch for her *tío*, she dashed out the door to catch the trolley clanking up Alameda Avenue. Jumping off at Magoffin Street, "I would run like a scared jackrabbit as I heard the bell signaling the start of classes at Beall School three blocks away."

Sundays were a different story. Jovita was Grandma Albina's favorite grandchild. Doña Albina bought Jovita pretty dresses of organdy and velvet so she could accompany her to Guardian Angels Church every weekend. Doña Albina loved ceremony: "We sat through five or six masses every weekend just to enjoy the weddings," says Jovita. Sunday evenings don Antonio took Jovita downtown to see *zarzuelas* (musical comedies) or *títeres* (puppet shows). Jovita was a star student. She proudly wore the required uniform of bloomers and middie top and even today remembers the school song set to the tune of *The Battle Hymn of the Republic*:

Glory, glory, glory, Beall School
Glory, glory, glory, Beall School
Glory, glory, glory, Beall School
B - E - A - Double L

Every morning Tio Antonio gave Jovita five cents for lunch. With this she could buy a large bowl of *menudo* and cup of delicious *chocolate*. Occasionally she added another five cents to that stipend by doing schoolwork for her best friend, Anita Romero. Unfortunately, this left Anita at a loss when the teacher called her to the chalkboard to work out math problems.

Tía Severa continued to make every effort to take Jovita out of school. One day, a mounted policeman overtook Jovita as she ran an errand.

"Why aren't you in school?" he asked. Terrified, Jovita told him her aunt wouldn't let her go to school any more. "We'll just see about that," said the policeman. He took her home and told her aunt that Jovita must attend school one more year, at least through fifth grade.

Tía Severa took Jovita out of school for good at age eleven. Cooking, housecleaning, washing, and ironing became her daily routine:

> In May of 1927, after my grandmother died, we came to the beet fields of Ovid, Colorado. We had many boys in the family, so we could earn much money. My tío would light the stove for me at 3 A.M. and I would wake up to make a hearty breakfast for everyone working at thinning and topping the beets. After breakfast, at about 4 A.M., I would also go out to the fields to work, but not before making a large stack of tortillas and putting beans to cook. I would return at noon to help my tía prepare the noon meal. While the boys rested in the shade, I would wash dishes and then return to the fields with them until it got dark. After dinner, I ironed clothes, finally going to bed at 11 P.M. Oh, those were tough times, so many boys in the family, so many clothes to wash and iron.

Most of the early Mexican immigrants who came north seeking to better their economic condition came from the agrarian states of Guanajuato, Jalisco, San Luis Potosí, Michoacan, and Aguascalientes. Though Great Western preferred to contract families because of their stability, an increasing number of the Mexican immigrants were single males between the ages of eighteen and thirty. Marciano Aguayo fit the typical profile exactly.

Aguayo left an abusive father and the grinding poverty of their tiny *rancho* in *La Barranca de las Cabras* (Goat Canyon), Aguascalientes, at age fifteen. Geronimo Aguayo was accustomed to leaving young Marciano to protect the distant *milpas*, cornfields, from birds and rodents for days at a time. Marciano, desperate at times, was forced to roast the immature corn and squash to satisfy his gnawing hunger. Their rancho, isolated in a spectacularly scenic canyon, barely produced enough food to sustain the Aguayo family. The scarcity of food, perhaps, compelled grandmother Maria Hernandez to lasso the towering *peñascos*, escarpments, and climb up to savor the delicious *tunas*, cactus fruit, growing high above the canyon. There too were honeycombs she wrested from the protesting bees.

One by one, the Aguayo family left *La Barranca de las Cabras* for the capital city of Aguascalientes, where there was more opportunity. Following his older brother Ciriaco to Aguascalientes, Marciano first worked as a blacksmith in the railroad roundhouse. He was too young to be hired officially, but Ciriaco convinced the foreman that Marciano was a hard worker. The foreman gave him a job but told him, "On payday, when the superintendent comes around, I want you to hide behind the locomotives."

Though railway workers were noncombatants, they played an important role in the revolution. They had to keep the trains that transported troops from city to city rolling. Pancho Villa often used more than a dozen trains to carry his troops into battle. At the roundhouse Aguayo learned to operate monstrous steam-powered hammers to shape replacement parts for the steam locomotives. This experience may account for his lifelong fascination with the railroad.

In Aguascalientes, near the end of the war, railroad workers including Aguayo petitioned victorious general Alvaro Obregon to make good the paper money issued to them by Villa's administration in northern Mexico. Obregon contemptuously replied, "When this arm that I lost to Villa's artillery grows back, I will make good that money." Aguayo's foreman was confident that President Carranza would eventually pay their back wages and urged him to stay, but Aguayo left Mexico for good about 1919. Penniless when he arrived at the border, he could only look hungrily at the bread in bakery windows. He spent a cold and hungry night before crossing the border the next morning.

Prosperity was not there for the taking in El Paso, although conditions were certainly better than what Aguayo had abandoned. The average daily wage in Mexico had been about eighty centavos (.80 pesos). Farm laborers in the United States earned five times that at $2.02 dollars per day (4.04 pesos at the current exchange rate of two pesos to the dollar). Anxious to again join his brother Ciriaco, who had preceded him to the United States, Marciano went north to Tyler, Texas, where he worked for a few months on the railroad extra gang at $1.25 per day. Moving on, he lingered awhile in Blackwell, Oklahoma, cutting four and a half cords of firewood daily at twenty-five cents a cord. He eventually teamed up with Ciriaco again in Pueblo, Colorado. Together they "worked the beets" near Sugar City on the Arkansas River. Compatriots returning to Mexico lavishly described the opportunity for high wages in the South Platte Valley, so, like hobos, they rode the truss rods of freight cars, jumping off near Merino, Colorado, in the spring of 1921.

Not all of the beet laborers were recruited by the sugar company. Some, like the Aguayos, approached the growers directly and negotiated their own contracts.

Tending sugar beets is a cyclical task requiring several "passes" over the same acreage. In *My Childhood on the Prairie*, Clara Hilderman Erlich describes the phases of sugar beet growing in 1904. The seed is planted in spring using a horse-drawn, four-row beet drill. It is planted generously to ensure a good stand. The seed germinates by the time school is out in early June. When the plant develops four leaves it is time for thinning—*el desaihe* to Mexican laborers. The field is "blocked" by cutting out plants in the rows with a hoe so that clusters or blocks of plants are evenly spaced about eight to twelve inches apart. Next, thinning of blocks by hand or again with the hoe removes all but one plant from each cluster. As the plants mature, two passes are made to remove weeds and any double plants missed in the thinning—*la limpia*. The field is then furrowed to prepare it for irrigation and machine cultivated to keep the dirt around the furrows loose. In late September, a special plow is set to cut deep down, severing the taproot and loosening the dirt so that the beet can be pulled out with one hand and the leaves or top cut with a long knife held in the other—*el tapéo*. Topped beets are piled and then loaded into wagons, transporting one and a half to two tons at a time directly to the sugar factory or to beet dumps located near the railroad for transport by rail car. The leaves are left in the field as nutritious feed for cattle.

In later years Marciano Aguayo often paid farmers to allow him to turn his small herds of cattle into the harvested beet fields to fatten on the beet tops. In poor health just before his death in 1979, Aguayo lamented the fact that he could no longer tend the cattle and pigs that he always managed to have around for extra income. "Since I was a small child, I have tended animals," he wrote in a letter to his son. "Now they are taking that joy away from me."

To maximize production and efficiency, Great Western compared the tending of sugar beet acreage among the various ethnic groups of laborers, passing on their findings to the contracted growers. According to the studies, a German Russian family could efficiently tend twelve acres of beets from thinning to topping. Japanese and Mexican "solos" could tend seven acres.

Using various incentives, Great Western attempted to increase the quality and quantity of field work. The company advised growers to "hold back" some of the wages from thinning and cleaning the fields in the spring to ensure that the contract laborer would remain to do the topping in the fall. Laborers accused growers of excessive "hold back," or of neglecting to pay at harvest time the earnings held in escrow, and the practice was outlawed in 1930. Another incentive was bonuses to laborers for tonnage harvested above the district's average. This incentive also discouraged excessive or sloppy thinning of the beet crop in the spring—a practice attributed to laborers wanting to lighten their workload when the beets were pulled in the fall.

The company conducted its operations like athletic competitions: the factory processing season from October to March was called a "campaign," and factories vied to win the "pennant" for highest production. Marciano Aguayo held many certificates of merit issued by Great Western as incentives to help maximize the beet crop and to identify, for the growers, laborers who were reliable and efficient. Aguayo's certificates, dated 1925 to 1931, indicate that he was an exceptional beet laborer, tending from nineteen to twenty-six acres per season with a quality-of-work grade of "A."

Everyone wanted to be Aguayo's partner. The family of Jovita Ortega, Aguayo's future wife, urged relatives to work with him because "*es muy trabajador*"—he is a hard worker. Aguayo was proud of his reputation and, in later years, told his children how hard he worked to earn it:

> I was accustomed to waking up at 3 A.M. every morning. I walked to the fields, arriving by first light when one was just able to see the individual beet plants. I would walk in the furrow between rows, thinning and hoeing two at a time. I continued this pace until well past dark, lighting my way with a carbide lamp mounted on a miner's cap. I was home by 10 P.M. every night to catch a few short hours of sleep before repeating the routine all over again.

Beetworkers' wages varied considerably from year to year and from one district to another. Magdalena Arellano remembers being paid eighteen dollars per acre in the Fort Collins factory district in 1923. Marciano Aguayo's receipts in the Ovid factory district show a breakdown of wages for 1929 of seven dollars per acre for thinning, two dollars per acre for hoeing, and nine dollars per acre for topping, with an additional bonus at harvest of $.775 per acre for exceptional production. Aguayo's earnings for the 1929 sugar beet season totaled just four hundred eighty-two dollars. Before he married, similar amounts had to last through the winter, for he had made the decision early on to make the United States his home. With his seasonal earnings he could purchase a hundred pounds each of beans, potatoes, and flour and a bit of lard, sugar, and coffee. In later years, Aguayo demonstrated the skill at making tortillas he developed as a bachelor. Even Jovita, an award-winning tortilla maker herself, acknowledged that his perfectly round, thin, and fluffy tortillas were better than those made by most women!

After beet harvest, Aguayo augmented his winter survival fund and earned a little "fun money" by picking corn in the hills rising south of the Platte River at Sedgwick. Aguayo and two or three companions would pile into his 1926 Model T Ford and drive to Denver. "We stayed in the best hotel—the Shirley Savoy," he would later tell his children. He would point to a studio photograph of two young *Mexicanos* in cowboy garb and say, "I bought this fine hat, a John B. Stetson, at the Daniels & Fisher store." Then, laughing, he would continue, "After one of these trips, a friend and I were determined to return to Mexico. We started out, catching a south-bound Rio Grande freight train. But outside of Denver we were robbed at gunpoint. The robber took my friend's new shoes, leaving as replacement the smelliest pair of boots imaginable. After this incident, I decided that I would stay in the United States."

Spanish Americans and Mexicans alike measured their early years in Colorado by the names of farmers for whom they worked: "Those were the years that I worked for *la Señora Frink*," or "*Cuando viviamos en el rancho del Toyne*." They were not any more welcome as permanent residents than the German Russians who preceded them. To the white farmers they were all immigrant Mexicans—no matter that some of their ancestors had settled the Southwest more than four hundred years earlier. As they put down roots in Fort Collins, Greeley, Longmont, Brighton, Eaton, Loveland, and other beet-growing towns in northern Colorado, they also began to leave the fields and farm-labor shacks to settle in previously all-white communities. They learned the language, laws, and customs of their adopted land.

When they purchased homes, they were usually shunted to the fringes of the community, it seems, to live among "their own kind." These neighborhoods, and the clusters of houses subsidized by Great Western on land near its factories, became the Mexican *colonias* of Colorado.

Initially, immigrant laborers lived in housing provided by the farmers with whom they contracted. The housing was nearly always substandard and inadequate for sheltering large extended families. Jovita Ortega, newly married to Marciano Aguayo in 1929, recalls crowding into a one-room labor shack with another couple and Marciano's brother Ciriaco. The sparse furnishings included an iron bedstead and a wood-burning stove. A later home was somewhat better—two rooms made of brick—but Jovita had to place their two infant daughters in a washtub balanced on two chairs to keep them safe from rats as big as house cats.

In *Through the Leaves,* the sugar company, recognizing the critical role played by Mexican labor in its operations, implored growers to provide better housing: "Do not expect a high class of labor if you have a poor place for them to live."

One benefit of working on a farm was the patch of land provided by the farmer on which to grow vegetables that could be canned to last through the winter. The Aguayos kept a large garden, eventually taking up half a town block, throughout their lives. When their children came to Sedgwick on summer visits in later years, bags of fresh cucumbers, tomatoes, chiles, and melons went home with them to Greeley and Denver. Marciano and Jovita's garden produce were perennial first-place winners at Sedgwick's annual harvest festival. The Aguayos were justly proud of the relatively bountiful life that the garden represented. Marciano delighted in taking the newest grandchildren to see and taste the powerful *chorro* (stream) of water pumped from his thirty-foot-deep, hand-dug well.

Great Western created a program for beet laborers to build their own houses of adobe. Laborers were issued building materials on credit against earnings from the next growing season. Purchase of the land on which they built could be extended over a four-year period. The company newsletter even carried information about construction technology, including how to make adobe—recommending it for its insulating qualities and economy and noting its familiarity to the Mexican and Spanish American beet labor force.

Colonias sprang up in Greeley, Kersey, Loveland, Hudson, Brush, Fort Morgan, Brighton, Fort Collins, and Ovid. Some were no more than a cluster of two or three houses. Most were viewed by the white population as an appropriate means of keeping the Mexicans together. Even Spanish American families, who managed to edge into the fringe of the white communities, sometimes looked down at their compatriots living in the colonias.

Magdalena Arellano bought a house on Howe Street in Fort Collins for five hundred dollars. She arranged for the loan and made several payments from her earnings as a domestic before her husband was even aware that they were becoming homeowners. Marciano Aguayo traded his Model T for some land and a one-room, tarpaper shack on the outskirts of Sedgwick. A few years later, he used a team of draft horses to drag a two-room clapboard building from Main Street to attach to the shack. This was the Aguayo family home until the 1970s, when Marciano and Jovita moved into the more genteel center of the small community.

Mexican laborers faced many obstacles in their adopted land.

Marciano Aguayo's personal files are filled with letters he wrote to the Mexican consulate in Denver requesting investigations of dishonest practices by company fieldmen. Some accused the fieldmen of favoring growers by shortchanging unsuspecting laborers when measuring the beet acreage they tended. Other growers allegedly refused to pay wages held back from the laborers' spring earnings. Local merchants were suspected of overcharging laborers for goods and services and conspiring with growers to deduct these exorbitant store charges before paychecks were distributed to them. Because most Mexican laborers did not speak English and did not understand the laws of the United States, it was easy to defraud them. They relied on compatriots like Aguayo, who learned to speak English and gained a working knowledge of the local economic and legal systems to communicate their concerns to the appropriate authorities. Aguayo also served as intermediary for Mexican laborers being repatriated during the 1930s and helped locate the families of single laborers who died in northern Colorado, far from their homes in Mexico.

As further defense against prejudice and exploitation, Mexican immigrants in northern Colorado formed mutual aid societies like the Comisión Honorífica. Spanish Americans, especially in southern Colorado, formed Sociedad Protección Mutua de Trabajadores Unidos chapters for similar purposes. The primary function of these organizations was to build solidarity within the Mexican and Spanish American communities, to educate their members about the laws and institutions of the United States, to welcome new arrivals to the communities, and to plead cases of injustice before the appropriate authorities. Comisión Honoríficas also organized festivals and social gatherings designed to build pride in their heritage, to reinforce loyalty to their homeland, and as a means to meet and visit. The Aguayo brothers led organizers of festivals on two important Mexican national holidays, Cinco de Mayo (Fifth of May) and Diez y Seis de Septiembre (Sixteenth of September).

Patriotic red, white, and green posters printed in Denver announced the festivals held in Sedgwick and Ovid throughout the 1920s. Candidates for festival queen rode on elaborately decorated farm trucks with both the Mexican and American flags flying. Programs for celebrations in Fort Collins and Sedgwick listed musical presentations, poetry recitals, and waltz, polka, and two-step dances. Red, white, and green and red, white, and blue strings of bulbs lighted the rented halls above Jankovsky's Store for the events in Sedgwick. These were memorable celebrations, where people of Spanish and Mexican descent could express pride in their heritage while acknowledging loyalty to the United States. More than a few marriages, including Jovita Ortega's to Marciano Aguayo, resulted from introductions at these festivals.

The Aguayos and Arellanos were among those who found ways to establish themselves permanently within the white communities. In 1941, after years of applying, Marciano Aguayo was finally able to land a job with the Union Pacific Railroad section gang in Sedgwick. In characteristic fashion, he worked hard maintaining the railroad right-of-way from Ovid to Crook. He was already forty-three, but this stocky, muscular man could hoist an eighty-pound railroad cross-tie onto each shoulder and run to place them in position. He never missed a day of work in thirty-two years with Union Pacific, no matter if he was ill or how severe the weather. Aguayo's children remember running to meet his sheepskin overcoated figure as he walked home on cold and snowy winter days, his eyelids nearly frozen shut.

Working somewhat regular hours for the railroad left Aguayo time in the evening to entertain his children with stories of his childhood in Mexico. He was a talented raconteur, and his accounts of village *brujas* (witches), buried treasure, and the Mexican Revolution created vivid images. One could almost see his horrified cousin bringing the ascending *brujas* crashing to earth with her cry, "*Ave María purisima!*"—hail blessed mother—instead of what she had been instructed to say: "*Sin Dios y sin Santa María*," without God and without the Holy Mother. He painted a vivid verbal picture of the old woman who admonished him against entering her *casita* to search among her personal belongings. What more incentive could you give a curious young boy? As soon as she left, Marciano would enter and examine the little jars inside the house filled with pin-pierced dolls that bore a striking resemblance to crippled villagers whom he knew. Aguayo attributed the poverty of his childhood years to his father's superstitious nature. According to Aguayo, his father failed at recovery of several buried treasures. He would begin to dig at the sites, but imagining he heard the screams of armed conflict, he would hurriedly refill the excavations. Finally, there were accounts of Villa's mounted revolutionaries coursing for hours through Aguascalientes in endless dusty columns, then toppling from their horses in the distance as they furiously charged the enemy.

Aguayo was an amalgamation of Chichimecan *caciques* (chiefs) and unknown Spanish forebears. As a young boy, he accompanied his abuelo Pedro Aguayo on horseback to collect land titles entrusted to Pedro by the indigenous village of Jesus María because he was a cacique of that congregation of Indians. The Spanish side of his ancestry was, perhaps, inextricably tangled in the exploits of the colonial Marqueses de Aguayo. Though he and Jovita proudly became citizens of the United States in the 1950s, he always maintained and instilled in his children a fierce loyalty to Mexico and their *mestizo*—Indian and Spanish—heritage.

Also in the 1950s, when a workforce reduction caused him to transfer to the Crook, Colorado, section of the Union Pacific, Aguayo faced unusual hardship in order to maintain his family. Always obsessed with punctuality, Aguayo rose at 4 A.M. (as he had when he worked in the beet fields) to ride "el loco," the local Union Pacific freight train, the seven miles to Crook. Arriving before anyone was stirring in the small community, he would curl up in the cement water troughs at the abandoned stockyard to catch a bit more sleep before reporting for work at 7:30 A.M. El loco took him back to Sedgwick well after dark. Grateful for the relatively steady employment, he never complained. One day in the 1970s, Aguayo suffered a heart attack while returning to Sedgwick on the section gang motorcar. The foreman merely braked the motorcar long enough for him to dismount. Aguayo rested awhile beside the track before walking to the Sedgwick Lumber Company to ask for help.

All beet laborers, Spanish American or Mexican, suffered the prejudice, intolerance, and discrimination seemingly always directed toward the most recently arrived ethnic group. The Mexicans, perhaps, suffered more because they looked different and spoke a different language as well. In northern Colorado during the 1920s, it was not uncommon to see signs posted in public places stating "No dogs or Mexicans allowed" and "We cater to the white trade only." Filigonio Arellano often said, "During wartime and when they need votes, white people call me an American; if I need a loan, I am Spanish; and if I am applying for a job they call me Mexican." Arellano's ancestors, of course, became citizens at the end of the Mexican War in 1848, when nearly half the Mexican Republic, including what would later be the states of Texas, New Mexico, Arizona, Nevada, California, and parts of Colorado and Utah, was ceded to the United States.

The children of beet laborers were unwelcome in northern Colorado schools. School boards characterized Mexicans as unsanitary and proposed separate schools or classrooms to protect white students from this misperceived health hazard. No extra effort was made to ensure that immigrant children attended school in compliance with the law. According to some white educators, Mexicans lacked ambition and possessed limited intellect. School administrators in Larimer and Weld counties made it easy for families to keep their children out of school for the spring beet thinning and fall harvest seasons. They made it extremely difficult for Mexican children to feel that they belonged in school, let alone to compete or excel.

None of this deterred Jovita Aguayo. She brought to Colorado her love of learning, developed in the schools in El Paso, Texas. Some of the older children born to her and Marciano Aguayo worked in the fields, but they did so only when school was out. While Marciano worked on the railroad, Jovita and some of the older children picked potatoes to earn extra money for school clothes. None of her children would be deprived of an education: there were few illnesses and no event important enough to keep anyone out of school. The Aguayo children nearly always brought home perfect attendance certificates. All learned from these outstanding and hardworking parents the value of education, graduating at the top of their high school classes and earning one Ph.D. and five Master of Arts degrees among them. Still, the Aguayos are not unique. Many Mexicans and Spanish Americans of the war years generation overcame the obstacles placed in their path and succeeded in various professional careers.

Today, the descendants of Colorado's Spanish American and Mexican beetworkers are fully assimilated. The sugar beet industry in Colorado is just a shadow of what it once was. What little land is planted in sugar beets is tended completely by machinery. The sugar factories that vitalized the communities along the South Platte River stand empty except for those in Loveland, Greeley, and Fort Morgan. Still, Colorado's Hispanics and Chicanos appreciate the hardships and obstacles overcome by their parents and grandparents so that they could capture a share of the American Dream. And many are thankful for the rich legacy of social and moral values carried down to them by their indigenous and Spanish forebears.

Mexican Migrant Workers in Depression-era Colorado

Tanya W. Kulkosky

ABOUT THE AUTHOR

Tanya W. Kulkosky received her Bachelor of Arts in history (magna cum laude) from the University of Southern Colorado in Pueblo in 1995. She will receive a Master of Arts in history from the University of Colorado at Colorado Springs in December 1998. In 1996, she completed the research manuscript which placed Pueblo Mountain Park on the National Register of Historic Places.

THE HISTORY OF migratory farm work in the southwestern United States dates back to at least 1870 with the use of Chinese labor. At that time, an "open door" policy allowed the free flow of immigration into this country. In 1882, however, Congress passed the Chinese Exclusion Act, which prompted southwestern farmers to look to Mexico for inexpensive, temporary field hands who could be attracted across a virtually open border.

Political division, religious suppression, and a poor economy in Mexico resulted in cycles of Mexican immigration into the southwestern United States after the Mexican Revolution in 1917. By the 1920s, Mexican nationals had begun immigrating into the United States in large numbers. World War I and the subsequent prosperity of the 1920s had created a shortage of labor north of the border, and American farmers and businessmen were pleased to have access to a large labor supply at such close proximity. Soon Mexican enclaves were found in cities offering employment throughout the United States, most notably in the five southwestern states of California, Arizona, Texas, New Mexico, and Colorado.

In Colorado, Mexican migrant workers found employment in the railroad gangs and sugar beet fields. Although a restrictive immigration law was in place (the Immigration Act of 1917), it was loosely applied with regard to Mexican migration.[1]

Early immigration laws, most notably the Alien Contract Labor Act of 1885, prohibited the contracting of temporary migratory workers from any country. However, a provision of exception in the Immigration Act of 1917 allowed for a massive influx of Mexican migrant workers. This was enhanced by the Immigration Act of 1924, which caused the exclusion of Asian immigrants and thus increased the demand for Mexican labor.[2]

The legacy of the Mexican migratory worker in Colorado is largely tied to agriculture. By 1900, Colorado's soil had proven itself fertile for sugar beet farming, and the state soon led the nation in sugar manufacture.[3] Large-scale sugar mills developed in the southeastern Colorado counties of Otero, Bent, and Prowers around the towns of Rocky Ford, La Junta, Lamar, Holly, and, of course, Sugar City. The area had seen a shortage of temporary labor since about 1900.[4] Sugar beet farming was labor intensive, and factories in the Arkansas Valley constantly competed for sources of cheap field labor. Germans from Russia, Mexican immigrants, Japanese immigrants, and Native Americans were solicited to work in the fields.[5] Mexican migrant workers, due to need, cost, and proximity, quickly filled the void. By the 1920s, four very profitable sugar beet mills in southeastern Colorado were using primarily Mexican migratory workers as their source of labor. State legislative attempts to restrict Mexican immigration were successfully lobbied against by the large-scale growers, sugar companies, and industrial concerns.[6]

Beet farmers and sugar factories encouraged migrations from Mexico in order to have a long-term supply of inexpensive labor. Local Anglo and Spanish citizens themselves encouraged it because it was work they were unwilling to do for the price. Thus, Mexican migrant workers had long been welcomed in the area until the severity of the Depression put some twelve million Americans out of work.

For a number of reasons, certainly low wages, the Mexican migrant worker was quickly preferred over the native Spanish-speaker who lived in this area of Colorado's vast sugar beet fields. However, indigenous Spanish-speaking people would soon be called back into the Colorado fields when nativist policies forced Mexican migrants out during a 1936 repatriation.

Because of the seasonal nature and low pay of work in the beet fields, migrant workers often could not afford the cost of transport back to Mexico. They were thus forced to spend the off-season in Denver's slums and Pueblo's barrios. There they looked for low-paying work or went on relief for the winter.[7] Historian Daniel Elazar wrote of Colorado migrant workers:

> Kept segregated and relegated to subcitizen status, it would be another generation before they (or their children) would begin to enter Colorado's political life. Their neighborhoods in Denver and their barrios located around Pueblo and the state's smaller cities became Colorado's equivalent of the black ghettos of the east.[8]

Apparently, however, the sugar beet companies tried to keep their seasonal Mexican workers in the area. If not forced outright to stay in the area during the winter due to debt, they were certainly encouraged to stay. Often their final contract pay was withheld, making them virtual slaves in a foreign country. It is easy to see why the sugar beet companies preferred the "unspoiled Mexican," for they were able to treat them little better than cattle.[9]

By the end of the 1930s many thousands of Mexican immigrants considered America and Colorado their home. Many had borne children here, who automatically became U.S. citizens under the Fourteenth Amendment. It is difficult today to estimate the number of Mexican immigrants who either crossed the border temporarily or stayed in the United States, as there was constant legal and illegal movement back and forth. It was a small matter to report oneself at a border station, and immigrants moved around the United States as they settled into different communities during the 1920s and 1930s. The U.S. Census Bureau also tended not to distinguish between generations-old Spanish American citizens and Mexican nationals, preferring to lump them together as one cultural group. This changed, however, with the 1930 census, which specified Mexican as a race unto itself.[10]

Once here, the Mexican immigrant, due to his immigrant status, generally remained locked into low-paying, unskilled labor or farm work. But there was also a great deal of reluctance on the part of Mexican immigrants to become naturalized American citizens. Like other immigrants to the United States, many Mexican nationals believed they would eventually return to Mexico. Others did not become citizens because they felt they would not receive adequate justice at the hands of the Anglos as "lower-class" Mexican American citizens as they would as citizens of Mexico.[11]

With the onset of the Great Depression, there began a "national call" to repatriate the roughly four hundred thousand illegal aliens in the country.[12] As historian Abraham Hoffman states, "Repatriation means a return to one's homeland—more than a return—a sending back."[13] In the 1940s, many went back because they *wanted* to go back; they had always intended to go back and may have been encouraged to do so by the improving Mexican economy. The thinly-veiled border made it easy to go back and forth.

But in the Depression the Bureau of Immigration, under Secretary of Labor William N. Doak, set out to locate, arrest, and deport the aliens. This early "Doak campaign" was based in southern California.[14] Thousands of Spanish-speaking people were viciously rounded up and shipped back to Mexico by train. This was Doak's grand plan to reduce unemployment during the Depression.[15] Doak's contention about the purpose of his campaign was contradictory, however, as many of the aliens he deported were themselves unemployed and on relief. Doak carried on despite strong criticism from immigration officials and the Wickersham Commission.[16] Between June 1930 and June 1931, the federal government moved almost thirty thousand aliens out of the United States.[17] Some left voluntarily, and some were deported. Some had lived in the United States for as many as ten years.[18]

By 1932, however, long-term immigrant residents of the United States began to resist repatriation to Mexico, since stricter immigration laws were making it harder to return to the United States once gone. According to Hoffmann, "Mexicans whose economic status had fared better than others were not therefore tempted to make the move. Once the New Deal programs were inaugurated, reluctance among poor Mexican nationals to return to Mexico became more pronounced."[19]

While the sugar beet companies generally prospered during this period, certainly with the help of the cheap availability of Mexican labor, the social climate changed drastically. With some twelve million unemployed, western farmers began an embargo against Mexican labor. Two years into the Depression, in 1931, a wave of American nativism against Mexican national migrant workers and immigrants had manifested itself as Americans desperately sought employment.

Nativism during the Depression was extended to all poorer classes regardless of ethnicity: the older migrant class from Mexico and the new class created by the tenant farm worker of the Midwest and the South. In addition, the government of Mexico was calling its native sons home. There were offers of free land, and the Mexican government's anti-religious campaign, the "Cristero Revolt," had ended.[20]

By 1933, at the height of the Depression, many migrant workers who had lived and worked in Colorado for ten years or more had repatriated themselves to Mexico in response to the Mexican government's new land distribution policy. Thousands from around the nation returned voluntarily by the free-rail transport the Mexican government had offered in 1930 and 1931.[21] Many of these immigrants were eligible to become naturalized U.S. citizens, having been here for over ten years. But sensing that they would remain second-class citizens and because "it was next to impossible to establish proof of legal residence in the United States,"[22] they decided to return. Those who stayed, like the displaced Oklahoma tenant farmers, roamed the Southwest throughout the 1930s. Mexican migrants "were among the poorest of the poor."[23]

According to historian Gerald Nash, "The tendency of so many migrant workers to stay near the sugar beet fields was the result of various factors. Often they were in debt, for car, food, or medical bills, and so remained in a particular locality to work off their debts."[24] Proximity to schools, hospitals, and other services also kept them settled. By the time the Depression had hit hard, just about everyone was on relief, and migrant workers tended to stay in the areas where they were provided relief and basic services.[25] Nevertheless, the poverty these Mexican migrant workers experienced as a result of the Depression proved intense in both rural and urban areas. All over the Southwest, migrant workers were forced to live in bare shacks hardly fit for an animal. This was true to no smaller degree in Pueblo, the urban center of southeastern Colorado. A number of factors contributed to the migration of Arkansas Valley workers from the rural valley to urban Pueblo. "Pueblo," as Elazar writes, was ". . . situated at an important crossroads between east and west . . . in the mainstream of the nation's westward movement."[26]

Pueblo was also in "dust bowl" country. As Nash states, "as if the woes of the Depression were not bad enough, the worst weather in over a century came to plague the Great Plains in the thirties."[27] By 1933, many small farmers in the Midwest who had suffered through the dust bowl and the Depression and had lost their farms began to migrate to the vast farmlands of California, Colorado, and other western states in hopes of securing at least temporary employment as farm field hands. But agricultural and economic crises had brought about the near collapse of the sugar industry in southeastern Colorado. The Sugar Act of 1934 (written by Senator Edward P. Costigan of Colorado), high sugar tariffs, and the exclusion of Asian immigration all contributed to a second wave of Mexican migration into Colorado in the mid-1930s and a "propping-up" of the Colorado sugar beet industry.[28] Still, the industry struggled. This fact, no doubt, along with the seasonal nature of the work, contributed to a significant migrant worker influx into the barrios of Denver and Pueblo in the mid-1930s. The accompanying swelling of relief rolls by both unemployed Anglo and Spanish-speaking peoples created tensions as citizens and aliens competed to survive in close proximity.[29]

The migrant-worker issue was quite alive in Pueblo in 1935. A local charitable organization, the Family Service Society, had been instrumental in repatriating migrant workers voluntarily returning to Mexico from Pueblo. The society then proposed that a colony be constructed outside the city limits in order to place another two hundred to two hundred fifty Spanish-speaking families. The society believed that the migrant workers could go off relief by living in a self-sustaining, segregated colony. People would survive by gardening and selling handmade crafts, "trinkets," and pottery to tourists. It would become, essentially, both a homestead and trading post.

The plan received national attention by Works Progress Administration (WPA) administrator Harry Hopkins, who gave his tentative approval through the Federal Emergency Relief Administration.[30] The plan thus became part of a national relief housing movement. According to the

Pueblo Chieftain, "the village would house 200 of the 'better-type' families now dependent on the community."[31] The families would be able to continue their low-paying jobs at the steel mill or their seasonal migratory farm work and could work on handicrafts at their leisure in the evening. Extreme opposition to the plan came from farmers and landowners on St. Charles Mesa.[32] The dissenters suggested an alternate site that had been proposed for a "homestead project" north of the Colorado state fairgrounds.[33]

In April 1935, the issue of deporting Mexican aliens came to a head in Pueblo when a public debate on the issue was held at City Hall in response to questions over the number of migrant workers on the city's relief rolls. Local leaders with "expertise" in the area publicly addressed the question, "Shall We Deport the Aliens?" before a crowd of three hundred Puebloans, with many turned back at the door for lack of room. The debate featured speakers whose beliefs ranged from unbiased humanitarian aid to opposition of those aliens who refused to assimilate themselves to the "American way of life" by becoming naturalized citizens. Others argued in response that the citizen exam requirements were too difficult. Still others argued against racist implications made by some locals and Governor Edwin C. Johnson in the newspaper, implications that they believed were only the result of the poor economic climate. One panel member placed the blame on the railroads and sugar beet industries who had brought the Mexican work force into the Pueblo area in the first place. Another panel member, a twenty-year educator and minister, thought that the problem stemmed from the segregated barrios or *colonias*, which, he argued, should be decentralized in order to allow aliens to assimilate into the local community. This same person felt that many foreign-born aliens were openly hostile to taking citizenship and should be deported.[34]

Governor Johnson, a Democrat running for re-election but long a foe of Roosevelt's New Deal, was facing intense political opposition on both state and national levels. Johnson's fervor over Mexican aliens was so great that, according to a *Chieftain* report in May 1935, he sent a wire to the sheriff of Trinidad ordering him to arrest twenty-seven aliens whom he had heard were heading north, possibly with old temporary labor passports. Johnson was rebuked by the Mexican consul in Denver, since only federal immigration authorities had the right to arrest suspected illegal aliens.[35]

The year 1936 was pivotal for Mexican migrant workers in southeastern Colorado. Editorials that spring echoed the national sentiment supporting deportation of Mexican nationals. Pueblo itself became pivotal because of its proximity to the sugar beet factories and its centrality as the largest urban area in southern Colorado. It was also the southeastern Colorado district headquarters for the WPA. Thus, millions of WPA dollars were being pumped into southern Colorado, and administrators in Pueblo did the hiring. But continued WPA funding was in question in 1936, a situation that was no doubt a useful tool to anyone in power in an election year. For whatever reason, Johnson used the editors of the *Pueblo Chieftain* to help promote and stir nativistic, anti-immigrant fervor in the area. Migrant workers in the Arkansas Valley and Pueblo saw themselves increasingly attacked as unwelcome interlopers in a state that had begged them to immigrate for the last ten years. Still, many preferred the peonage of the beet fields to going on relief.

The culmination of this nativist bickering was Governor Johnson's declaration of martial law on April 20, 1936. The governor called the Colorado National Guard to the New Mexico border in an attempt to hold back the "hordes" of migrant workers who were "trying to storm the Colorado beet-fields" and perhaps get themselves a WPA job or federal relief. At Johnson's behest,

> . . . the National Guard set up barriers against possible incursions of migrant workers and began to stop trains, trucks, buses, and automobiles to inquire into the origins and assets of the occupants. Acting under martial law, they were instructed to "prevent and repel the further invasion of . . . aliens, indigent persons, or invaders." In more common parlance the barrier was referred to as the "bum blockade."[36]

In the end, Johnson's martial law was declared unconstitutional and did little but infuriate the state of New Mexico. New Mexicans were incensed that he considered them "undesirable."[37]

Throughout 1935 and 1936, Johnson helped fan the nativistic flames that ran throughout the region. Another factor that may have motivated him politically in this election year, however, was the threatened cutoff of WPA funds in Colorado. Johnson fought constantly with Harry Hopkins, head of the WPA in Washington, D.C., and Paul D. Shriver, head of the Colorado WPA. Johnson, though a Democrat, was a fierce states' rights advocate who deeply resented any federal interference in state matters. Thus, he strongly opposed Roosevelt's New Deal programs and fought with Hopkins his entire term of governor. (Ultimately, Johnson failed to stop New Deal money from flowing into Colorado.) Despite this open conflict, however, in early 1936 both Hopkins and Johnson spoke against the employment of aliens in Colorado.[38]

Governor Johnson's calls to deport the aliens in 1935 and 1936 stirred public opinion among a variety of sources in Pueblo. Native Spanish Americans, whose ancestors in the area pre-dated U.S. acquisition of northern Mexico during the Mexican War, were put on the defense. In February 1936, according to an editorial in the *Pueblo Chieftain*, the local chapter of the American Citizens of Spanish Descent criticized the fact that migrant workers were getting New Deal jobs or relief when Spanish American citizens could not even get on relief.[39] By March, this same group wrote an open letter to Governor Johnson to express support of the governor's call to prevent more migrants from coming into Colorado from other states.[40] What is not mentioned in the letter is the fact that new WPA guidelines had prohibited anyone who had not previously been on relief from securing WPA employment.

Another group of indigenous Spanish Americans in Pueblo also spoke out. The president of the Pueblo Mexican Honorary Committee wrote, in defense of the Spanish-American citizens, that "Mexicans" were not overrunning the WPA program.[41] The spokesman for the committee reported that, in 1932, three hundred eighty families in Pueblo had repatriated to Mexico, many with the aid of the Family Service Society and others via their own funds. He added that between 1932 and 1936 many families in Pueblo had returned to Mexico voluntarily, and many more were waiting to do so as soon as they could afford it.[42] Sadly, the effect of the committee's statement was that the group appeared to align itself against the Mexican migrant workers.

Thus was the plight of the Mexican migrant worker in Pueblo and southeastern Colorado during the Great Depression. Governor Johnson continued his attack on minorities throughout the rest of his political career, including an endorsement of concentration camps in Colorado for Japanese Americans during World War II.[43]

In Pueblo and southeastern Colorado, many migrant workers eventually became naturalized citizens. When the WPA was first formed, there were no restrictions whatsoever on citizens and aliens receiving employment. But by the time the wave of nativism ran through Colorado and the rest of the country, WPA employment was highly coveted as a result of six years of depression. Beginning in 1936, hearings held before a Senate committee in Washington considered the issue of aliens on WPA payrolls. From 1936 to 1939, the issue remained controversial, and anti-alien legislation was enacted each of those years through the Emergency Relief Administration acts.[44] By 1939, legal restrictions on WPA employment had grown tighter, effectively forcing naturalization on aliens wishing WPA employment. No doubt this had an effect in Pueblo, for by the end of the 1930s the WPA was a major employer in the city.

That year, Congress demanded the removal of all aliens from WPA rolls, including those who had applied for naturalization. By March of 1939, all WPA workers in Pueblo were required by federal law to show proof of citizenship by filing affidavits at WPA headquarters in City Hall.[45] This was the government's attempt to weed out Mexican nationals. Only seven Mexican aliens were found on WPA rolls in Pueblo among thou-sands of workers.[46] Undoubtedly, federal legislation against aliens on WPA payrolls contributed to increased naturalization attempts by Mexican nationals in Pueblo at the end of the 1930s. The *Chieftain* reported a record number of local cases (some fifty to seventy families) in April of 1941 that were to come before the naturalization examiner and the federal judge.[47]

The percentage of Pueblo's Hispanic community that inherited the legacy of migratory farm work in the United States would be difficult to calculate. Third and fourth generation descendants retain much of their ancestors' rich cultural heritage from Mexico. Cycles of migratory workers coming from Mexico continued through the 1960s, when the United States and Mexico signed the so-called "Bracero" program, setting new standards to protect the migrant worker from U.S. exploitation. (The improvements had begun back in the Depression when the Sugar Act of 1937 prohibited child labor.) The heritage of the United States' treatment of Mexican national migrant workers is not as rich; it is, rather, yet another piece of our collective shame. Perhaps the shared crisis of the Depression helps explain why we later came to treat immigrants more humanely.

Notes

1
Abraham Hoffman, *Unwanted Mexican Americans in the Great Depression: Repatriation Pressures 1929–1939* (Tucson: University of Arizona Press, 1974), 9.

2
Carney Clark Crisler, "The Mexican Bracero Program with Special Reference to Colorado" (Master's thesis, University of Denver, 1968), 13.

3
Dena S. Markoff, "A Bittersweet Saga: The Arkansas Valley Beet Sugar Industry 1900–1979," *The Colorado Magazine* 56 (Summer/Fall 1979), 161.

4
Ibid., 162.

5
Ibid.

6
Hoffman, *Unwanted Mexican Americans*, 28.

7
James A. Atkins, *Human Relations in Colorado: A Historical Record*, Byron W. Hansford, ed. (Denver: Colorado Department of Education, 1968), 100.

8
Daniel J. Elazar, *Cities of the Prairie: The Metropolitan Frontier and American Politics* (New York: Basic Books, Inc., 1970), 343.

9
Atkins, *Human Relations in Colorado*, 100.

10
Hoffman, *Unwanted Mexican Americans*, 13.

11
Ibid., 19.

12
Ibid., 39.

13
Ibid., 24.

14
Ibid., 41.

15
Ibid., 39.

16
Ibid., 40. Things were so bad in California that the state was also barring Oklahoma tenant farmers. The largest number of repatriates in 1931 returned to Mexico from California.

17
Ibid., 82.

18
Ibid., 93.

19
Ibid., 131.

20
Abraham Hoffman, "Mexican Repatriation Statistics: Some Suggested Alternatives to Carey McWilliams," *Western Historical Quarterly* 3 (October 1972), 401.

21
Hoffman, *Unwanted Mexican Americans*, 36.

22
Atkins, *Human Relations in Colorado*, 102.

23
Gerald D. Nash, *The American West in the Twentieth Century: A Short History of an Urban Oasis* (Englewood Cliffs: Prentice-Hall, Inc., 1973), 154.

24
Ibid.

25
William Wilson Bundy, "The Mexican Minority Problem in Otero County, Colorado" (Master's thesis, University of Colorado, 1936), 4.

26
Elazar, *Cities of the Prairie*, 95.

27
Nash, *The American West*, 158.

28
Markoff, "A Bittersweet Saga," 167.

29
Pueblo's Spanish-speaking community derives from two primary sources. Spanish Americans with land grants had been in the Pueblo area since 1840. Pueblo was the northernmost boundary of "Old Mexico" until the Treaty of Guadalupe Hidalgo changed the boundaries in 1848. The second source of population influx from Mexico originated with the migrant workers of the 1920s and 1930s who stayed. But the legacy of the Spanish Americans in Pueblo and southwestern Colorado was generations old. Their ancestors had explored the area since the sixteenth century. Yet during the nativist cycles of the 1920s and 1930s, public prejudice against them became almost as strong as that against the Mexican immigrant.

30
Pueblo Chieftain (hereinafter referred to as *PC*), January 21, 1935.

31
PC, January 6, 1935.

32
PC, January 26, 1935.

33
Apparently, it was this alternate plan that was later adopted. The housing units, built in Pueblo in the early 1940s under federal housing acts, became known as "the projects."

34
PC, April 7, 1935.

35
PC, May 8, 1935.

36
Robert G. Athearn, *The Coloradans* (Albuquerque: University of New Mexico Press, 1976), 280.

37
Ibid., 281.

38
Within the myriad state and local conjecture over issues such as New Deal money in this 1936 election year, a second cycle of Mexican repatriation in southeastern Colorado can be detected. This cycle appears to be tied more to politics and economics than were earlier cycles of partial voluntary repatriation by the Mexican government or relief-roll concerns of 1931.

In 1936, states vied for New Deal–generated programs, jobs, and money. Colorado politicians used these issues as a political battleground in southern Colorado. The victim was anyone of Spanish-speaking descent.

39
PC, February 5, 1936.

40
PC, March 14, 1936.

41
PC, March 5, 1936.

42
Ibid.

43
Richard D. Lamm and Duane A. Smith, *Pioneers and Politicians: Ten Colorado Governors in Profile* (Boulder: Pruett Publishing Company, 1984), 143.

44
Donald Howard, *The WPA and Federal Relief Policy* (New York: DeCapo Press, 1973), 303.

45
PC, February 7, 1939.

46
PC, March 4, 1939.

47
PC, April 30, 1939.

The Valdez Rug Project:
A Depression-era Craft Rediscovered

Katie Davis Gardner

ABOUT THE AUTHOR

Katie Davis Gardner is the curator of the Colorado Springs Museum and formerly assistant curator of material culture at the Colorado Historical Society. She has written previously about Valdez rugs and Hispanic textiles in "Colorado's Valdez Rugs," *Colorado Heritage News*, March 1989, and "Woven Across Time," *Colorado Heritage*, 1988, issue 3. Gardner curated the Colorado Historical Society exhibition *Woven Across Time: Colorado's Hispanic Textile Tradition*, a portion of which has been incorporated into the current *La Gente: Hispanos in Colorado* and which has also traveled to El Pueblo Museum and the Colorado Springs Museum.

N 1931 THE Colorado State Vocational Education Department, the Las Animas County School District 61, and the Young Men's Christian Association cooperated with one of Colorado's largest and most powerful corporations, the Colorado Fuel and Iron Company, to develop one of the most progressive and innovative worker-training projects in the West. Colorado Fuel and Iron (CF&I) in southern Colorado trained its out-of-work miners to weave rugs and blankets in an effort to stave off the effects of the country's economic depression and to create a cottage industry that could sustain the miners while the mines were closed.

The company hired José Ramón Ortega, a well-known Hispanic weaver from Chimayó, New Mexico, for a six-month contract to teach the miners to weave. The company heralded the Valdez Rug Project as a "new industry" that would eventually provide the miners with a home-based occupation in "summer months and other slack periods in the coal mining communities."[1] This remarkable project preceded by five years the federally-funded Works Progress Administration (WPA) weaving projects implemented in southern Colorado and New Mexico.

The Valdez project ended in 1933 when the mines reopened and the weavers were called back to work. During its successful two-year run, between two and three hundred rugs, blankets, car seat covers, and special orders were woven and sold in Denver and Pueblo through CF&I company stores and other outlets. The Valdez Rug Project continued to promote traditional Hispanic weaving and self-sufficiency long after the project itself had officially ended.

Part of a larger, multifaceted corporate relief effort, the Valdez Rug Project was directed through CF&I's Employee Services Department under George M. Kirk. The project's funding, managed by state director of vocational education H. A. Tiemann, was made available through the Smith-Hughes Act, which had provided federal dollars to CF&I since 1916 for the vocational training of industrial workers.[2] All activities were held at the Young Men's Christian Association (YMCA) building in the small company-owned coal camp of Valdez, Colorado, about ten miles west of Trinidad.

In 1931, the demand for coal was slow. The Depression made it difficult for people to buy consumer goods, and many large coal-fueled factories closed. The southern Colorado mines that were not shut down altogether were worked only sporadically. The largest coal mine in Colorado, the Frederick in Valdez, was one of these. Miners from the

The YMCA building in Valdez where weaving classes were conducted. Photograph taken February 1960; courtesy Colorado Fuel and Iron Company.

smaller adjoining coal camps of Primero, Segundo, and Morley were affected—hundreds were out of work. These miners were the target of CF&I's unemployment relief program. Thus, in November, classes in traditional Hispanic-style weaving began under the guidance of master weaver José Ramón Ortega, whose family had been renowned for generations for its high-quality Río Grande–style weaving.[3]

Forty students enrolled in the one-and-a-half-hour classes held five days a week, four times daily.[4] Two men worked at each of the five looms. Weaver Gilbert Fernandez recalled that one would weave while the other watched; then they would trade places. There was a waiting list for the classes—no wonder, since announcements of the class had been reported in the CF&I *Blast*, the company's weekly newspaper, since October 1931. Weaving was expected to begin on the looms November 1, but construc-

Detail of tag affixed to all woven products marketed by CF&I. Author's collection; photograph by David D. Guerrero for the Colorado Historical Society (F32,709).

tion of the looms themselves took longer than anticipated, and no classes could be undertaken without them. The looms were built under the direction of W. C. Nel, apprentice instructor at the Pueblo steel mill, who traveled to the area with blueprints and materials for their construction.[5] Some parts were fabricated at the steel mill machine shops in Pueblo; most parts were made of salvaged materials.[6] Originally, twelve looms were planned, but the number was reduced to six. Finally, classes began with only five looms completed. The looms were installed at the Valdez YMCA building, the town's "community" building, where a variety of classes, church activities and social events took place. Ortega's classes began on Monday, November 30, 1931, with five looms made of scrap lumber, gears, and wire.

By April 1, 1932, the state school board was satisfied with the progress of the classes: approximately fifteen men had become skilled at weaving and had expressed their commitment to weaving independently of the school once they "graduated." Las Animas school board members approved the funds necessary to construct looms for use in the houses of the graduates after the classes ended in May.[7] Classes continued under Ortega's instruction through the week of May 10, when an open house, featuring a weaving demonstration and an exhibition of the finished woven pieces, was held at the YMCA.[8]

Gilbert Fernandez at his loom in Weston, Colorado, March 1988. Photograph by the author.

At this time, CF&I made a business of the weavings, marketing them through various means and paying the weavers to produce rugs. Gilbert Fernandez remembers that ten men were actively weaving, five with looms at home and five on the looms at the YMCA. The *Blast* reported that all finished items were being placed for sale at CF&I's retail sales department in Denver. A small pamphlet was produced, describing the weaving process as well as the Valdez program and its benefits for the miners. A tag was affixed to each item, depicting a rug with *Valdez* woven into it and informing potential buyers of the item's pattern, size, and price; the tag also announced that "Valdez handwoven rugs and bath mats are made on handlooms in the homes of employees of The Colorado Fuel & Iron Company."[9]

As a result of CF&I's marketing campaign, Valdez rugs were taken to fairs and exhibits around the state. They were shown at Trinidad's Progress Day on June 17, 1932, where several of the weavers demonstrated their skills. "The walls and balcony were decorated with magnificent rugs of different design, clearly emphasizing that a new industry has been started in Las Animas County, supplementary to the coal industry itself."[10] The rugs were exhibited at a national convention of the Phi Delta Theta fraternity in Estes Park in August 1932 as part of the company's strategy to develop markets with organizations having moneyed members: dude ranches, college sororities and fraternities, and other groups. A photograph in the *Blast* shows several of the fraternity and sorority leaders holding a Valdez rug depicting the fraternity's letters in its colors of blue and white, with a mountain scene below.[11]

Weaver Gilbert Fernandez recalled that car seat covers were a popular item with the college crowd, and that the Colorado College's Sigma Chi fraternity placed an order for them. Unfortunately, Sigma Chi members from the 1932 alumni roster had no recollection of such purchases when interviewed in 1989.[12] It is likely that the fraternity was a test case for the marketing of the weavings, however, since George M. Kirk, manager of the project's sponsoring department, and his son, George M. Kirk, Jr., were both Sigma Chi members.

The Valdez rugs were exhibited at the Colorado State Fair in late summer of 1932. Fernandez recalls taking the loom to the fair on his truck. "People would visit and look, but no one was buying. It was the Depression." The *Blast* reported that, "The loom [was] operated by Gilbert Fernandez and Mike [*sic*] Tomsic, CF&I employees at Frederick Mine."[13] Additionally, the Carter, Rice and Carpenter Paper Company in Denver agreed to sell a supply of the rugs through its floor-covering divi-

Valdez Rugs Go Collegiate at Convention

• • •   • • •

Phi Delts, Sig Eps, and Sigma Chi

Social Agencies T
Seek United Relie
Program for Regio

Efforts Being Made to Inaugura
Thorough Red Cross Re-
lief Activity Here

Every effort is being made by
ficials of the Pueblo county cha
ter of the American Red Cross, c

Fraternity and sorority leaders hold a Valdez rug. From the CF&I Blast, *September 2, 1932.*

Gilbert Fernandez and John Tomsic demonstrate weaving techniques at the 1932 Colorado State Fair amongst a display of their weavings. From the CF&I Blast, *September 16, 1932.*

sion. The company arranged a large display of rugs with college and university colors and fraternity letters in the Sixteenth Street display window of the Daniels and Fisher department store in Denver.[14]

CF&I encouraged its employees to purchase the weavings by providing an extended payment plan. Using the *Blast* to announce and advertise the plan, the company set up a display of the weavings in the technical library at the Pueblo Steelworks YMCA to promote sales.[15]

The rugs were about four feet by five feet and sold for $8.50 to $9.50, depending on the weight—one of the weavers remembers trying to weave the rugs as tightly as possible to make them heavier.[16] In addition to rugs and car seat covers, the weavers also wove lap robes. All were made from the highest available grade of Germantown wool yarn, a type known for its heavy weight and thickness. The warp (vertical yarns threaded onto the loom) was cotton, as was typical of Chimayó weaving at that time. In an effort to reduce prices, project officials considered the use of local wool, which would have to be cleaned and spun; that suggestion evidently was never implemented.[17] From the beginning, the rugs' designs were very close to traditional Chimayó and Río Grande (Hispanic) patterns. Often this was a central geometric "southwestern" design on a solid color field with a striped pattern on both ends of the rug. Gilbert Fernandez described a typical pattern as being "regular Chimayó designs." With the expansion of the market into college fraternities and sororities, however, the weavers became interested in new designs. By November, the *Blast* could report that "new designs have been developed and the Indian influence has been discarded. A distinctive effect is being secured in the commercial rugs by the use of two-tone blends. These rugs have proven very popular."[18]

Shortly before the coal mines reopened, the CF&I retail fuel store at 1620 Stout Street in Denver displayed handmade clothing, goods, and food produced by CF&I miners and their families. This was part of an effort to draw attention to the needs of the out-of-work miners and to show their "ingenuity and self-helpfulness."[19] Among the items displayed were canned food from the miners' gardens, planted with seed furnished by the company's relief fund. The CF&I Employee Services Department considered the home gardens and the Valdez project exemplary programs with, in the words of George M. Kirk, "special significance." The projects, Kirk wrote,

. . . symbolize the spirit which has ever motivated the directors and managers of this company since its beginning: the consistent and faithful desire to plant and nourish the seeds of good will and mutual understanding, and perchance to weave out of the rapidly changing conditions of life and labor a better fabric of relationships between capital, management, workers and the community at large.[20]

Indeed, CF&I did have a progressive approach to employee services, beginning with the appointment of Dr. R. W. Corwin to its Sociological Department, formed in 1901. Corwin, formerly superintendent at the Minnequa (later Corwin) Hospital, formed the department to oversee education, recreation, and vocational and technical training for workers.[21] The department initiated a variety of projects that included circulating libraries, children's groups and kindergartens, musical bands, English classes for foreign language speakers, and home economics classes for the workers' wives.[22] "One only needs to read the issues of *Camp and Plant*, a company organ instituted by the Sociological Department of the last decade of the old century by Dr. Corwin and his associates," Kirk wrote, "to understand the place that welfare and education held in the lives of all connected with the company from management down to the humblest worker."[23]

Despite the paternalistic overtones of the company's efforts and the mildly propagandistic slant of Kirk's article, CF&I was, in fact, a pioneer in employee benefits and educational support. Up to 1901, conditions at the mines were appalling—with long hours, dangerous work, the inability of foreign laborers to communicate with one another, and most miners working off debts to the company store rather than making money to send to their families abroad.[24] Prompted by the 1901 coal miners' strike, the Sociological Department was formed, not only for the benefit of the workers, but for that of the company as well.[25] Corwin set about implementing changes in the workers' lives by offering programs in education and vocational training, housing, and communications.

When the country was plunged into the Great Depression after the economic crash of the 1920s, CF&I's Sociological Department was well established and fully prepared to provide support to its large work force. In fact, the company's "Industrial Home" in Pueblo had been offering manufacturing jobs to injured workers and the widows and children of former workers for years prior to the Valdez weaving project.[26] Various items were manufactured there, including rugs, carpets, other textiles, mattresses, brooms, and furniture. The items were sold locally, enabling the workers to provide an income for themselves. Other precedents for the

Valdez weaving project were conducted in the mining towns themselves: both lace manufacturing and basket weaving were developed at Engleville, El Moro, and Primero, towns located near Valdez.[27]

Twenty-year-old miner Gilbert Fernandez (1911–90) became so adept at weaving during the Valdez project that he was soon designing for the teacher and helping instruct. "I had the knack of designing in my head," Fernandez said. "I fell in love with it."[28] He was the best weaver in the class and essentially took over for Ortega in May 1932 when the class ended.

Paid by CF&I and the school district as the weaving supervisor, Fernandez continued weaving, designing, and overseeing the designs of the other weavers who stayed with the project. He distributed yarn to the weavers and collected their finished pieces. He wove at home from 4:00 to 7:30 A.M., then ate and reported to the mine office in Valdez. There, the other weavers picked up their yarn from him and he helped them with their designs "if they got stuck." Weavers who were fast and dedicated wove one rug a day; those who were less interested wove one a week. One weaver, John Tomsic, estimated that he wove a total of about twenty rugs during the project.

George Kirk came to Valdez periodically to load his truck with the weavings and take them to Pueblo. Fernandez recalled that he never knew exactly where the rugs were sold: he knew that CF&I had a department store in Pueblo, but he did not know where the weavings ultimately ended up. He remembered that, due to the Depression, they did not sell well.

Fernandez built himself a loom at home, while also continuing to use one at the YMCA building. Later, when his loom broke, he kept parts from it with which he repaired the CF&I loom. At the conclusion of the Valdez project, CF&I gave him one of the looms. When last interviewed in 1989, Fernandez was still using the green CF&I loom in his home weaving shop.

Fernandez remembered that the other weavers wove throw rugs almost exclusively. He always wove the special orders himself, usually weaving the larger items at home.[29] A standard throw rug was twenty-seven by fifty-four inches (about two and a quarter by four and a half feet). Car seat covers were fifty-four by sixty inches (three and a half by five feet). Tomsic recalls that CF&I paid the weavers a dollar per pound, which averaged out to about two dollars per rug. They always wove them with a double selvage edge and on a two-harness loom. The rugs had fringe on the ends, rather than being turned under at the ends and sewn.

Together, CF&I and the school district paid Fernandez a total of sixty dollars a month, which he considered good money for the Depression. At the time, he was single and living at home, supporting his brothers and sisters. His father had died young, and although Fernandez was not the oldest child, he was nevertheless responsible for supporting the family by working in the mine. It was critical that he continue to earn a steady income while the mine was closed.

When CF&I discontinued the project after the mines reopened, Fernandez bought all the leftover yarn and continued to weave blankets. He also returned to work the mines in 1933. He worked the coal mining machinery on his knees throughout World War II, wearing knee pads, but it "got so I could barely get up in the morning," he recalled. In 1945 he started "fire bossing"—checking for danger in the mines before the crew went in. He went to work at 1:00 A.M. and returned home by 9:00 or 10:00 A.M. He slept until noon, then went to the YMCA building, where he wove until 3:00 P.M. He returned home to chop wood and meet his children when they came home from school.

Fernandez described the wage cuts before the actual mine closures: "There was no union in the thirties—we worked under the Rockefeller Plan."[30] A meeting held in December of 1930 announced the wage cut for "company men" of one dollar a day, from $5.25 to $4.25, and miners took a fifteen-cent-per-ton wage cut. He worked at that time digging coal for fifty-nine cents a ton, after the cut earning only three to four dollars a day.

Fernandez worked on the CF&I loom at the YMCA for thirty years. He continued to weave as a hobby while working in the mines. He and his family lived in Valdez until June 17, 1961, when the Valdez mine was finally closed for good. After transferring him to the Allen mine for six months, CF&I laid Fernandez off, giving him a "shut down" pension. He opened his first privately owned weaving shop in 1963 and a second in 1965 when he bought property in Weston, Colorado, a few miles west of Valdez. Fernandez wove professionally from that time until about 1989, when he, in his words, began to "slow down," weaving only three or four hours a day. His legs bothered him and he could no longer stand at the loom for several hours at a time. Although he was concerned about the diminishing quality and lack of variety in the colors of yarn offered by his yarn supplier, the Buscilla company, he continued to use the same yarn because it was washable without fading, and the weight and thickness of another brand would not match exactly. Taxes took much of his business profit, and as taxes continued to climb, he sold fewer weavings every year. When interviewed in 1988 he figured he had enough yarn to weave for another year; in January of 1989 he was still weaving.

In the years after he retired from the mine and before his "retirement" from weaving, Fernandez wove as many as fourteen hours a day on his home loom, with coal-oil lamps on either side. The newspapers noted his success many times,[31] and his weavings—mainly his popular "thunderbird" rugs—were included in Colorado Springs Fine Arts Center exhibitions. He took prizes at the Los Angeles County Fair in 1952 and the Colorado State Fair in 1954.[32] In 1949 CF&I published a pamphlet that featured Fernandez and his work in an article entitled "A Fireboss Weaves a Blanket." The article reported that because of his talent he had been asked to repair valuable Navajo blankets, "an art in itself."[33] Fernandez was so well respected among longtime weavers that José Ramón Ortega asked him to come to Chimayó to design for his weaving shop, but Fernandez declined, saying he wanted to both design and weave.

By 1988, most of the miners who had been involved in the Valdez project were no longer living. Fernandez was shown a list of weavers that a 1932 *Blast* claimed would "probably have looms in their homes at Valdez."[34] Included were Fernandez, Fred Rosetti, Paul Cordova, Chris Buscarino, Eliseo Amador (actually Eliseo "Lish" Abeyta, according to Fernandez), Ricardo Abeyta, Rupert Trujillo, Mose Sena, Mike (actually John) Tomsic, Thomas Guttierez, A. H. Tomez, Tony Madrigal, and James Brownrigg. Fernandez recalled that Fred Rosetti wove for a short time in Trinidad after the project, possibly for the Works Progress Administration. He mentioned Johnny Tomsic and Lish Abeyta as two of the only other weavers still living in 1988; Tomsic was subsequently interviewed, but he had not continued to weave after the project ended. Fernandez did not remember Thomas Guttierez as being in the class; A. H. Tomez and Tony Madrigal were in the class but did not weave for the company after the project ended; and James Brownrigg did not finish the class—"he got disgusted right away," said Fernandez. Tomsic said that he, Fred Rosetti, and Gil Fernandez were the only weavers he could recall who actually produced woven items for CF&I after the project.[35]

Weaving, an unlikely activity for professional miners, proved to be more than just a source of financial support during hard times. As part of the greater sheep ranching activity in nineteenth-century southern Colorado, loom weaving had traditionally been an economic mainstay of the area's Hispanic communities, but it had virtually died out in the Arkansas Valley by the 1930s. The Valdez weaving project provided a vehicle for both Hispanic and non-Hispanic miners to gain firsthand knowledge of a historically indigenous occupation with which they were unfamiliar. It proved to be so enjoyable that at least one miner, Gilbert Fernandez, continued to think of himself as a weaver and produced weavings into the late 1980s.

Similarly, CF&I seems an unlikely candidate for patron-of-the-arts status until its record of worker education and training in the early twentieth century is closely examined. In a business sense, the Valdez weaving project was never the successful "new industry" CF&I had anticipated, and the company and nearly everyone else quickly forgot about it as soon as the mines reopened. The finished weavings have been almost impossible to trace, with the exception of the beautiful rug woven by Gilbert Fernandez for project director George Kirk (see back cover). Nevertheless, economic necessity and a locale rich in Hispanic heritage combined to create a brief renaissance of traditional craft activity between 1931 and 1933 in the mining town of Valdez, Colorado.

Notes

The research for this essay was funded by a grant from the Colorado Endowment for the Humanities. Thanks also to Lee Scamehorn for introducing the author to the topic of the Valdez rugs.

1

Colorado Fuel and Iron Company, *Blast*, October 16, 1931, 1:6-7.

2

Ibid.

3

About twenty-two miles north of Santa Fe, Chimayó catered mainly to tourists in search of curios with a southwestern flavor. Because of the great popularity of Native American crafts such as pottery and rugs sold to tourists from about 1900 on, Hispanic weavers had begun to produce weavings that were "generic" or "pan-southwestern," incorporating both Hispanic and Indian motifs. This created great confusion as to the actual origins of Chimayó weaving, although the Hispanic technique of weaving on the European-style horizontal treadle looms created quite a different product than the vertical looms of the Navajos and Pueblos. Thus, confusion about this still arose in the literature produced to market the Valdez rugs, which referred to the rugs' "Indian" style. See Charlene Cerny and Christine Mather, "Textile Production in Twentieth-Century New Mexico," *Spanish Textile Tradition of New Mexico and Colorado*, Nora Fisher, ed. (Santa Fe: Museum of International Folk Art, 1979), 170-73.

A similar weaving project, also directed by Tiemann, had been implemented the year before in Fort Collins, Colorado, to generate alternative income for unemployed sugar beet workers; *Blast*, October 16, 1931, 1:6-7. Ortega had taught for this project as well. The program produced several weavers, some of whom together eventually opened their own shop in Fort Collins, the "Spanish Industrial Weaving Shop." One of the weavers, Flavio Salas, continued to weave in Denver as a hobby even after he went almost totally blind. Flavio Salas, personal interview, September 11, 1989 (Tape recording, Colorado Historical Society, Denver).

4

Gilbert Fernandez recalled that the classes were one and a half hours long; the CF&I *Blast* reported that they were two hours long. Gilbert Fernandez, personal interview, March 26, 1988 (Tape recording, Colorado Historical Society, Denver).

5

Blast, November 6, 1931, 1:1.

6

Blast, November 20, 1931, 1:6-7.

7

Blast, April 1, 1932, 8:3.

8

Blast, May 13, 1932, 8:2.

9

Valdez pamphlet, collection of the author. The tag also reads, "Many of the best weavers are descendants of the early Spanish settlers, and have shown an adaptability to this art truly characteristic of the Spanish-American, and they are his expression of the influence of the colorful Sangre de Cristo Mountains," a statement that demonstrates the marketing department's understanding of the weavings' Hispanic origins, even if *Blast* reporters did not.

10
Blast, June 24, 1932, 1:6-7.

11
Blast, September 2, 1932.

12
Colorado College Sigma Chi members, personal interviews, 1988.

13
Blast, September 9, 1932. John Tomsic, not Mike Tomsic, operated the loom. Tomsic recalled that Mike Tomsic was the assistant secretary at the YMCA, and he did not weave. John Tomsic, personal interview, August 5, 1989 (Tape recording, Colorado Historical Society, Denver).

14
Blast, September 2, 1932, 1:3-4; November 25, 1932, 2:2.

15
Blast, September 23, 1932, 1:1-2.

16
John Tomsic, personal interview, August 5, 1989.

17
Blast, April 1, 1932.

18
Blast, November 25, 1932, 2:2.

19
Blast, December 2, 1932, 1:1.

20
Blast, April 15, 1932, 14.

21
Sylvia Ruland, *The Lion of Redstone* (Boulder, Colo.: Johnson Books, 1981), 49.

22
H. Lee Scamehorn, *Pioneer Steelmaker in the West: The Colorado Fuel and Iron Company, 1872–1903* (Boulder: Pruett Publishing Company, 1976), 150.

23
Blast, April 15, 1932.

24
Ruland notes in *The Lion of Redstone* that the system of recruiting workers from the Mediterranean was considered by many to be a deliberate effort to keep the miners from understanding one another or communicating with the union. Ruland, *Lion of Redstone*, 49.

25
Scamehorn, *Pioneer Steelmaker in the West*, 149.

26
Ibid., 152.

27
Ibid.

28
Gilbert Fernandez, personal interview, March 26, 1988.

29
Fernandez wove very large blankets only after he went into business for himself.

30
The Rockefeller Plan was an alternative

to the union and a system of representation for both workers and employers, where topics such as wages and benefits could be discussed. It was implemented in 1915 in response to violence in the southern Colorado mines over the previous few years. See Scamehorn, *Pioneer Steelmaker in the West*, 172.

31
See for example *The Denver Post*, March 14, 1954, *Empire Magazine*; *Pueblo Star-Journal and Sunday Chieftain*, December 29, 1968, February 2, 1967; *Trinidad Chronicle News* 86, no. 214 (September 12, 1963); *Blast*, November 19, 1948.

32
William Wroth, ed., *Hispanic Crafts of the Southwest* (Colorado Springs: The Taylor Museum of the Colorado Springs Fine Arts Center, 1977), 101.

33
Pamphlet in the collection of the Gilbert Fernandez family.

34
Blast, April 1, 1932, 1:1.

35
John Tomsic, personal interview, August 5, 1989.

GROWING DIVERSITY, 1945–PRESENT

Rodolfo Gonzales and the Advent of the Crusade for Justice

Ernesto Vigil

ABOUT THE AUTHOR

Ernesto B. Vigil was born in Denver and was a Crusade for Justice member from 1968 until his resignation in 1981, when he was the group's vice-chairperson. He served as co-chairperson of the Crusade's legal defense committee, associate editor of its newspaper, and history and social studies instructor for its school. *Los Vigiles* have roots going back over three hundred years in the region. Pedro Cosio, his maternal grandfather, was born in Chihuahua, Mexico.

Portions of this essay have been incorporated into Vigil's book, The Crusade for Justice: The Chicano Movement in Denver, *forthcoming for December 1998 from the University of Wisconsin Press.*

I N 1960, MORE THAN sixty thousand Spanish-surnamed residents lived in the Denver metropolitan area, forty-three thousand in the city of Denver proper.[1] In Colorado, 9 percent of the population (157,173) was Spanish-surnamed; of them, 79 percent lived in urban areas, 76 percent of the males in the labor force were manual laborers, and 31 percent of all families earned yearly incomes of $3,000 or less.

As their population grew, Spanish-surnamed residents became the focus of demographic studies—studies that confirmed what some saw as obvious. In a 1968 study of Denver's poverty area (which comprised a fifth of the city), a University of Colorado economics professor found:

1) The area's Spanish-surnamed population grew 46 percent between 1960 and 1967, with the Spanish-surnamed having the largest families and the lowest incomes in the area.

2) The schools in the poverty area were 50 percent Spanish-surnamed, 26 percent African American, and 24 percent white.

3) While the national unemployment figure was 2.7 percent, Denver's poverty area showed overall rates of 11.5 percent unemployment and 23.6 percent underemployment. Unemployment figures for Chicanos, African Americans, and whites were 15 percent, 14.5 percent, and 8.4 percent, respectively.[2]

Data gathered by the Colorado Department of Education revealed that the Denver school district ranked as the third worst district in the state with a projected 40.4 percent dropout rate. In contrast, the suburban school districts of Cherry Creek, Littleton, Boulder Valley, and Jefferson County projected three-year dropout rates of under 10 percent each. Denver's dropout rate varied from school to school: predominantly white high schools projected three-year dropout rates of under 13 percent each, while the dropout rates of high schools with predominantly African American and Chicano enrollment ranged between 46 and 57 percent.[3]

In response to these conditions, Chicano communities in the Southwest blossomed in a period of political activism known as the "Chicano movement." Though Colorado's Mexican-origin population was smaller than that of those states which bordered with Mexico, Colorado's impact on this movement was far out of proportion to the size and percentage of its

Mexican-origin population. The exemplar of the movement in Colorado was the Crusade for Justice under the guidance of Rodolfo "Corky" Gonzales, whose charismatic leadership of this powerful organization influenced the entire movement. Gonzales hoped the Crusade would be a national model for organizing urban Chicanos to resolve chronic problems and achieve self-determination.

Though the Crusade's influence was not solely dependent on the charisma of its founder, it would never have risen to prominence without his guidance. The Crusade grew from a small, male-dominated group in the mid-1960s into a multifaceted, multi-issue organization with hundreds of members before its fortunes wavered and then declined in the mid-1970s. Because its achievements are poorly chronicled, the Crusade is often recalled for the controversies in which it was embroiled rather than for its many accomplishments in the face of adversity.

"We Are Bringing this Matter to Your Attention . . ."

On July 7, 1962, Edward Larry Romero, age nineteen, was shot and killed in northeast Denver by off-duty police officer Gordon L. Thomas. Romero was reportedly involved in an altercation with Thomas and officer Charles Cullen at the Cowboy Drive Inn near closing time. As the officers led Romero out of the bar, he broke away and ran. Thomas chased him, and as Romero turned a corner Thomas claimed someone yelled, "Look out, he's got a gun!" A police spokesperson later reported that Thomas "thought he heard a shot."[4] Romero fled to an alley behind the 3200 block of Curtis Street and ran between two houses. Thomas said he fired a warning shot, then fired a second shot which struck Romero, who died later in the ambulance.

The Denver Post reported that Romero had been shot in the chest, and chief of detectives James Schumate said, "To the best of my knowledge, the officer took every precaution possible before he fired at the boy."[5] But no gun was found on Romero, and the next day's *Post* revealed a crucial point: Romero had been shot in the back. Thomas claimed, however, that he had shot "toward the legs."[6]

Two cousins, Tony Trujillo and David Cordova, seventeen and sixteen, were in one of the two houses between which Romero had fled. According to the *Post*, Trujillo was in the kitchen when he heard three shots and later recounted, "As soon as we heard that guy [Romero] fall, we turned out the lights and went into the parlor." The *Post* reported that the cousins looked out the window and saw Romero and Officer Thomas. They heard Romero say, "What did you shoot me for? I didn't do nothin'." Thomas

Gonzales addresses demonstrators at the State Capitol in Denver, ca 1980. Colorado Historical Society, courtesy Juan Espinosa.

responded, "If you didn't do nothing, what did you run for?" Trujillo said Romero then "tried to talk to the policeman, but he just couldn't."[7]

In response to protests over Eddie Romero's death, mayoral candidate Thomas Guida Currigan promised to create an independent review board to investigate such killings if he were elected. Rodolfo Gonzales, motivated by this promise, campaigned on Currigan's behalf in the 1963 mayoral election. After Currigan won, however, he failed to establish a review board. He explained that the prototype, the Philadelphia Police Advisory Board, had proven ineffective. Still, activists were angered that he had rescinded his promise.

One year and eight months after the Romero shooting, a similar incident occurred in Denver's Westwood neighborhood. On March 7, 1964, officers Michael Dowd and Warren Beard were working at the Westway, another 3.2 beer establishment. In the midst of a commotion, an officer struck nineteen-year-old Alfred Salazar with his nightstick and arrested the young man for disturbance and resisting arrest. Salazar's friends claimed that Salazar was not involved in the commotion and had been struck needlessly.

Salazar was booked at city jail around 1 A.M. on March 8. He complained that his head hurt, but no injury was found. His parents went to Rodolfo Gonzales's bail bond company and arranged for Salazar's release. The family, accompanied by Gonzales, went to the jail to take Salazar home, but found him incoherent and unable to sign his name. He was taken to Denver General Hospital, where doctors discovered that his skull had been fractured. He died that night. One of Salazar's jail mates told *The Denver Post* that jailers had struck the youth and that sheriffs had thrown him into a cell. The autopsy showed that Salazar's skull was exceptionally thin, half the thickness of an average skull. Largely because of this, the grand jury ruled his death accidental and cleared the officer who had hit him.

The incident aroused protest among several local groups, including Denver chapters of the American GI Forum and the Congress of Racial Equality (CORE) as well as the Denver Luncheon Club, the Committee Against Police Brutality, the United Mothers, and Los Voluntarios—the precursor to the Crusade for Justice. Los Voluntarios was a mainstream organization, not a "radical" group, founded in the spring of 1963 specifically to advocate for "the Spanish-speaking people of Colorado."[8]

Under Gonzales's leadership, Los Voluntarios took the forefront in the Salazar controversy, as recounted in Los Voluntarios' newspaper, *Viva! The Battle Cry of Truth*. On May 5, 1964, Gonzales headed a community meeting at labor union headquarters at Third Avenue and Acoma Street. City and state government representatives were among the attendees. *Viva!* reported that the five hundred who attended "proclaimed in a single voice that the investigation of purported police brutality remains an issue for the people to see and hear until just action had been taken."[9] Gonzales said, "We are regarded as a voting block and if in four days we can raise 500 people to show up here, we can raise 5,000 when we march on City Hall."[10]

The grand jury that had investigated Salazar's death recommended the abolishment of the police Internal Affairs Bureau. The jury further proposed a city charter amendment to create a citizens' board which would hear charges of police misconduct.[11] The mayor, however, believed misconduct should be investigated by the Internal Affairs Bureau and the Commission on Community Relations, each acting as a check on the other.

Unsatisfied with Currigan's position, Gonzales addressed matters in clear terms in a letter to Currigan. He stated that, "Since it is our experience that your mayor's citizens and City and County Employee Commission has no legal powers to investigate, subpoena, or enforce any action against policemen who use unnecessary force, we are bringing this matter to your attention for immediate action on these incidents."[12] Citing incidents of alleged brutality that occurred in June 1964, he wrote, "We suggest immediate suspension or removal of those officers involved. A complete investigation by an independent investigator and attorney to be selected by civil rights organizations such as SNCC (Student Nonviolent Coordinating Committee), CORE (Congress of Racial Equality) and Los Voluntarios. We must have an objective and thorough investigation. Only then can we expect positive results."[13]

Gonzales reminded Currigan of the May 1964 grand jury recommendations to abolish the police Internal Affairs Bureau "and to establish a citizens review board." The letter concludes:

> Our first approach is to seek redress in a diplomatic fashion; the weight of positive decisions lies in your hands. Once before I advised you that relief for those who are abused and mistreated cannot be expected unless you as mayor and head of this city take the initiative and use the position of your office to insure maximum safety for the citizens of this city and that you use your position as chief of this city to reprimand and penalize those officers guilty of misconduct. The community can no longer wait patiently while their complaints are aired by anemic boards appointed by the mayor to absorb and confuse issues. It is time for positive and responsible action.[14]

During his campaign, Currigan had stated,

> In fairness to both the officer and the citizen involved in such a complaint [of brutality], it would seem that a body completely separated from the police department could receive and hear grievances with greater detachment than a unit of the police force. I would strongly urge the creation of such a board in Denver and feel that it would not only protect the policeman from unfair charges, but give the public an opportunity to present grievances against improper police action.[15]

Viva! reprinted part of an April 22 *Denver Post* article by Tom Gavin detailing the mayor's 1963 campaign promise to establish an independent police review board. In the article, Gavin states that Currigan's "promises to the spokesmen of the groups in question have not been kept and these people are justifiably angry."

Though he was a political maverick, Gonzales was a popular community leader and a force within the Democratic Party. Voter registration drives conducted by Los Voluntarios and the turnout of Denver's Spanish-sur-named voters in the 1960 presidential election were so successful that no one was surprised when, on September 1, 1965, Currigan appointed Gonzales to head the Denver War on Poverty, the keystone program of the social reform agenda of the late President Kennedy.

Gonzales was thirty-seven years old and, as usual, had something quotable to say about his new job: "I'm an agitator and a trouble-maker. That's my reputation and that's what I'm going to be. They didn't buy me when they put me in this job."[16] The *Rocky Mountain News* article reporting his appointment was accompanied by a photo of Gonzales with Lady Bird and Lynda Bird Johnson, the wife and daughter of President Lyndon Baines Johnson. In the article, Gonzales criticized those whom he described as "coyotes" and "generals of the banquet table." In support of Pueblo Chicanos who thought it inappropriate for an Anglo appointee to direct Pueblo's War on Poverty—Pueblo was nearly half Chicano—Gonzales suggested organizing a Denver contingent to picket on their behalf.

Gonzales was optimistic about the War on Poverty, though he had critical comments about it as well:

> [Poverty programs] only scratch the surface, sure. But there's kind of a mass hypnosis. Somebody makes it, and those around them see them make it and want to make it themselves. They begin to see how you do it. Just like in politics, where you throw a job to your brother or your uncle—these people get a job through the poverty program and learn how to go about wrangling a job for a brother or a man from the community. . . . We have to keep an eye on the agencies and make sure they hire people from the community. All over the country, the poverty jobs and the administration have gone to the professionals, and nothing has trickled down to the people. That's not the way. You have to get people involved, and the way to do that is to live among the people, to hear what they are saying, and to agitate them.[17]

He took to heart the anti-poverty guidelines of the Washington, D.C., office of Sargent Shriver, the national head of the Office on Economic Opportunity. The guidelines promoted the "maximum feasible participation of the residents of the area or neighborhood in which the program will be carried out and of the members of the groups that it will serve [to] allow residents (of poverty areas) to influence the ways in which policy decisions are made and carried out."[18]

Gonzales's responsibilities in the anti-poverty effort included raising local matching funds. He realized that the local private sector would have to add to the $7 million in tax revenues Denver would receive. He expressed hopes that, "Maybe that's where a mass rally of the poor would come in—in waking people up."[19]

The War on Poverty stirred controversy throughout the nation. Community involvement in decision-making meant shifting local balances of power, and ruling elites had interests at stake. Gonzales's vision of community empowerment made many uncomfortable. One such doubter of Gonzales's role was A. Edgar Benton, a War on Poverty board member who had voted against Gonzales's appointment as chairperson. Benton said, "Aura is not irrelevant. There is the basic issue of one's reputation in the community, which I find here to be a disqualifying factor . . . . The legislation calls for the local contribution to step up from 10 percent now to 50 percent next August. I question whether Gonzales can relate to the community at large in such a way as to win a local commitment of such funds."[20] Benton apparently recognized the contradiction of an anti-poverty leader conducting marches against local government and business while raising funds from them.

"I Made Them White People, and They Like It"

Controversy over racial terminology in police records further strained relations between the Chicano community and the Denver city administration in early 1966. Chicano suspects were designated as "Spanish," "Mexican American," or "Latin American," indicating to many that police did not see Mexican-origin people as citizens but as primarily Spanish, Mexican, or Latin rather than "American." The February 17 *Denver Post* reported,

> Safety Manager Al Capra announced Wednesday afternoon, effective immediately, persons of Spanish descent will be classified "White" or "Caucasian" on police arrest records. Until Wednesday, police had listed such persons as "Spanish American" or "Latin American." Capra said police will use only three designations of race on police booking slips: Mongolian, Caucasian, and Negro. "We will now use the term *race* in its scientific connotation," he said, "and as far as I'm concerned, Spanish Americans are now a member of the white race."[21]

Mayor Currigan commended the decision, commenting that the terms "Spanish-American" and "Latin American" were irrelevant to law enforcement. But Bert Gallegos, a member of the Denver Luncheon Club and a former state representative, called the move an "idle gesture." Gallegos further insisted that Currigan "'has been talking out of both sides of his mouth' on this question and cited recent conflicting orders over whether county jail escapees will be identified by race or ethnic group. Gallegos said the new policy 'is merely a token thing for publicity purposes. It doesn't begin to touch the problem.' Gallegos said Currigan probably made the announcement because he—Currigan—plans to run for re-election next year."[22]

Public criticism might have subsided but for Capra's subsequent remarks. On February 23, public defender Edward Sherman requested that Capra post in the city jail a Spanish-language advisement of constitutional rights. Capra refused Sherman's request, saying, "Just a week ago I liberated these people . . . . I made them white people, and they like it."[23] When an outcry arose over Capra's "humor," he modified his statement: "As to making them white men, no one of course can make anybody a white man. . . . I merely insisted they be designated as members of the white race on public records." In the end, the Spanish language advisement was not posted at the city jail because Capra reasoned this "would be like throwing salt into an open wound."[24] Interestingly, no community protest resulted when the advisement was not posted.

If Chicanos were sensitive about racial terminology, chief Harold Dill was equally sensitive about charges of racism against his department. "We have no riots, no problems, and a respect for the law," Dill said. "There are a lot of good [Spanish Americans] who have been tremendous help to us. We have some on the police department, and you can't get finer men."[25]

Though Dill was unable to get "finer men," he had not hired many of them. In 1967, a year after Dill's remarks, the police department had employed only thirteen Spanish-surnamed police out of more than eight hundred officers in a city that was 10 percent Spanish-surnamed. Only three held command positions: one was a lieutenant and two were sergeants.[26]

Conservative Anglos, including Rev. James Miller of Montclair Community Church, resented criticism of police by minorities. Miller, a local John Birch Society leader, wrote that "All this [criticism of police] sounds too much like what the Communists have achieved in China and Vietnam and plan to instigate between Negro and White in our country— American fighting American with only the Communists standing a chance to gain."[27]

"We Can No Longer Be Exploited . . ."

Though Gonzales was not the sole critic of police behavior, his well-publicized activism brought him into conflict with the party for which he worked. Though he consciously employed pressure tactics through Los Voluntarios, Gonzales's strategy was to work through the system to build a voting bloc that would ultimately make the Democratic Party and local government responsive to community needs. His strategy of working within the system, however, was about to change.

Gonzales's vocal criticism of the status quo was embarrassing to Mayor Currigan and the Democratic Party. Gonzales was a rising star in the party, but, as he advanced politically, his criticism of the establishment did not subside. In addition, the party's failure to address concerns he raised caused him to reexamine his work-through-the-system strategy.

On April 23, 1966, Gonzales spoke to a liberal coalition at the Denver headquarters of the American Federation of Labor/Congress of Industrial Organizations (AFL/CIO). Gonzales said that he had "canvassed the community, both the leadership and the grassroots," and could effectively "speak from my own personal feelings and observations what the feelings and attitudes are of a majority of our people." He felt "mixed emotions, torn between the intense desire to involve myself in a new and dramatic move to unite the strength of groups who would work towards the goal of better government, and my dedication to my own ethnic group . . . ."[28] Gonzales, however, was now guided by a new vision in which ethnic solidarity and urban organizing took priority over coalition-building and electoral strategies involving politicians and processes he deemed untrustworthy or unworkable. He had decided to create an autonomous, grassroots movement separate from the coalitions already in place. In his announcement, Gonzales stated:

> We are bound to no one . . . we cannot dilute our strength . . . we will be a bargaining power committed to the economic, social, and academic betterment of the Spanish-named people in the state of Colorado. We can no longer be exploited or taken for granted by any political party, city, state, or federal agency . . . . We must struggle to unite the factions within our own group and we must guarantee to ourselves and the people in the entire community that we are one group, united and strong. It is at this time, in good conscience, that I cannot bring myself to ask my group to commit themselves to this new exciting idea . . . . I also want to make it clear that our reluctance at this time not be construed as a negative decision, but that we will support the objectives

and goals of organized labor, we will support the programs and legislation to aid the aged. We are still committed to fight for equality for the Negro, all races, ethnic, or religious groups.[29]

The philosophical underpinnings of the Crusade for Justice were now in place, but the time to form the organization had not yet come. Gonzales's break with the establishment was fast approaching, and the setting for this break involved his administration of the Neighborhood Youth Corps (NYC). A *Rocky Mountain News* article insinuated that Gonzales's administration favored Chicanos over other youth by placing their names higher on an NYC waiting list. In effect, Gonzales—a minority spokesperson—was being charged with discrimination. When his administrative assistant, Peter Papageorgiou, asserted that the NYC suffered from disorganization and mismanagement, Gonzales countered that Papageorgiou lacked "administrative ability." He contested the charge of bypassing names on the waiting list, saying that "if a kid comes along from a family of ten children where the income is $2,000, he gets a job quicker than a kid from a family of four with a $4,000 income. If that's favoritism, then let it be that way."[30] This alleged bias resulted, according to the *News*, in officials "keeping a wary eye" on Gonzales. Gonzales called for a newspaper boycott and organized a picket against the newspaper—conduct Mayor Currigan declared improper for a public official.

On April 24, 1966, Currigan fired Gonzales as NYC director. Gonzales said Currigan's decision was "a gutless, weak-minded decision. But you have to remember—he's easily influenced and led. He can't stand up to pressure because he's got very little courage."[31] Gonzales pointed out that Currigan had recently praised the NYC in a letter to Sargent Shriver, head of the War on Poverty. "Then," Gonzales said, "he terminates me. I think the real reason I was fired was because of my calling the boycott on the *News* . . . . I told Mayor Currigan when I took the Youth Corps job that he was not buying me. I said I would always express my views as a private citizen. I guess I'm the cannon fodder who has to pay the price because I didn't agree with the power structure."[32]

Gonzales and his associates organized a rally at Denver's Civic Center, at which he proclaimed to the twelve hundred in attendance, "This meeting is only the spark of a crusade for justice which we are going to carry into every city in Colorado."[33] A rejection of mainstream politics now paved the way for a strategy of militant grassroots organizing and independent political action in which Chicanos were to decide their destiny independent of institutions controlled by others.

A scathing letter Gonzales would write a year later to the Democratic Party's county chairman, Dale Tooley, reveals a continuing disappointment with party politics:

> After having spoken to you last summer I was impressed by your seemingly dedicated, liberal, and progressive views. I watched for some time to see if there would be any changes in the party under your leadership. I looked hopefully for the restoration of dignity and respect for the individual and maybe, much too idealistically, a change in the status quo and conventional attitudes which the Democratic Party has been guilty of in the past. It is clearly apparent that the party has not progressed on any of the pre-mentioned planes but instead, has regressed so far back that the Party is certainly in jeopardy of antagonizing those people who have accepted the party with open arms, induced by a tradition of social progress and humanistic philosophies initiated by such men as Roosevelt, Truman, and J. F. Kennedy. From my point of view, party politics have traveled backward instead of forward. The individual who makes his way through the political muck of today's world—and more so the minority representatives—suffer from such a loss of soul and dignity that the end results are as rewarding as a heart attack, castration, or cancer![34]

Gonzales criticized Tooley for "arrogant intimidation of career service city employees to vote for the mayor on the threat of not being promoted, placed, or employed," saying that Tooley pressured party members with city jobs to "pay part of their earnings to the campaign of the Mayor." He wrote that Tooley, as a party official,

> . . . chose to appoint to party leadership in the districts, except for one grassroots person, Barbara Santistevan, a blue ribbon crew of Uncle Toms and political hacks to represent people who they do not communicate with, let alone identify with . . . . You and your cohorts have been accomplices to the destruction of moral man in this society. I can only visualize that your goal is the complete emasculation of manhood, sterilization of human dignity, and that you not only conscientiously but purposely are creating a world of lackeys, political bootlickers, and prostitutes.[35]

". . . The Conduct of a Wanton, Ruthless War"
Gonzales's evolving consciousness included international views and an

economic critique of society, as seen in his August 1966 speech condemn-
ing the Vietnam War, in which he charged that American society was run
for, and by, "the ruthless financial lords of Wall Street" and "great and
powerful corporations."[36] Gonzales's departure from mainstream politics
also coincided with his entry into the files of the FBI. Gonzales and the
Crusade for Justice were linked with the Black Power movement, a development the FBI noted.

On January 6, 1966, Denver police arrested a group of protestors at
the FBI office in Denver's federal building. The protestors, identified as
the Denver Friends of the Student Nonviolent Coordinating Committee
(SNCC), were protesting the slaying of Samuel Younge, Jr., in Tuskegee,
Alabama; Younge had been killed by an angry racist when he attempted to
use a segregated facility. In county court on May 4, the Denver protestors
were found guilty of disturbance, and later appeared for sentencing. When
the defendants left the courtroom, the FBI reported, "they were joined
by several persons who had been spectators in the courtroom, as well as
Rudolph (Corky) Gonzales and some of his followers. They all joined
hands and sang, 'We Shall Overcome.'"[37]

While monitoring a meeting of the Denver Friends of SNCC at Denver's
Mount Girard Church, the FBI noted that "the Reverend Clifton Whitley
of the Democratic Freedom Party in Mississippi" was the guest speaker
and that the discussion included a new term: "Black Power." The FBI
reported Rev. Whitley as stating that "Negroes in Denver should work with
[Gonzales] to form a united front with the Spanish-American people."[38]

Wary of political dissent, the Denver FBI field office reported on a
speech Gonzales made at a Vietnam War protest rally on August 6. The
report noted the presence of members of the Denver Communist Party and
the Denver Branch of the Socialist Workers Party.[39] In his speech, Gonzales
was guided by a new vision in which ethnic solidarity and urban organizing
took priority over coalition-building and electoral strategies involving politicians and processes he deemed untrustworthy or unworkable. Gonzales
stated:

> My feelings and emotions are aroused by the complete disregard of
> our present society for the rights, dignity, and lives of not only people
> of other nations but our own unfortunate young men who die for an
> abstract cause, war, that cannot be honestly justified by any of our
> present leaders . . . . The American people are daily faced with news
> that attempts to brainwash them into approving of a war that can only
> bring shame and disgrace to the most powerful nation in the world

along with misery and destruction to weak and helpless people. Would it not be more noble to portray our great country as a humanitarian nation with the honest intentions of aiding and advising the weak rather than to be recognized as a military power and hostile enforcer of our political aims? What the American people should recognize and evaluate is that political doctrine is not the issue in Vietnam. It is not the real issue here at home. The real issue is economics. At present the economic stabilization of our country is dependent upon the war in Vietnam. The ruthless financial lords of Wall Street are the only real recipients of the tremendous profits to be made by the conduct of a wanton, ruthless war. The great and powerful corporations who control our industries, who control the purse strings of the nation, calmly play a chess game trading the lives of innocent American boys, confused and bewildered Vietnamese men, women, and children for green dollars that do not show the red stain of blood, the anguish and torment of grieving parents, the guilt for rape of a weaker nation . . . . Who reaps the profits? If in essence we are sharing in this prosperity by our own personal good life, then we are prospering at the expense of the blood and bones of fellow human beings. If our own economic gain must be earned by such a grisly trade, then we are truly a very sick society.[40]

Gonzales's 1966 antiwar speech found its way into FBI files in a 1968 summary of his activity. As the summary also reported,

[Gonzales] was quoted as saying that he had been accelerating his efforts to organize the Spanish-speaking community and stated he hoped that the May 21, 1966, rally "will be the biggest rally in the history of the state." Gonzales was quoted as saying that the May 21, 1966, rally would be held under a "Crusade for Justice" organizational blanket which would include a number of participating organizations. He stated he hoped to have as a speaker, Caesar [sic] Chavez, leader of the National Farm Workers Association Strike Against the Grape Growers in California's Delano County.[41]

The Crusade's ideas antagonized not only the FBI but also local reactionary groups. One such group was the "Soldiers of the Cross," which harassed Denver's early anti-war marchers. The Crusade's anti-war politics, however, were not pacifist; its members would fight back. Esequiel "Kelly" Lovato, Jr., son of Esequiel and Eloisa Lovato and a founding member of the Crusade, wrote in *El Gallo* of a confrontation at a 1967 protest at the state capitol. Lovato equated police officers with right-wing fascists, pointing out that when Crusade members attempted to talk with the Soldiers of the Cross, the police halted them. Later, however, chief R. D. Potter led the Soldiers to the podium in an attempt to end the rally. Lovato concluded his article with a call to "Wake up minorities; unite!" for "war has many forms." From his perspective, the government that sent its citizens to fight in Vietnam was disregarding the rights of Chicanos, and the responsibility for righting these injustices lay in the hands of minorities.[42]

"The People of New Mexico Have Moved Together . . ."

To the FBI, Gonzales's anti-war politics and ties to Black Power activists, leftists, and progressives were overshadowed by his association with Reies Lopez Tijerina and the dramatic New Mexico land-grant struggle. Tijerina and his organization, the Alianza Federal de Mercedes, sought to reclaim millions of acres taken by force and fraud from native New Mexicans after the 1846–48 Mexican War. The Alianza, founded in 1963, sought the return of these lands based on provisions of the Treaty of Guadalupe Hidalgo, which formalized the war's end. Gonzales attended the Alianza's 1966 convention, and an informal alliance based on a spirit of common struggle soon evolved. As the Alianza's efforts to recover land grants escalated, it met with increasing hostility from local officials. At stake were millions of acres in two hundred seventy-seven Spanish and Mexican land grants.

After breaking with the Democratic Party, Gonzales—in the spring of 1967—campaigned as an independent mayoral candidate against Mayor Currigan. As Gonzales had anticipated, Currigan was reelected. After the election, Gonzales's attorneys—Walter Gerash, Harry Nier, and Eugene Deikman—sued Currigan for violating the city's $1,000 charter campaign expenditure limit, which was established by city charter in 1913. As campaign costs mounted over the years, candidates had routinely ignored this restriction. Currigan thus became the first candidate required to defend himself against the previously ignored violations. As the case wound through the courts, events in New Mexico took a dramatic turn in June 1967—events set in motion the previous year.

In October 1966, the Alianza had dramatized its demands by gathering at the Echo Amphitheater, part of U.S. Forest Service holdings and—more importantly for the Alianza—originally part of the San Joaquin del Río del Chama Land Grant. When forest rangers arrived at the scene, they were "arrested," "tried," and "convicted" for trespassing, then released. The

Alianzistas, in turn, were arrested on assault charges. Six months later, Reies Lopez Tijerina sent Gonzales a letter alerting him that the "Sons of San Joaquin" planned to reclaim San Joaquin del Río del Chama "once and for all," and inviting a Crusade representative to witness and report on the takeover:

> The people of New Mexico have moved together in a miraculous manner which causes joy in the soul of the natives but great fear and terror in the strangers who arrived in New Mexico but yesterday. The taking of San Joaquin del Río del Chama will be about the third day of June. And those valiant ones from Denver who wish to be present are invited and can personally see the valor of the "Sons of San Joaquin."[43]

New Mexico authorities tried to forestall the Alianza by arresting its members who gathered in Coyote, New Mexico, on June 3. But the arrests infuriated other Alianzistas, and on June 5, angry Alianzistas stormed the Tierra Amarilla courthouse to make a citizens' arrest of district attorney Alfonso Sanchez, who had ordered the initial arrests. The attempt ended in a confrontation in which gunfire wounded two officials. The Alianzistas fled into the surrounding countryside and were later captured. National Guard troops, with armored personnel carriers, flooded the area. The courthouse raid drew national attention to the cause and methods of the Alianzistas.

Though the Crusade sent no observers in response to Tijerina's March 25 invitation, it monitored these developments. Gonzales and a small Colorado delegation quickly visited New Mexico on June 8 for a firsthand view. Returning to Denver on June 9, Gonzales discovered that Tijerina too had been arrested. In response, he "drafted a telegram to President Johnson, Attorney General Ramsey Clark, Civil Rights Commission Director William Taylor, New Mexico Governor Cargo, and Río Arriba County District Attorney Alfonso Sanchez."[44] The telegram stated:

> It is with great concern that we ask your immediate consideration and attention to afford fair and impartial administration of justice to those individuals arrested and now in custody . . . . Areas of concern are fair and reasonable bond, legal aid, and a thorough investigation of the legality of all arrests, warrants, interrogation, search and seizure procedures, etc. . . . It is of imperative importance that the incidents, long-standing problems, and complete disregard of the law [i.e., the Treaty of Guadalupe Hidalgo] be thoroughly studied, evaluated, and acted

upon in order to prevent future problems and misunderstandings . . . .[45]

At a June 10 rally at Denver's Sunken Gardens Park, Gonzales called for "dedicated and concerned members of our community . . . not only in Denver but in the entire Southwest . . . to support a just and honorable cause."[46] A Denver FBI report chronicled developments in Denver and New Mexico, referring to Alianzistas as "armed desperadoes" and to Tijerina as a "terrorist leader."[47]

Two days later, Gonzales and the Crusade organized a caravan to New Mexico to support the Alianza and assist it during the absence of its leadership.

Crusade members were present when arrested Alianzistas appeared in court in Santa Fe. The June 23 premiere edition of the Crusade's newspaper, *El Gallo*, recounted that cries of "*Viva Tijerina!*" went up as Tijerina, in handcuffs, was led through the hallway into the courtroom. Charges against his brother, Anselmo, were dropped. When asked how it felt to be free, Anselmo answered, "It is no different being out here than in the penitentiary. Our people are still not free."[48] During this time, Tijerina supporters welcomed Crusade members into their homes, and a "new spirit of confidence prevailed over the past few days of gloom. . . . People were now talking freely and refused to be intimidated as they had been by the arrests, questioning, and harassment instigated by the D.A. of Santa Fe."[49]

On June 28 Gonzales reported on the New Mexico trips at a Crusade-sponsored meeting at Denver's Santa Fe Theatre. He announced that Tijerina had authorized Gonzales to take over the New Mexico Alianza movement. Tijerina asked the Alianza's branches to cooperate with Gonzales, who promised, "I will offer as much advice as I can on such things as organizing and moving forward with the movement there. . . . The United States government itself is part of a criminal conspiracy in taking these people's lands, making out fraudulent titles, and selling the land to others."[50] Gonzales stayed in New Mexico from July 12 to July 22, operating from Alianza headquarters.[51] On July 23, Tijerina was released on bond and announced that the Alianza would hold a national conference for land grant heirs in Albuquerque the following month.

Some New Mexicans appreciated the Crusade's support, while others found it meddlesome. Jailed Alianzista Jose Madril of Velarde, New Mexico, wrote to Juanita Dominguez of the Crusade. Acknowledging the common struggle, Madril wrote:

I can't find the words to express the great feeling that came to our hearts when we heard inside the prison that the Crusade for Justice was supporting us . . . . This morning . . . I met Mr. Corky Gonzales for the first time and I wished we could have more people like him and the ones that are helping us . . . . I will close my letter with this, give me liberty or give me death. *Y que viva la justicia!* May God bless each and all of you.[52]

But Garcedan Madrid of Chaperito, New Mexico, denounced the Crusade's involvement:

We from New Mexico have never attempted to solve your people's problems . . . . Why, then, should people from your great state try to stick their noses into affairs which are strictly New Mexico's? . . . We have competent people in New Mexico capable of handling any and all situations. We strongly resent intrusions and assure you that yours is neither desired, needed, nor appreciated.[53]

Waldo Benavidez of the Crusade responded with his own letter:

Most of the people who went to Santa Fe are originally from New Mexico, knowing of the problems, and not outsiders, and even if they were, they still believe in a common cause and the human rights of all people . . . . I might add that the "competent people" Madrid mentions are probably the same ones that have created this situation in the first place. They have sold out their pride and honor to the highest bidder for money, positions, etc. Now they are desperately trying to regain a semblance of leadership, but the people are no longer buying this.[54]

". . . Piñedo Was Shot in the Back"

During Gonzales's absence from Colorado, further killings by Denver police roused public protest and Crusade ire. Louis Piñedo, age eighteen, was killed on July 12, 1967; around the same time, the death of a young African American, Eugene Cook, angered the African American community as well. The Crusade for Justice, the Black Panther Party, and others converged on police headquarters. Crusade and Black Panther representatives sought march permits. The manager of safety granted the Black Panthers a permit but refused to give a Westside Crusade contingent permission to march. The explanation was that the march would interfere with traffic.

On July 23, one hundred twenty-five African American and Chicano protestors converged in a two-pronged march on police headquarters, demanding to talk with chief Harold Dill. Chief Dill, with division chief Clifford Stanley and eight helmeted officers, pushed the crowd from the door.[55] Emilio "Zapata" Dominguez, Crusade vice-chairperson, stated: "This will be the last time we come here in peace; we want to do right, but we're not left alone. Our people are shot in the back." He meant this literally, for while newspaper accounts of Piñedo's death claimed that Piñedo had been shot in the chest, an *El Gallo* article stated, ". . . the coroner's report proves that Piñedo was shot in the back."[56]

The press reported that Officer Cain had killed Louis Piñedo when he found Piñedo stealing car parts from an auto dealership. Piñedo allegedly stabbed Cain with a sharp metal object (a knife or a screwdriver) and in defense, Cain shot Piñedo. Desiderio "Desi" De Herrera, a former town sheriff from southern Colorado, went to the coroner's office on behalf of the Crusade and insisted on a copy of the death certificate. After much resistance, the document was given to De Herrera. Three words clearly revealed the cause of death: "gunshot wound, back."[57]

Though the Crusade demanded action, an *El Gallo* editorial shows the organization's skepticism that anything would be done:

In 1964 demonstrations were held against the Denver Police Department for the killing of Eddie Romero and Alfred Salazar. A Grand Jury investigation was held in connection with the Salazar death. The officers were vindicated [and] although the Grand Jury recommendations [for an independent review board] were objective and meaningful, they have since gathered dust in the vault of Denver's district court. Now comes the killing of Louis Piñedo and Eugene Cook. . . . What now? Another grand jury investigation to handle the hot potato long enough to cool the situation down? Or complete disregard by the Police Department, District Attorney, and city administration? . . . The time has come for action . . . . Our people who are hiding behind closed doors hypnotized by TV sets, trying to identify with Anglo success figures, had better come awake and start fighting their brother's battle. The power structure, meaning this society, only recognizes reaction or power, and action produces both. Where are you?[58]

Shooting controversies did not subside. On August 20, 1967, off-duty officer Harold McMillan critically wounded twenty-three-year-old Andres Garcia at a local tavern. *El Gallo* reported that McMillan had shot Garcia for allegedly stabbing him:

> Witnesses interviewed by Crusade for Justice Police Board Chairman, D. C. De Herrera, claimed Garcia was shot as he ran from the officer and then after falling, Officer McMillan clubbed him with his pistol until it went off a second time. A number of calls came into the editorial office of *El Gallo*, telling of past incidents in which Officer Harold McMillan has been involved . . . . Denver has had no riots to date, but the toll of injured and killed in the Mexican American community continues to climb. The people contacted in the neighborhoods, scoff at what they term "phony meetings with the Mayor." The Police Community Relations Division is considered a public relations division and that the Man is encouraged to, rather [than] discouraged from, assaulting Mexicans.[59]

In a harshly worded editorial, Gonzales chastised the community for its passivity:

> So what now, or rather, just "So what?" Andres Garcia gets shot and pistol-whipped by a policeman acting as a paid bouncer while he wears a police uniform, badge, and the authority vested in him by the city and county of Denver. The minorities look at each other and say, "What now?" Do we picket? Do we demonstrate? Do we force a grand jury investigation so that the recommendations gather dust in the district court? Shall we have police command-community leaders conferences; shall we hold hands and play ring-a-round-the-rosy? Shall we just keep watching our TV sets, drinking our beer, and say, "It's his problem, not mine"? Shall we pretend it didn't happen and turn our other cheek just in case it really did? After seeing what is happening across the nation, the Denver Mexican Americans should start analyzing the situation. Police are not afraid of us. They can mistreat one Chicano, and a hundred looking on won't make a move. We fight each other at the drop of a hat. The young tough cats shoot each other down, cut each other up, and don't blink an eye. The policemen are not afraid of Mexican Americans and, until they are, they will never respect us.[60]

New Mexico's controversies now surfaced in Denver as well. On September 12 Danny Tijerina, son of Reies Lopez Tijerina, was arrested at Denver's West High School. Danny, age fifteen, was staying with his mother in Denver when he was arrested on a warrant issued by the district

attorney of Santa Fe and charged with assault with intent to commit murder and kidnaping at the Tierra Amarilla raid. Adamant *El Gallo* writers
reported:

> Young Tijerina was arrested by juvenile authorities and placed in
> Juvenile Hall. . . . When interviewed by *El Gallo* representatives, Danny
> said he was never given an explanation of rights or advised about secur-
> ing an attorney. Maria Escobar, Danny's mother, contacted the Crusade
> for Justice office who called on Eugene Deikman, one of Denver's fin-
> est attorneys, to represent the Tijerina boy . . . . Deikman said, "The
> public should know what the District Attorney of New Mexico is try-
> ing to do." Certified papers and amended warrant had not yet been
> received although [Danny] had been arrested and held in custody and
> brought before the court . . . . Danny said that he was not at the Tierra
> Amarilla when the shooting started June 5. He   remained in camp
> at Canjilon, eleven miles from Tierra Amarilla,   with forty others.
> It was at Canjilon where the state National Guard kept them hostage
> in a sheep pen.[61]

Danny's extradition proceedings were scheduled for October 2, but
the Denver district attorney's office requested a continuance to seek more
information from Santa Fe. The Crusade felt the grounds for extradition
were flimsy, and *El Gallo* reported that juvenile judge Ted Rubin agreed
that juvenile court had no jurisdiction over Tijerina.[62]

With Tijerina's extradition dropped, the Crusade's focus shifted when
young Robert Gene Castro was killed by detective Paul Montoya, one of
Denver's few Spanish-surnamed police officers. Controversy now erupted
in another public forum, as recorded in FBI files. Intelligence reports sent
to Washington, D.C., claimed that Crusade members, including Gonzales,
interrupted a meeting regarding police relations with the community:

> [Gonzales] and other members of his Crusade for Justice organization
> entered and disrupted the meeting by shouting "police-brutality" type
> insults at the police officers who were on the panel. . . . Several of
> Gonzales's group started to shout, "Shoot them all!" Gonzales himself
> started to shout about revolution and stated that his group would arm
> themselves, if necessary. At this point almost everyone in the meeting
> began shouting insults back and forth at each other which approached
> an actual disturbance.[63]

On October 6, Gonzales wrote a letter to the mayor and police chief demanding the firing of five policemen for brutality. "Because we no longer intend to use the meaningless methods of attempting to gain redress for the injuries sustained by our people," Gonzales wrote, "we demand the immediate dismissal of the . . . officers (please do not confuse dismissal with suspension). We expect immediate action. Patience and time is running out. Awaiting an immediate reply."[64]

The takeover of the October 3 conference may or may not have "approached an actual disturbance," but it was doubtlessly prompted by the Crusade's anger, desire for direct action, and feeling that community grievances had been neither heard nor heeded. Anger was also directed at unnamed persons derided as "worn-out race horses that are still listening to the bugle of the past and still dancing to the tune of the power structure for their daily bread."[65]

Members of the Crusade heaped invectives on these figures because the unnamed "race horses" were previous members of Los Voluntarios. Gonzales felt they reaped jobs, political appointments, and other benefits via Los Voluntarios, things they were unwilling to jeopardize in protests. Gonzales wrote:

> They went through the same pretension that they had in the past and will in the future. They shadowboxed, growled ferociously, pledged undying brotherhood, fawned over each other, and strutted like gladiators. Only there is one thing wrong. They never finish in the winners circle. In fact, they'll never finish the race. Weren't those the same faces that tried to form a council of Latin American groups some years back? It flopped! How many of those people were members of Los Voluntarios, an organization that was comprised of a cross section of the community? Los Voluntarios, a political organization [that was] the fore-runner of the Crusade for Justice, was the initiating or employment bridge for almost every self-acclaimed leader in Denver's "Spanish-surnamed" community. That's why sounds of demonstration, riot, and militancy coming from people who ran like thieves when Los Voluntarios took up the cause against police brutality sounds not only ridiculous, but impossible. [66]

He further described them as "old left-wingers who now fear the mention of red, the old bulls who were castrated years ago . . . the young, ambitious status seekers, the bootlickers and the malinches of our times." He predicted that they would "be scorned and cast out by a social revolution led by the young who will not buy hypocrisy or be bought by money . . . . It is no wonder that the young shy away from politics and phony meetings. They just aren't buying it."

The Crusade did not believe that the courts provided remedies, as evidenced in the October 18 acquittal of Officer Cain for first degree murder in the death of Louis Piñedo. Attorney Eugene Deikman wrote that the trial had been unfair to Piñedo from the beginning. Jurors were biased, Chicanos were barred from the courtroom while Anglos were not, and the prosecutor had failed to mention the crux of the argument: that Piñedo was shot from behind.[67] Deikman's article discounted the testimony of Officer Vandervelde, Cain's partner, who had not seen the actual shooting. According to *El Gallo*, Cain had said to him, "I've been stabbed. You'd better call an ambulance." While Cain and Vandervelde discussed Cain's half-inch wound, Piñedo was writhing on the ground, bleeding profusely. Vandervelde called an ambulance and tended to Cain, ignoring the dying boy. According to Deikman:

> Later, when the court dismissed the murder charge against Cain, the victim's brother, Henry, furious and humiliated by this travesty, spat full in Cain's face as Cain slunk past him near the courtroom. Vandervelde jumped Henry Piñedo and brutally handcuffed him. "He's my brother," Henry gasped. Vandervelde sneered, "He was your brother." "You're proud of what you've done aren't you?" Henry screamed. Vandervelde smiled and spat in Henry's face.[68]

". . . By Concentrating Manpower on Direct Political Action"

Police controversies were not the only focus of Gonzales's energy. On August 31, 1967, Gonzales—accompanied by Crusade vice-chairperson Emilio Dominguez—was invited to Chicago to attend the National Conference for New Politics. Conference organizers held the meeting "to enable those who work for peace, civil rights, and an end to poverty to register the greatest impact by concentrating manpower on direct political action."[69] (The conference was thoroughly infiltrated by government informers.[70]) Gonzales intended to develop ties with other Latino groups at the conference, although Latinos were scarce—numbering about two dozen. Mexican population was concentrated in the Southwest, but national political, financial, and media centers were located in eastern seaboard cities and the industrial Midwest, factors Gonzales felt impeded Latinos' impact at the Chicago conference. He noted the clout wielded by African Americans, but he felt whites had little sense of who Chicanos and

Latinos were. Todd Gitlin's book, *The Sixties*, recounts that "at the chaotic National Conference for New Politics convention in a Chicago hotel over Labor Day weekend, some three hundred blacks in a conference of two or three thousand demanded—and in an orgy of white guilt were granted—half the votes on all resolutions."[71] Gitlin's book, significantly, makes no mention of Latino issues or activism.

Whether or not black impact was tied to white guilt, which did not concern him, Gonzales felt Latino impact was tied to unity on a regional and national level, so he proposed that Latinos operate as a caucus at the convention. He also called for a national Latino gathering for the spring of 1968 to lay the groundwork for unity. Latino activists responded enthusiastically, and the Crusade committed to host the gathering.[72] Though the gathering was subsequently postponed, the proposal to hold it drew the attention of FBI informers. Though Gonzales was never again involved with the National Conference for New Politics organizers, Crusade member Eloy Espinoza attended a follow-up meeting in Chicago. The FBI reported that Gonzales was in attendance, apparently confusing the two.[73]

The FBI had closely monitored Gonzales's activity since the spring of 1967, especially his association with Reies Tijerina and the Alianza. Tijerina had appeared in November of 1967 before the first anniversary celebration of the Crusade for Justice. Approximately five hundred individuals, including Gonzales, were present at the meeting.[74] Tijerina was quoted as saying that the land grant dispute would be taken to the United Nations by some nation, even Castro's Cuba, if necessary. Though Cuba's mention interested the FBI and local media, *El Gallo's* account of Tijerina's visit merely recorded his itinerary in the Denver area.[75]

Gonzales traveled extensively in October and November to speak to groups such as the United Mexican-American Students at California State College and the Peace Action Council. The eyes and ears of the FBI followed:

On October 12, 1967, a meeting sponsored by the United Mexican-American Students at California State College at Los Angeles was held and approximately 200 individuals were present at this meeting. . . . In his speech before the crowd . . . Gonzales called for all Mexican Americans to rebel from the present standard way of life. Gonzales stated that the widespread frustration of the Mexican Americans of the southwest United States will eventually lead to violence . . . that large-scale violence would be resorted to unless the federal government changes its ways . . . [and that] there would be large-scale rebellion unless the government provides basic needs of the Mexican-American people.[76]

On October 20 Gonzales attended an Albuquerque conference sponsored by the Alianza. Also attending were Jose Angel Gutierrez of the Mexican American Youth Organization, Ralph Featherstone and Ethel Minor of SNCC, *La Raza*'s Eliezer Risco, Maulana Ron Karenga of US, Hopi traditionalist Thomas Banyacya, Bert Corona of the Mexican American Political Association, James Dennis of CORE, Anthony Babu of the Black Panther Party and the Black Student Union, and the Los Angeles Black Congress's Walter Bremond. The Albuquerque gathering was Tijerina's attempt to broaden the Alianza's support among people of color and to draw activists from throughout the nation to conservative Albuquerque. The conference closed with participants signing the symbolic Treaty of Peace, Harmony and Mutual Assistance, which led to no formal alliance. Gonzales did not sign the treaty, but was soon involved in another conference that was reported in FBI files.

". . . Brave Words, Promises, Motions—and No Action"

On October 27, 1967, a public meeting was held at the Sacred Heart Gymnasium, El Paso, Texas, in connection with the travel to El Paso by President Gustavo Diaz Ordaz of Mexico. [Gonzales] was one of the speakers at this meeting, and he told the group that the Mexican Americans in the Southwest would demand their rights and obtain justice for all. Also a speaker on that date was Reies Lopez Tijerina.

FBI Internal Security File 105-176910.[77]

A public meeting was held in El Paso to protest the Cabinet Committee Hearings on Mexican American Affairs, which were sponsored by the federal Inter-Agency Committee on Mexican American Affairs. The hearings were highlighted by a visit from Mexican president Gustavo Diaz-Ordaz and by the return to Mexico of a parcel of land due to a change in the course of the Río Grande. The return of this land, known as the Chamizal, was to symbolize the United States' good intentions toward its southern neighbor. The hearings, however, were called in response to a walkout by activists at the meeting of the Equal Employment Opportunity Commission in Albuquerque in March 1966. Gonzales had participated in the walkout, which was held in protest of the government's neglect of civil rights concerns in Mexican communities.

President Johnson had promised to hold a White House conference for Chicano leaders in response to the Albuquerque protest, but that conference never materialized because Johnson feared another walkout. Instead, the El Paso hearings were held to demonstrate government concern, but activists like Gonzales, Cesar Chavez, and Tijerina were not invited.

The Johnson administration's concern with the growth of militancy was evident in its efforts to defuse it. The planning in Washington, D.C., for the public meeting in El Paso took place in secret. The *Rocky Mountain News* related:

> Although reporters were barred from the [planning] meeting, reports of dissension among the delegates from Colorado, New Mexico, and Texas leaked out . . . . The White House reportedly decided to split up the meetings to keep harmony between more militant Spanish-American groups and more moderate members of the Southwest's Spanish-speaking communities. A source said there was fear one large pre-conference session might produce a repeat of last year's meeting of the Equal Employment Opportunity Council in Albuquerque. Militant Spanish-Americans including Rudolph "Corky" Gonzales marched out of that conference. The planned White House conference grew out of a promise by President Johnson to take up Spanish-American problems and complaints this fall . . . [and was] in response to criticism for not including Spanish-Americans in a national White House civil rights conference last summer. Spanish-Americans long have complained about treatment they have received from government officials who, they charge, court them only around election time . . . . But the White House in recent months has become increasingly alarmed by what seems to be a growing move among Spanish Americans in the Southwest, where they are the largest minority, to abandon their traditional support for the Democratic Party.[78]

The protestors' declaration, the *Plan de La Raza Unida*, was more moderate than subsequent Chicano rhetoric and blended patriotism with anger over American racism. The proclamation's more militant signers included the Crusade for Justice, the Alianza, the UCLA United Mexican American Students (UMAS) chapter, Chicago's Latin American Defense Organization (LADO), and northern California's Mexican American Student Confederation (MASC). The American GI Forum and others represented more moderate activists. The proclamation demanded housing, education, and labor rights, an end to police abuse, and "the strong enforcement of all sections of the treaty of Guadalupe Hidalgo, particularly the sections dealing with land grants and bilingual guarantees." The proclamation states:

> On this historic day, October 28, 1967, La Raza Unida organized in El Paso, Texas, proclaims the time of subjugation, exploitation, and abuse of human rights of La Raza in the United States is hereby ended forever . . . . We have demonstrated and proven and again affirm our loyalty to the constitutional democracy of the United States of America and to the religious and cultural tradition we all share. We accept the framework of constitutional democracy and freedom within which to establish our own independent organizations among our people in pursuit of justice and equality and redress of grievances. La Raza Unida pledges to join with all our courageous people organizing in the fields and barrios. We commit ourselves to La Raza, at whatever cost.[79]

The United Steelworkers of America's Maclovio Barraza signed the proclamation, participated in the picket, and attended the government conference, where he stated:

> In the programs of the federal government directed against poverty there is increasing emphasis on the need for the poor to be represented. It is logical that it takes the poor to understand the problems of the poor and to be involved in the plans and decisions aimed at the solution. It is equally true that one has to be a Mexican American living in the Southwest to know and understand the problems of this people, who today are among the most disadvantaged segment of our society and for whom the door of opportunity is, in most instances, more tightly shut than even [for] the American Negro. . . . While I personally welcome the invitation to present my views, I cannot refrain from informing you that several important organizations equally concerned with the problems of the Mexican Americans view this conference with suspicion. They hold little or no expectation that it will result in anything meaningful for the Mexican Americans. These groups consider this meeting as being politically motivated at a time when the Federal election season approaches. They charge that the conference is structured so as to have only the "safe" Mexicans participating.[80]

El Gallo recorded the Crusade's sentiments and the organization's role in the protest: "Twelve Crusaders traveled to El Paso to take part in La

Raza conference, which took place at the same time as the President's Conference on Mexican American Affairs. Yes, we picketed, we demonstrated, we marched, and we're still mad. A crowd of 300 out-of-state delegates led by Reies Tijerina and Rodolfo (Corky) Gonzales marched through the streets of downtown El Paso to a meeting of 1,000 people at the Sacred Heart Gym. Unity was the pledge."[81]

The Crusade contingent, however, encountered peculiar difficulties prior to the march in downtown El Paso. Despite their arrangements to stay inexpensively at a church, nobody responded to their knock when they arrived. When they called Tijerina's hotel, the woman who answered claimed that Tijerina was not in, when in fact he was. Crusade members continued on to Juarez, where their bus and cars were searched. The proprietor of a hotel refused them rooms, citing fear of Mexican authorities. Nobody in Juarez wanted to shelter *Mexicanos Norteamericanos*. Finally, they crossed over to El Paso and stayed at the YMCA.[82]

After resting for the night and getting their bearings, Gonzales and the Crusade delegation led a march to Texas Western University, where vice-president Hubert Humphrey was addressing the conference. Farm workers from Laredo, Texas, were picketing the conference when the Crusaders arrived and joined them. Texas Rangers barred the protestors from entering, but Crusade members challenged them on the grounds that, since they were Mexican Americans attending a conference on Mexican American affairs, they should be allowed to demonstrate for justice. As reported in *El Gallo*:

> We marched into the campus directly to the auditorium and demonstrated. All of the O.E.O., Labor, and government agency employees went out the side doors and got in buses rather than walk through the front to see their brothers who were demanding justice.[83]

Gonzales felt the conference lacked "any positive direction or militant action and rehabilitation. What resulted was a lot of brave words, promises, motions—and no action."[84] A little-noted resolution by young Crusade member Manuel Martinez criticized conference participants ("opportunists, *tío tomases*, coyotes") and educational shortcomings affecting Mexican Americans. His resolution stated, "We . . . support those leaders who truly represent the feelings of the poor and who have taken a public stand denouncing the war in Vietnam. Furthermore, we support them in their efforts to secure justice with dignity for our people. Two of these leaders being, and I say with pride, Reies Tijerina of New Mexico and Rodolfo 'Corky' Gonzales of Colorado."[85]

"The Individual Then Becomes a 'Revolutionist' . . ."

Gonzales's travel continued into November 1967, and his speeches denounced the war in Vietnam. Though as an individual he had publicly criticized the war a year earlier, his criticism now reflected the official Crusade position. The FBI reported,

> On November 5, 1967, the *People's World* (West Coast communist newspaper) held its annual fund-raising banquet at the Miramar Hotel, Santa Monica, California. [Gonzales] was one of the featured speakers at this banquet. In his speech Gonzales dwelled on the oppression of the Mexican Americans in the United States by the "Anglos." He traced the history of the Mexican Americans . . . . He stated that the young people should be told the truth about the racist policies of the U.S. government. He stated that the battle in Vietnam is really an extension of the imperialistic racist policies of the United States. Gonzales further stated that the "battle" should be [in] Los Angeles, in Denver, in Albuquerque, and throughout the Southwest. He stated that the "battle" should be in the Southwest and not in Vietnam.[86]

The FBI monitored Gonzales's involvement with cultural events as well as his speeches to communist audiences. Teatro Campesino, a theater troupe that worked with Cesar Chavez's farmworkers union, gave its first Denver performance at the Santa Fe Theatre on August 8, 1967, sponsored by the Crusade. In addition to Teatro Campesino's performance, Crusade troupers performed *The Revolutionist*, a play by Gonzales.

As the FBI reported,

> On August 7, 1967, there was showing of a play called "The Revolutionist," written by [Gonzales] at a theatre in Denver. Among those present were members of the Denver C[ommunist] P[arty]. "The Revolutionist" is a play about a typical Mexican American coming into a large city with a great deal of ambition and finding that willingness to work is not enough to get along in the city. The individual then becomes a "revolutionist" when he finds himself an outcast.[87]

In December, the Crusade sponsored Chavez's first visit to Colorado. Though this was his first visit, Chavez's union was already represented in Denver by Louis Melendrez, who was provided housing at Crusade headquarters at 1265 Cherokee Street. The headquarters, a small apartment building owned by Gonzales, was used as office space for the Crusade, one unit serving as a combination coffee house/crash pad for young artists and activists. Chavez stayed with Melendrez during his visit. Chavez arrived on December 20 and was busy with interviews the following day, which culminated with a dinner in his honor at Annunciation Church in northeast Denver. In his presentation that night, Chavez briefly addressed the issue of police brutality, saying, "For those who have never suffered police brutality, it was impossible to discuss the problem and, for those who had, nothing was more degrading and barbarous than police brutality."[88]

The first Crusade-sponsored visits to Denver by Tijerina, the Teatro Campesino, and Chavez demonstrate Gonzales's contacts, talents, and political contributions in the Crusade's early years. Gonzales was not merely a participant in political activity: he was often its initiator. He was a leader who could speak to the powerful and voice the outrage of the powerless. Those he criticized sought to minimize his words, beliefs, and sentiments as unrepresentative of the community—as though the pressures exerted by Gonzales and the Crusade were insignificant. Community pressure, however, was an undeniable factor in chief Harold Dill's resignation in November 1967.

"Harold, I Want You to Resign . . ."

At 4:00 P.M. on November 17, 1967, Denver police chief Harold A. Dill met with Denver mayor Tom Currigan. Also present was manager of safety Hugh McClearn, Dill's immediate superior. Currigan had sent for Dill, and the mayor had bad news: "McClearn is going to resign and is going back into private practice. Getting down to the meat of it, Harold, I want you to resign, too."[89]

Dill later recounted that the mayor was anxious for Dill to set the date of his departure within a week. On November 21 Dill announced his resignation, effective December 31, thus ending a career that began in 1935. The *Rocky Mountain News* wrote:

> While [Currigan and Dill] are reluctant to discuss their differences, it's generally believed the split between the former friends stems from one boiling issue. The issue isn't one of Denver concern alone. It extends to state and national levels of government. It touches every city which has persons classified as the minority—those who are hungry, jobless, poverty-stricken. When these minority groups rebel over their years of frustration, their first target is the police—symbols of authority with whom they are in the most frequent contact. The dispute between the Chief and his boss stemmed over how this explosive problem should be handled.[90]

Articles by reporter Al Nakkula—who was provided documents reflecting the rift between Currigan and Dill—revealed that the mayor wanted this "problem" handled "with kid gloves," while Dill "insisted on maintaining full police powers as the symbol of authority."[91] The mayor's own words described the situation as one in which the two were poles apart.

A three-page, single-spaced letter to Safety Manager McClearn depicted Currigan's emotional stresses as he dealt with a situation he feared could lead to riots. Another document revealed the mayor's concern about three confrontations involving the police and minority communities, with two of the incidents occurring in Park Hill, an African American neighborhood. In one incident, Dill was present and police car windows were broken. Unnamed community leaders felt the police presence incited the anger of the crowd and urged Dill to withdraw his men, a suggestion Dill rejected as police prepared to maintain control through force. The third incident was the Crusade for Justice–Black Panther Party protest at police headquarters over the deaths of Louis Piñedo and Eugene Cook on June 23.[92]

The Crusade was unsympathetic to Currigan's stress and Dill's resignation. A front-page cartoon in *El Gallo* lampooned the two: Dill, offering the mayor his resignation, is shown with a big retirement check protruding from his pocket, his left hand's index and middle fingers crossed to indicate unwillingness to tell the truth. In the background, unnoticed by the two, policemen beat an elderly, cane-carrying *Mexicano*.[93] The Crusade's views are further reflected in an *El Gallo* editorial titled "Change or Exchange?"

Police Chief Dill has resigned or, as those supporters of the Mayor would say, "Currigan fired him." Now what? Is he replaced by another career cop who has been with the DPD for 20, 25, or 30 years, like Dill? If so, the same attitudes toward minorities and humanity will prevail that prevailed 20, 25, and 30 years ago in our fair city of conservative moths who scream from their cocoons that police brutality, harassment, and inhumanity is only a figment of the poor people's imagination . . . . There is a new cry arising from the Mexican American areas of Denver, and it has changed from a cry of pain to a cry of anger. "An eye for an eye and a tooth for a tooth, bullet for bullet; instead of cracked skulls, bullets in the back, justice in the alley." As [Dill and Currigan] go their separate ways, tight-lipped about each other's problems, Dill will receive vacation pay, back pay, and retirement pay. [Currigan] will remain on as mayor, praised by the Uncle Tom Negroes and the Tio Taco Vanishing Spanish Americans who retain their jobs and are in the good social graces with the patron . . . .[94]

An ugly confrontation at a public forum held a week before Currigan summoned Dill to his office may have influenced Currigan to seek Dill's resignation. The meeting was to be moderated by Herrick Roth, the Colorado Labor Council president; another participant, Ted Yoder, was to provide the discussion format. McClearn was involved, and division chief Ralph Potter and police technician Al Nieto represented the police department. The meeting was disrupted when Desiderio de Herrera of the Crusade went to the stage, took control of the microphone from Yoder, and denounced the police department. An unnamed Crusade member also spoke, angrily saying that,

> "If you shoot our kids in the back, we're going to shoot policemen in the back." Herrick Roth then invited Rodolfo "Corky" Gonzales to speak. Gonzales supported the militant spokesman 100% and then let the Police Department know that the Mexican American would no longer take insult, abuse, harassment, beating, or killing from the police. "If it takes retaliation and violence to gain justice and equality, that's what is going to be."[95]

These words drew FBI scrutiny and are cited in subsequent FBI reports. The Crusade's speakers, however, may have felt they merely spoke the truth: society respected neither Chicanos' rights nor their lives, and if the only option to gain those rights and respect was to take to arms in self-defense, or in retaliation, they stood ready.

Were these words, deeds, and beliefs justified? And were other questions in need of asking and answering? Did police routinely abuse people and, sometimes, murder them? Did politicians lie and cover up due to convenience, incompetence, or racism? Who—or what—was at fault? Though the answers to these questions may not be clear, it seems safe to say that circumstances were now reaching critical mass.

"Policemen Are Going to Have to Get Smart . . ."

The firing, or "retirement," of Harold Dill led to his replacement by George L. Seaton. Chief Seaton, who rose through the ranks like his predecessor, was appointed on December 29, 1967, and sworn in on January 2, 1968; Dill's absence at the ceremony was conspicuous. News accounts trumpeted the media's high opinion of the new chief. *Denver Post* editorials proclaimed, "Chief Seaton Off to a Good Start" and "Seaton Impresses

Minority Leaders." The "leaders" went unnamed.[96] Additionally, attorney Francis K. Salazar wrote the *Post*'s editor, urging minority support for Seaton:

> I have read the comments of Denver's new Police Chief, George L. Seaton, and he sounds almost too good to be true. He sounds sincere, educated, and enlightened . . . . As sick as it may sound, there are people who hope that [Seaton] fails in his very difficult undertaking . . . . There are others who hope to profit by strife and riot, would-be-leaders who do not care about the consequences of their reckless statements . . . . Currigan's actions in changing Police Chiefs were courageous and right: he suffered with dignity and restraint a great deal of unjust and unwarranted criticism.[97]

Chief Seaton realigned the department's policy and command structure, saying: "We are aiming at human relations, with everyone we serve, and legalities and trying to dispel any suspicion and hostility that may exist among them. Policemen are going to have to get smart . . . . Many times, by what he says, a police officer gets himself in trouble . . . . I hope to release men from less critical areas for community relations and delinquency control."[98] Similarly, the *Rocky Mountain News* reported that Seaton's "key [administrative] appointments appear in line with Seaton's previously stated intent to emphasize improvement of community relations . . . and a heavily accelerated war on juvenile crime."[99]

Though a new chief was in place, the Crusade continued its forceful protests. On January 28, a Denver chapter of the American GI Forum hosted a panel discussion at the Denver City Auditorium titled "Will the Mexican American Riot?" Among the panelists were Armando Rodriguez of the Mexican American Affairs Unit of the Department of Education; Dr. Phil Montez, identified as a California dentist; and Dr. Ralph Guzman of Los Angeles. As with the November 1967 forum, the discussion did not go as planned.

As the panel began, a large Crusade contingent arrived in no mood to hear out-of-town speakers: they were tired of panels, discussions, and experts. According to *The Denver Post*, "Gonzales and his group of vocal supporters made their presence known quickly . . . . Shouts demanding that Gonzales be allowed to speak had interrupted panelists, and when it was agreed that Gonzales should come to the speakers rostrum, cries of 'Viva! Viva!' went up."[100] Though Gonzales did not predict riots, the *Post* reported he said, "I don't think that there won't be people who will be

putting names on lists" and that the Southwest would see "guerilla warfare."

The *Post* reported that Gonzales linked the government's Vietnam
policy to domestic racism, saying Chicano casualties made possible "the
millions and millions of dollars being made on Vietnam by the industrial-
ists and politicians." He called American society racist, adding that "if
we say we want to be a part of this society, then we are sick because this
society is sick and corrupt." In contrast, a *News* article quoted three of
the eleven panelists without reporting that the Crusade commandeered the
event. Gonzales and the Crusade, in fact, were not mentioned at all.[101]

" . . . A Threat to the Internal Security of the United States"

Gonzales traveled to California three weeks later to attend a rally at the
Los Angeles Sports Arena. As the FBI reported, "Approximately 5,000
people were in attendance. STOKELY CARMICHAEL and H. RAP
BROWN, militant black nationalist leaders, were the main speakers.
[Gonzales] was introduced and spoke in favor of REIES TIJERINA."[102]
Gonzales, in company with Tijerina, subsequently spoke at a press conference at the New Left School in Los Angeles. According to the FBI,
Gonzales said he was "training the young people there on the idea of who
their enemy is and how they can be taught this principle instead of being
'brainwashed' and being 'used' to go to Vietnam, to fight the battle 'here'
instead of in Vietnam. They must learn to operate in the 'open' instead of
underground methods."[103]

On January 22, 1968, the Denver FBI sent Hoover's office a
Nonprosecutive Summary Report on Gonzales. Hoover's office responded
on February 7, stating that the FBI should continue to investigate him
because Hoover considered Gonzales "a likely candidate for leadership [of
the Alianza]" if its leadership was sent to prison.[104] A letter three weeks
later added that Gonzales "has been approved for inclusion on the Rabble
Rouser Index . . . . There seems to be no question that his activities pose
a threat to the internal security of the United States."[105] After judging
Gonzales's activism a security threat, Hoover's office took the next logical
step and targeted the entire Crusade organization. On February 29 FBI
headquarters instructed its Denver office to investigate the Crusade to
determine the "true nature of the organization."[106]

Correspondence from the Chicago FBI to the office of J. Edgar Hoover
in 1968 indicates the extent of the bureau's concern over the Latino gathering that Gonzales first proposed in Chicago in August 1967. This correspondence, called an "Airtel" in FBI jargon, is heavily edited, but it is

clear that numerous Latinos at the gathering were subject to surveillance after the Chicago gathering.[107] Memos show that the bureau considered the proposed gathering an "internal security" matter. By the spring of 1968, the Crusade had refocused its efforts on the Washington, D.C.–based Poor People's Campaign, and the national gathering was postponed. But the FBI did not know this, and in May 1968 Denver, Chicago, and Washington, D.C., FBI offices searched unsuccessfully for the conference location.[108]

"Yesterday's Militants, Boomerang Chicanos, Limb-Swingers"

The federal government responded to growing social discontent with more social programs. In 1968, President Johnson asked Congress to provide $6.3 billion for new housing for the poor, rent supplements, mass transit planning, and anti-poverty efforts for American cities. Among the goals he set was the provision of six million housing units for the poor, to be built within ten years.

While conservatives decried these liberal policies and the growth of the "welfare state," Gonzales criticized liberals and conservatives alike. As the former head of the Denver War on Poverty, Gonzales's experiences led him to a jaundiced view of efforts to reform society through established channels. He believed that racism motivated conservative opposition to social programs: the real welfare recipients, he reasoned, included conservative farmers who received subsidies not to grow food while the poor went hungry. Democrats and Republicans routinely supported such subsidies in Congress.

Gonzales considered the war in Vietnam a mechanism for providing profit to corporations for airplanes, ships, and weaponry while poor and minority soldiers paid the price in blood; meanwhile, the Vietnamese landscape and people were laid waste in a war supported by Republicans and Democrats alike. This, he felt, was a welfare state for war contractors and wealthy corporations.

His criticism of liberal politicians and programs was equally scathing. He felt money allocated for poverty programs served as patronage for the Democrats to dole out to subservient community "leaders" in programs where more money went to administrative salaries and overhead costs than trickled down to the poor. With this money came dependent "leaders" and control, not reform.

Distribution of food commodities served to buy and distribute excess production from conservative farmers—commodities that were mere crumbs tossed to the poor, who were then despised and stigmatized as though they deserved their misfortunes. Rent subsidies passed through the hands of the poor and back into municipal public housing bureaucracies. Food stamps were given to the poor and redeemed by chain stores where the poor shopped. Who was really on welfare: the poor, the rich, or the bureaucrats?

He felt these programs were mild concessions to the protest movements of the poor, rather than remedies for social inequality. According to Gonzales, poverty programs were the establishment's mechanisms to pacify communities without empowering them. The patronage dispensed by the system served to buy minority "leaders" with jobs and social prestige. Gonzales frequently said, "Yesterday's militant is today's government employee." He referred to people who returned to the community as government-funded leaders as "boomerang Chicanos." As program administrators went from one government job to another, Gonzales likened them to monkeys swinging from tree limb to tree limb, calling them "limb-swingers."

Government-funded programs (and the emergence of a government-funded leadership class) were not the sole response to festering social problems. National foundations also "discovered" Mexicans. The Ford Foundation, for example, made a $221,164 grant to the System Development Corporation to expand a pilot study project of Spanish-surnamed students in Los Angeles; Dr. Julian Zamora, of the University of Notre Dame, used Ford Foundation money to study U.S.-Mexico border issues; and the foundation made available $150,000 to increase the number of Spanish-surnamed attorneys in the Rocky Mountain region in response to a finding that 9 percent of the area's population was Spanish-surnamed "but of over 2,000 lawyers in the [Denver] metropolitan area, less than 10 are of Spanish-American descent."[109] Some people in neighboring New Mexico, however, criticized Ford's apparent generosity:

According to one well-placed Ford man: "Ford's first direct contact in New Mexico was in the spring of 1967. The key (Ford) man here was Bill Watts, who was active head of the Office of Government and Law. Ford was very anxious even at that point to build some reasonable alternative to Tijerina and the Alianza. Within a month after the raid at Tierra Amarilla, a team was dispatched to New Mexico. Their purpose was to create as quickly as possible a leadership structure alternative to Tijerina.

"Actually, the team had two objectives: The first was to divert attention from Tijerina and the land question by creating an alternative

leader, someone to whom they could point as a spokesman for the
Mexican Americans in New Mexico. The HELP [Home Education
Livelihood Program] was existent, under the direction of Alex Mercure,
so Ford decided to make Mercure that leader. A few months after the
team was sent to New Mexico, Ford approved a $453,450 R & D
(research and development) grant to HELP as part of the program
to knock Tijerina and create this alternative leadership structure."
After Ford's initial $453,450 grant . . . Mercure became known as
"The Empire Builder" among his poverty program colleagues and
was named to national commissions, advisory boards and panels as a
"Mexican American leader." When Congress called hearings after the
Tierra Amarilla incident . . . it called Mercure to testify, not Tijerina
or Alianzistas. . . . Watts is no longer with Ford; at last report he was
working as a staff secretary of the National Security Council in the
Nixon Administration under Henry Kissinger, an old personal friend of
Ford Foundation President McGeorge Bundy. . . . In the fall of 1967,
Ford moved, under a $21,839 grant, to bring together a select group of
Mexican Americans at a meeting in Los Angeles. Out of that gathering eventually came the Southwest Council of la Raza, designed as an
umbrella organization covering the Southwest, funded by Ford to the
tune of $630,000 in February 1968. The Council's first executive direc-
tor was Herman Gallegos, who resigned his job as a Ford Foundation
consultant to accept the new position. Alex Mercure was immediately
appointed to the Council's Board of Directors.[110]

"Gonzales and Tijerina Met with Dr. King . . ."

Rodolfo Gonzales, on March 12, 1968, in a KBTR radio interview,
announced that he was going to Atlanta, Georgia, to meet with Rev.
Martin Luther King, Jr., regarding Southern Christian Leadership
Conference plans to march on Washington, D.C. The Denver FBI reported
to director J. Edgar Hoover, "Gonzales hopes to have poor Spanish-
Americans join King's march, along with poor Negroes."[111] As *The Denver
Post* related, Gonzales "was in Atlanta Thursday to confer with [King] on
the role the Southwest will play in a national demonstration of the poor in
Washington, D.C., April 22."[112]

The Denver FBI sent an eighteen-page report to Washington headquarters, as well as to the State Department, the Secret Service, the 113th
Military Intelligence Group, and the CIA. The report states:

On March 14, 1968, Reverend Martin Luther King, Jr., President of the

Southern Christian Leadership Conference (SCLC) attended a meeting of representatives of minority groups held at Paschal's Motor Hotel, Atlanta, Georgia. The purpose of Reverend King's address was to solicit support of minority groups for the SCLC's Washington Spring Project. In connection with the above meeting, the public relations office of the SCLC prepared a press release. This release showed that at the meeting a "National Poor People's Steering Committee" was selected. The name "RODOLFO CORKY GONZALES, Crusade for Justice, Denver, Colorado," was shown as a member of this committee.[113]

The report then cites the April 9, 1968, *Denver Post*:

Rodolpho (Corky) Gonzales, chairman of the Crusade for Justice, a Spanish-American civil rights organization, flew to Atlanta, Ga., Tuesday for the funeral of the Rev. Dr. Martin Luther King, Jr. Gonzales said he would confer in Atlanta with Reies Lopez Tijerina. . . . Gonzales and Tijerina had met with Dr. King to plan Mexican American involvement in Dr. Kings's "poor people's march" on Washington.[114]

The strategy for the Poor People's Campaign was to make demands to the federal government on poor people's behalf and to bring Washington to a standstill by militant civil disobedience if the government did not respond. King's assassination deprived the SCLC of its most able, inspiring leader. The civil disobedience anticipated in Washington never occurred on the scale some feared and others hoped for. The SCLC continued organizing for the campaign after King's assassination, and Gonzales and Tijerina's support boosted Mexican and Native American participation in the southwestern contingent to Washington.

It is tempting to probe the implications of Gonzales's social critique for questions needed to be asked—and resolved—about the organization, tactics, and strategy necessary to bring about social change in this crusade for justice. What was the nature of the struggle, and the basis of oppression? What was the role of a leader, and how should the oppressed, themselves, win freedom and recoup their dignity and humanity? Though Gonzales and the Crusade never fully resolved the questions posed by the dilemma of oppression, his words now described an inherently oppressive society divided by class, race, and nationality.

Notes

1
Viva! The Battle Cry of Truth (hereinafter referred to as *Viva!*), May 20,
1964. The figures are reported from
the 1960 U.S. Census.

2
This three-part study was conducted
by Dr. Reuben Zubrow for the Denver
Model Cities program and was
reported in the *Rocky Mountain News*
(hereinafter referred to as *RMN*), May
10, 1968.

3
The Denver Post (hereinafter referred
to as *DP*), November 12, 1968.

4
DP, July 7, 1962.

5
Ibid.

6
DP, July 8, 1962.

7
Ibid.

8
Viva!, May 20, 1964. The preamble
of Los Voluntarios' charter stated,
"We, the members of Los Voluntarios,
realizing that the Spanish-speaking
people of Colorado are in need of an
active political organization dedicated
to its complete social, economic, and
political advancement, do hereby join
together to establish a state organization to be known as Los Voluntarios."
Charles C. Vigil wrote, "[the] group
was formed from among leaders of
various cultural, educational, and fra-
ternal groups as well as those who had

political party affiliation." Vigil
recounted that Los Voluntarios gave
its support to the candidates who
pledged the most to the community
only to find, "A promise made is a
debt unpaid." Los Voluntarios and
its newspaper, *Viva!*, were precur-
sors of the Crusade for Justice and *El
Gallo*. *Viva!* reports it was founded
because "of frustration and determina-
tion for the truth. . . . This newspaper
will not only inform, but advise the
public on political issues, educational
advantages, social acceptance. Where
there is a cause to be fought and there
is no leadership, this newspaper will
champion that cause. Where there is
ignorance, this newspaper will educate.
Where there is misunderstanding, this
news-paper will guide. Where there
is hypocrisy, this paper will tell the
truth."

9
Viva!, May 20, 1964.

10
Ibid.

11
Viva!, June 16, 1964.

12
The letterhead shows the first use of
the name "Crusade for Justice" and
used Gonzales's bail bond business
at 1961 Larimer Street as its address.
The Crusade, however, was not formally incorporated until 1966, and it
appears Gonzales used the Crusade
name to circumvent the need for
approval of the more moderate (and
more timid) middle-class elements
within Los Voluntarios who would be
reluctant to approve the highly critical

remarks found in the letter to Mayor Currigan.

13
Rodolfo "Corky" Gonzales to Mayor Thomas G. Currigan, July 5, 1964.

14
Ibid.

15
Viva!, May 20, 1964.

16
RMN, September 29, 1965. Gonzales was prosperously self-employed since the age of eighteen except for appointments to the directorship of Denver's War on Poverty (more formally called the Office of Economic Opportunity) and the Neighborhood Youth Corps, an employment program serving low-income youth. This history of self-employment was undoubtedly responsible for much of his sense of self-reliance and political independence.

17
Ibid.

18
Ibid.

19
Ibid.

20
Ibid.

21
DP, February 17, 1966. The official racial designation Capra first used for Asians was "Yellow." He then changed it to "Mongolian." A spokesperson in the mayor's office said the term used would be "Yellow." The Chicano community's sensitivity to racial terminology—and/or its confusion over its own identity—had been raised with Mayor Currigan in a meeting on police-community relations. The mayor had previously (in 1964) ordered police to desist from registering "Mex.," "Mexican," and "U.S. Mexican" on police records as part of the physical description of Chicanos. See *Viva!*, May 20, 1964.

22
RMN, February 17, 1966.

23
RMN, February 25, 1966.

24
Ibid. Beyond the crude sentiments implicit in Capra's remarks, it appears the issue generated emotion because it questioned who and what Chicanos were at a time of prevailing racial conservatism before the Chicano movement raised the words "Mexican" and "Chicano" as banners of ethnic pride. The May and June 1964 issues of *Viva!* give insight to the Chicano community's self-perception in the early 1960s. The two issues reveal the ambiguity and confusion of identity by using different names for the community: "Hispanic," "Chicano," "Mexican American," "Spanish American," "Spanish-speaking people," "Mexican," "Spanish," "Latino,"and "Latin American."

25
DP, February 25, 1966.

26
DP, August 24, 1967.

27
DP, March 2, 1966.

28
Rodolfo "Corky" Gonzales, "Address to Coalition" (mimeograph), Denver, April 23, 1966.

29
Ibid.

30
DP, February 14, 1966.

31
Cervi's Journal, April 27, 1966.

32
Ibid.

33
DP, April 30, 1966.

34
El Gallo (hereinafter referred to as *EG*), June 23, 1967. Though published in *El Gallo* in June, the letter was written to Tooley on May 15.

35
Ibid.

36
Denver FBI Special Agent in Charge (SAC) to J. Edgar Hoover, *Non-prosecutive Summary Report*, January 22, 1968, 7, Denver FBI field office, file 100-9290 (Rodolfo Gonzales), 9; filed in Hoover's office as BUFILE 105-176910. The "105" designates the matter as internal security.

37
Ibid. For a brief mention of the impact of the radicalization of black America on Gonzales, see *RMN*, September 11, 1977, where Gonzales states: "I learned from the Black movement. Look at Watts [the 1965 African American uprising in Los Angeles]. The day after the riots the government was dumping millions of dollars to help the people. They felt threatened so they give a little. They never give a lot, just a little. I've been taught that five loose fingers by themselves are nothing. Bring them together and you have a fist."

38
Denver FBI SAC to Hoover, *Nonprosecutive Summary Report*, January 22, 1968, 8.

39
Ibid. The FBI obtained a copy of Gonzales's three-page anti-war speech. Gonzales's opposition to the war grew as the war escalated: in the spring of 1965, 25,000 U.S. troops were in Vietnam. By the end of 1965 the number had grown to 184,000 and by the end of 1966, 385,000.

40
Ibid. It is not known exactly when, or how, Gonzales's anti-war position evolved. Though he was not a military veteran, Gonzales did belong to the American GI Forum. This was probably for social and political reasons since the GI Forum was founded as an advocacy group for Chicanos, not as an endorsement of militarism. The June 15, 1964, issue of *Viva!* pictures Gonzales standing with other Denver GI Forum officers behind Colorado governor John Love, who proclaimed June 15-21, 1964, "GI Forum Week." The proclamation notes that "more than half a million Spanish-Americans served in the United States armed forces during World War Two and the Korean conflict; . . . these brave men received more Congressional Medals of Honor than any other group of our great nation, and more than two hun-

dred and fifty thousand either lost their lives or were wounded on the field of battle." Ironically, the *Viva!* article about GI Forum Week appears with an article announcing a conference on "youth and morality in a nuclear age" sponsored by the pacifist American Friends Service Committee.

41
Denver FBI SAC to Hoover, *Nonprosecutive Summary Report,* January 22, 1968, 15.

42
EG, August 31, 1967.

43
Tijerina's letter to Gonzales was dated March 25, 1967, but the potential for conflict, confrontation, and legal entanglements was clear to Gonzales. There were times when publicity defused dangers and times when publicity was imprudent. Gonzales was carefully building the Crusade's core, so the invitation to send people to the takeover was interesting, though imprudent. Seasoned Crusade activists were guided by a saying: "The fish that gets caught is the one that opens its mouth." Tijerina's letter was published in *El Gallo* on June 23, 1967, when its contents would be of no use in giving advance notice to law enforcement authorities.

44
Peter Nabokov, *Tijerina and the Courthouse Raid* (Albuquerque: University of New Mexico Press, 1969), 150-51.

45
Ibid. By "disregard of the law," Gonzales referred to more than the preemptive arrests of Alianzistas

which prompted Alianza members to attempt the citizens' arrests at the Tierra Amarilla courthouse. The theft of land grants was a violation of the Constitution, because the Treaty of Guadalupe Hidalgo is on par with the Constitution as the "supreme law of the land" and its provisions safeguard the property of Mexicans who stayed in the conquered territory—provisions promptly violated upon conquest. This argument, fundamental to the Alianza's position, is based on the Constitution's Article VI, paragraph two: "This Constitution, and the Laws of the United States which shall be made in Pursuance thereof; *and all Treaties made, or which shall be made, under the Authority of the United states, shall be the supreme law of the land . . . ."*

Starting in the early 1600s, land grants were made by Spain, and then by Mexico, to entice settlers into Mexico's northernmost provinces—the present Southwest. There are 1,715 land grants in the United States, including those grants in Louisiana and Florida. The New Mexico grants, for which the Alianza fought, and southern Colorado's Mexican-era land grants, have been the most hotly contested. Indigenous nations in the Southwest have defended their land claims based on the treaty because Mexico recognized more extensive native landholdings than the United States. The legal argument based on Article VI applies to all treaties with native nations but would require that the government respect its own laws.

46
Ibid.

47
Denver FBI SAC to Hoover,

Nonprosecutive Summary Report, January 22, 1968, Denver FBI field office, file 100-9290 (Rodolfo Gonzales), 17.

48
EG, June 23, 1967.

49
Ibid. Crusade women organized a potluck dinner in Denver on July 17, 1967. Donations to the Alianza were solicited and $286.75 was raised. Present were "former members of the Alianza. The San Luis Valley Friendship Club was represented by their president, Lionel Ruybal and many of their members. Also present were many notable guests which included Los Valientes, the Crusaders who traveled to New Mexico and marched in Santa Fe." *El Gallo* listed the names of the Denver "valientes": Betty and Waldo Benavidez; Desiderio "D. C." De Herrera; Eugene Deikman; Emilio and Robbie Dominguez; Gary Garrison; Corky, Nita, Charlotte, and Rudy Gonzales; John Haro; Anthony and David Hermosillo; Amy Lizt; Bill Longley; Eloisa, Larry, Kelly and Sue Lovato; Don Martinez; Henry Montoya; Lorraine Quintana; Joe Perea, Jr.; Louis Ramirez; Richard Romero; Robert Trujillo; Al Sanchez; Bob Sandison; and Eloy Espinoza.

50
DP, June 29, 1967. This article was cited in the Denver FBI SAC *Nonprosecutive Summary Report* on Gonzales of January 22, 1968.

51
EG, July 28, 1967.

52
Ibid.

53
Ibid.

54
Ibid. The resurrection of the New Mexico land struggle affected Colorado. In November 1967, Colorado land grant heirs filed an unsuccessful suit in Denver's U.S. District Court over grants in southern Colorado and northern New Mexico. Also, southern Colorado's San Luis Valley is home to a land grant dispute dating from 1960, when J. T. Taylor, Jr., sought to purchase and clear title to 77,524 acres of the 1844 Sangre de Cristo Land Grant in Costilla County; Taylor closed access roads to locals who had hunted, fished, and gathered firewood on the communal lands. This land struggle led to some violence, and the legal struggle continues as of this writing. See Adeline Espinoza, Edward Espinoza, Pete Espinoza, Donny Lobato, Eugene Lobato, Norman Maestas, Eugene Martinez, Lucille Samelko, Emilio Lobato, Jr., Michael J. Vigil, plaintiffs, Corpus Gallegos, Zach Bernal, intervenors, versus Zachary Taylor, as executor of estate of Jack T. Taylor, Jr., deceased, et al., defendants, in the District Court, County of Costilla, State of Colorado, Civil Action 81CV5. See also *DP,* November 28, 1967.

55
DP, July 23, 1967. The Denver FBI field office cited the *Post* article in its *Nonprosecutive Summary Report* to J. Edgar Hoover in starting the internal security investigation on Gonzales and the Crusade for Justice's activities. The Denver FBI submitted the report to Hoover on January 22, 1968, when Gonzales was already listed on the local Rabble Rouser Index (RRI).

Hoover notified the Denver office on February 28 that Gonzales was approved for inclusion on the national RRI and stated, "His activities also warrant inclusion on the Security Index." Gonzales was now deemed a threat to the nation's internal security.

56
EG, July 28, 1967.

57
Ibid. *El Gallo* published a photo of Piñedo's death certificate showing the cause of death to have been a gunshot to the back.

58
Ibid.

59
EG, August 31, 1967.

60
Ibid.

61
EG, October 1, 1967.

62
EG, November 1967.

63
Denver FBI SAC, *Nonprosecutive Summary Report* to Hoover, January 22, 1968, 20.

64
EG, December 1967.

65
EG, October 1, 1967. One target of Gonzales's derision, "an old left-winger," was said to have been among the members of a communist-front organization in the early 1950s until the McCarthy era made things too

hot. The person was a Democrat who is now hailed for pioneering efforts in advocating for Denver's Spanish-sur-named community. Derision of those "still dancing to the tune of the power structure" is not new criticism of weak "leaders" who fail to squarely confront issues. Another such reference can be found nearly a generation earlier: "The working class Mexican who bears the brunt of police brutality cannot look for assistance to the self-styled Mex-ican leaders. Few of these middle-class Mexicans are able to face squarely the fact of police dereliction. . . . The middle-class Mexican, aspiring to leadership of the Mexican people, still feels so basically insecure in status that his primary concern is to demonstrate his own superiority to the Mexican masses." Lloyd H. Fisher, "Observ-ation on Race Conflict in Los Angeles: The Problem of Violence," *American Council on Race Relations* 14 (cited in Beatrice Griffith, *American Me*, 1948).

66
EG, October 1, 1967.

67
EG, November 1967.

68
Ibid. The same issue of *El Gallo* records the Crusade's anger over another police shooting that occurred within two weeks of Officer Vandervelde's acquittal. On October 27, 1967, twenty-year-old Richard Medina was shot three times by Denver officer Edwin James during a domestic dispute between Medina and his girlfriend in which Medina grabbed an unloaded rifle. When police arrived, his girlfriend reported, "I ran back into the bedroom and grabbed the gun away from Richard and threw

it on the bed and, while I was holding him, the policeman came in without any kind of warning and started
shooting. After he stopped, Richard
dropped from my arms onto the floor.
The police should have been able to
see that Richard no longer had the
gun." Medina survived and was held
for investigation of assault.

69
Denver FBI SAC, *Nonprosecutive
Summary Report*, 11.

70
Frank J. Donner, *The Age of
Surveillance: The Aims and Methods of
America's Political Intelligence System*
(New York: Alfred A. Knopf, 1980),
404, 430. The informers included
an operative from the Senate Internal
Security Subcommittee as well as those
from the Chicago Police Department
Intelligence Unit, people like David
Gumaer, a John Birch Society lecturer.
Files were stolen from the conference
organizers by Chicago police informers
and are now found in Chicago Police
Intelligence Unit archives held by
the Chicago Historical Society as the
result of a successful suit filed against
Chicago police.

71
Todd Gitlin, *The Sixties: Years of
Hope, Days of Rage* (New York:
Bantam Books, 1987), 245.

72
In December 1967, the Crusade con-
vened a national Chicano youth gathering in Denver, but a blizzard struck
and few attended. Two who attended
were Ignacio "Nacho" Perez of the
Mexican American Youth Organization (MAYO) in Texas and Francisco
Martinez of Los Angeles. This effort

was the forerunner of four national
youth conferences the Crusade organized. The chief focuses of the small
December 1967 gathering were the
development of an information center
and the planning of a national gathering of Chicano activists in the spring of
1968—the project that drew so much
FBI scrutiny when first proposed in
Chicago in August 1967. Very little
information is available on the December 1967 Denver gathering. *El Gallo*
refers to this meeting in January 1968
and April 1968.

73
Espinoza was sent to represent the
Crusade in Gonzales's place. A review
of these highly censored FBI documents indicates that the FBI mistook
Espinoza for Gonzales based on a few
physical similarities.

74
Denver FBI SAC, *Nonprosecutive
Summary Report*, 23.

75
EG, December 1967. At the anniversary dinner, two thirteen-year-old
boys recited *I Am Joaquin*, an epic
poem by Gonzales. A five-member
dance troupe—three of Gonzales's
daughters and two other danc-
ers—performed traditional Mexican
dances. New Mexico artists Cleofes
Vigil, John and Rini de Puy, and
Manuel Martinez of the Crusade
auctioned their work. Proceeds went
to the Crusade. Vigil, a farmer and
multitalented folk historian from San
Cristobal, New Mexico, was prevailed
upon to sing an *alabado* (a traditional
penitente song) to eighty-one-year-old
Teresina Romero, Gonzales's mother-
in-law. *El Gallo*'s article on Reies's
visit concluded with the names of

Crusaders who hosted Tijerina in his stay: Luis Ramirez, Eloisa Lovato, and John Haro.

76
Denver FBI SAC, *Nonprosecutive Summary Report*, 20-21.

77
Ibid., 21.

78
RMN, October 26, 1967.

79
"Plan de La Raza Unida Preamble" (mimeograph), El Paso, 1967, 1.

80
Cabinet Committee Hearings on Mexican American Affairs: Labor Standards (El Paso, Texas: Inter-agency Committee on Mexican American Affairs, 1967), 1-2.

81
EG, November 1967.

82
Ibid.

83
EG, December 1967.

84
Ibid.

85
Ibid.

86
Denver FBI SAC, *Nonprosecutive Summary Report*, 13-14.

87
Ibid., 20.

88
EG, January 1968.

89
RMN, January 1, 1968.

90
Ibid.

91
Ibid.

92
RMN, January 2, 1968. Another cause of the rift between Currigan and Dill was Dill's support for a police pay raise Currigan opposed. Dill had not backed down when confronted with the mayor's opposition.

93
EG, December 1967.

94
Ibid.

95
EG, November 1967.

96
DP, January 4, January 15, 1968.

97
DP, January 4, 1968.

98
RMN, January 4, 1968.

99
Ibid.

100
DP, January 29, 1968.

101
RMN, January 29, 1968.

102
Denver FBI field office, file 100-9290
(Rodolfo Gonzales), April 22, 1968.

103
Ibid.

104
Hoover to Denver FBI SAC, February
7, 1968, FBI headquarters, file 105-
176910 (Rodolfo Gonzales).

105
Hoover to Denver FBI SAC, February
28, 1968, FBI headquarters, file 105-
176910 (Rodolfo Gonzales). Though
the FBI's internal security investigation on Gonzales began in late 1967,
the January 22, 1968, *Nonprosecutive
Summary Report* shows the FBI gathered data on Gonzales as early as April
30, 1964, when he attended two meetings apparently related to the death of
Alfred Salazar. One meeting was sponsored by the Socialist Workers Party at
the Unitarian Church on Fourteenth
and Lafayette streets in Denver.

106
Hoover to Denver FBI SAC, February
29, 1968, FBI headquarters, file 105-
176910 (Rodolfo Gonzales).

107
Copies of the Chicago "Airtel" were
sent to FBI field offices in Albuquer-
que, Denver, El Paso, Los Angeles,
Milwaukee, Phoenix, Sacramento, San
Antonio, San Diego, San Francisco, and
Chicago.

108
A Denver FBI communication to
Hoover dated May 23, 1968 (copy sent
to Albuquerque FBI field office),

expressed interest in the possibility
that the Crusade owned a ranch in the
Southwest, apparently in New Mexico.
The Santa Fe district attorney claimed
on June 5, 1968, that the Alianza
had a guerrilla training in the Taos
area. Gonzales frequently visited San
Cristobal, New Mexico, just north of
Taos. It appears FBI suspicions were
related to reports written of Gonzales's
visits to San Cristobal by Alan Stang
in American Opinion, a John Birch
Society publication.

109
The Denver Clarion, November 10,
1967.

110
Rees Lloyd and Peter Montague,
"Ford's Pacification Program for La
Raza," *El Grito del Norte* (August
29, 1970), 8-11. The article was pub-
lished simultaneously by *El Grito* and
Ramparts magazine.

111
Denver FBI field office enciphered wire
to Hoover (March 13, 1968) with copies to Atlanta and Washington, D.C.,
field offices; Albuquerque field office
advised by mail.

112
DP, March 15, 1968.

113
Denver FBI field office to FBI headquarters, April 26, 1968, FBI headquarters, file 105-176910 (Rodolfo
Gonzales).

114
Ibid.

Internal Colonialism in Colorado: The Westside Coalition and Barrio Control

George Rivera, Jr., Aileen F. Lucero, and Richard Castro

ABOUT THE AUTHORS

George Rivera, Ph.D., is a faculty member in the Department of Fine Arts at the University of Colorado at Boulder. He received his doctorate in sociology at the State University of New York. He is a studio artist specializing in computer art, art and social change, and contemporary Chicano art. He has exhibited his work throughout the United States, Mexico, and Latin America.

Aileen F. Lucero, Ph.D., is a faculty member in the Department of Sociology, Anthropology, and Social Work at Metropolitan State College of Denver and is currently a member of the Census 2000 Advisory Committee on the Hispanic Population. She received her doctorate in sociology from the University of Colorado at Boulder and was an NIMH postdoctoral fellow in Social Problem Solving. She has published in the areas of the Chicano family, *curanderismo*, Latinos and AIDS, and demography.

Richard Castro was a Colorado state legislator for ten years and served a brief term as a member of the Denver School Board. The last position he held was in Denver mayor Federico Peña's administration as Director of Human Rights and Community Relations. He received his master's degree in social work at the University of Denver.

WITH THE EXCEPTION of minor editing, this paper is presented as it was originally written for the Rocky Mountain Social Science Association/Western Social Science Association, May 1–3, 1975, Denver, Colorado. As such, it represents a period piece of Colorado's Chicano history, written in the midst of the era it describes.

Though a number of studies have classified and described the activities of Chicano community organizations,[1] few have focused on community organizations that evolved as a result of the consciousness generated by the Chicano protest movement of the late 1960s and early 1970s. This paper examines the problems encountered by such a coalition, which attempted to organize Chicanos for the purpose of community, or barrio, control.

Chicano community organizations existed in the United States as early as the late 1800s.[2] Most of these early organizations offered mutual aid services to recent immigrants, but by the early 1900s organizations primarily concerned with assimilation began to emerge. After World War II, more politically oriented organizations began to surface, and by the early 1960s organizations closely tied to the Democratic Party were evident. By the late 1960s Chicano community organizations began to focus on the issue of community control.[3]

This study is rooted in the theoretical perspective that analyzes the barrio as an internal colony. Blauner popularized the application of this "Colonial Model" to racial and ethnic minorities in the United States by maintaining that the colonization complex is characterized by four basic components: 1) entry of the colonized into the dominant society is involuntary; 2) the colonizing power carries out a policy that constrains, transforms, or destroys indigenous values, orientations, and ways of life; 3) the lives of the subordinate group are administered by representatives of the dominant power; and 4) racism is a principle of social domination by which the colonized are seen as inferior or different in alleged biological characteristics and exploited, controlled, and oppressed socially and psychically by a superordinate group.[4]

Chicano social scientists have applied the Colonial Model to an analysis of Chicanos.[5] In particular, they argued that: 1) Mexicans entered American society as a result of war and land purchase (involuntary entry); 2) the development of Mexican culture, including the Spanish language, has been seriously impeded by an assimilationist orientation in American society (destruction of indigenous culture); 3) barrio homes, businesses, and social service agencies are owned and/or administered by members of the superordinate group (external control); and 4) racism has defined the Chicano as inferior. However, most of these studies have been theoretical in nature, and the model remained to be tested. We shall apply the colonial analogy to the activities of a Chicano community organization which attempted to reduce external control in the barrio.

The Principle of Colonial Community Domination

Fanon aptly described the colonial world as a "Manichean world"—a world divided into compartments.[6] Throughout the Southwest one will find rural and urban communities divided into sectors clearly defined as superordinate neighborhoods and subordinate ghettoes. Life in each sector is radically different. Gonzalez-Casanova has observed that the standards of life in the colonies differ from those in the world of the colonizer.[7] In the world of the superordinate group (the colonizer) economic conditions create less want and misery, but the world of the subordinate group (the colonized) is plagued by socioeconomic conditions of powerlessness. Consequently, the colonized world is often owned and controlled by the colonizer.

Blauner examined the issue of external control in minority communities and found ". . . a special relationship to the governmental bureaucracies or the legal order. . . . The colonized have the experience of being managed and manipulated by outsiders who look down on them."[8]

The dynamics of colonial community domination will be our major focus. We theorize that colonial community domination is maintained by three major mechanisms: socioeconomic powerlessness, intraethnic conflict, and external control (see figure 1).

Figure I

The Dynamic Relationship of Mechanisms in the Principle of Colonial Community Domination

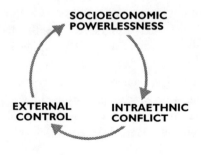

SOCIOECONOMIC
POWERLESSNESS

EXTERNAL
CONTROL

INTRAETHNIC
CONFLICT

Table I
Ethnic Composition of West Side and Total Population for
the City of Denver, 1970

| | AREA | | | |
| | WEST SIDE[a] | | DENVER CITY | |
Racial/Ethnic Composition	Number	Percent	Number	Percent
CHICANOS[b]	9904	62.1%	86345	16.8%
BLACKS	300	1.9%	47011	9.1%
WHITE	5745	36.0%	381322	74.1%
TOTAL	15949	100.0%	514678	100.0%

[a]The data from the three census tracts in the West Side (18, 19, and 21) have been summarized for the area known as the West Side.
[b]The census refers to this category as "Persons of Spanish Language or Spanish Surname," but we will refer to this category as "Chicanos."
Source: U.S. Bureau of the Census, Census of Population and Housing: 1970, Census Tracts, Final Report PHC (1) - 56, Denver Colorado SMSA, 1, 15-16, 132.

Though it can be argued that external control is a form of socioeconomic powerlessness, these two mechanisms are herein separated for purposes of analysis. External control is the structure of administrative management at the community level which results from socioeconomic powerlessness of roles at the individual level. Thus, occupational dependence (socioeconomic powerlessness) of the Chicano as a wage earner in low-status jobs creates conditions characterized by barrio property being owned and administered by Anglos (the colonizer) and/or a native bourgeoisie who acts as his/her liaison in the barrio.

The mechanisms of colonial community domination function in a cumulative fashion, but there is a primary order to the effect of the mechanisms. Socioeconomic powerlessness has the greatest effect on domination, and intraethnic conflict and external control exert secondary influences. When the system of community domination is in colonial equilibrium, all of the mechanisms have a maximum effect in influencing each other. Thus, socioeconomic powerlessness at the individual level greatly influences the degree of intraethnic conflict. As long as there is a differential distribution of rewards, conflict will be generated by competition for these perceived rewards by individuals or subgroups within the colonized. Furthermore, the cumulative effect of these two mechanisms greatly increases the colonizer's ability to externally control the colonized.

Since socioeconomic powerlessness has the greatest effect on community domination, any strategy for change must begin by reducing the effects of that powerlessness. Focus on any other mechanism will not substantially reduce colonial community domination. For example, focus on reducing intraethnic conflict will only produce temporary results because socioeconomic powerlessness will generate new conflicts along the same dimension or along other dimensions related to it. All too often, organizations seek to reduce domination by reducing external control, only to find that they have replaced it with a parallel mechanism. More often, these members of the colonized alienate themselves from the community by seeking to control rather than to liberate. This control, too, is often temporary because the loss of a community base erodes their legitimacy. Thus, the colonizer soon regains his position of external control through replacement or cooptation of those who sought to replace him.

We shall analyze the three major mechanisms of community domination in relation to a community organization that sought to reverse the effects of "the principle of colonial community domination." The Westside Coalition, a coalition of Chicano community organizations in the West Side neighborhood of Denver, Colorado, will be our unit of analysis.

The West Side Neighborhood
The West Side of Denver is an area of approximately one hundred sixty city blocks and houses more than fifteen thousand residents. The neighborhood is one of the oldest sections of the city and shows much evidence of deterioration and neighborhood decline. The area is located in the inner city, and small family homes predominate.

The West Side includes three census tracts: tracts 18 and 19 (Auraria Lincoln Park) and tract 21 (Baker Junior High area). In 1950 the West Side was predominantly an Anglo neighborhood, but by 1970 the ethnic profile of the area had changed in composition (see Table 1).

In 1970 Chicanos comprised 62.1 percent of the population in the West Side. There were a number of Anglos (36 percent) living in the West Side, and African Americans made up a very small percentage of the population (1.9 percent). Comparatively, the city of Denver had a much smaller percentage of Chicanos (16.8 percent), a larger percentage of African Americans (9.1 percent), and a majority of Anglos (74.1 percent). Though Chicanos were a numerical minority in Denver, they were a numerical majority in the West Side.

The Westside Coalition

The Westside Coalition was made up of organizations that primarily represented Chicanos in the West Side. The Coalition was formed in the wake
of a crisis in November 1969, when the City of Denver gave its approval,
through a bond issue, for the Auraria area (the northern area of the West
Side) to be the site of the new Auraria Higher Education Complex.[9]   A
central campus for Metropolitan State College, Community College of
Denver, and the University of Colorado–Denver Center was to be built,
and the campus was planned to serve fifty-five thousand students.

West Side residents were against the proposed site because it called
for the demolition of one hundred low-income residential structures,
which would necessitate the displacement of about three hundred families.
Residents argued that the land value would rise, forcing many low-income
renters to move. Residents were also fearful that the neighborhood would
become student populated and business oriented.

It was out of the struggle to combat Urban Renewal, the Denver
Planning Board, and the city of Denver that the Westside Coalition was
organized. The Coalition was formed for the purpose of bringing together
organizations and individuals in an effort to maintain and improve the
West Side as a family residential neighborhood. The Coalition would be
an advocate group for the West Side and would monitor street routes,
truck patterns, zoning, land use, and housing. Thus, future encroachment
by the city of Denver would not go unchecked.

The organizations which responded to the crisis created by the Auraria
Project included:

Auraria Community Center
Baker Junior High and West High School faculties
G.I. Forum, Mile High Chapter
G.I. Forum, Skyline Chapter
Greenlee Elementary School PTA
Inner City Parish
St. Joseph Parish Council
United Mexican American Students at Metropolitan State College
United Mexican American Students of University of Colorado–
   Denver Center
Westside Action Ministry
Westside Improvement Association

The Westside Coalition was composed of a mixture of residents and agency representatives. The board of directors was primarily Chicano, though about 25 percent were Anglos who represented Chicanos. In a few cases, board members were Anglos who represented Anglo constituencies in the West Side. Though some of the organizations and agencies had Anglo representatives, most of the resident representatives were Chicanos. The Coalition itself was primarily made up of Chicanos.

Socioeconomic Powerlessness

"Socioeconomic powerlessness" herein refers to the conditions of roles at the individual level. We assume that socioeconomic powerlessness created by occupational differences is the basis for the colonial relationship between the colonizer and the colonized. Almaguer points out that "Both the class and racial oppression of the Chicano, and of other colonized people of color, have stemmed from the organization of economic structure of U.S. capitalism and from the labor relationships that generate from that particular mode of production."[10] Moreover, Flores contends that the individual Chicano or Chicana is dependent as a worker in "socially permitted sources of employment in predominantly marginal sectors of the economy (especially low-status, unskilled and semi-skilled occupations) . . . ."[11] Barrera et al. best summarized this position by maintaining that "In essence, then, being an internal colony means existing in a condition of powerlessness."[12]

The West Side barrio can be analyzed as an internal colony. The socioeconomic conditions that existed exemplify the powerlessness barrio residents experienced as a colonized people. We shall examine three variables as indices of socioeconomic status: occupation, income, and education. The occupational status of Chicanos in the West Side can be found in Table 2.

The 1970 data on occupational status indicate that Chicano workers in the West Side were primarily blue collar workers (55.1 percent), whereas workers in the city of Denver were primarily white collar workers (58.3 percent). Furthermore, the occupational category with the second-highest percentage of Chicanos in the West Side was the service worker category (25.6 percent), while the city of Denver's second-highest category was blue collar workers (26.5 percent). Workers in the West Side differed from their Denver counterparts in occupational status by the fact that most Chicano workers occupied lower-status jobs.

Another variable closely related to occupation is income. If Chicanos in the West Side were clustered toward the bottom of the occupational ladder, we would also expect income differentials to be evident. The median

Table 2
Occupational Status of Chicanos in the West Side
and total population for the city of Denver, 1970

	AREA			
	WEST SIDE[a]		DENVER CITY	
Occupational Status	Number	Percent	Number	Percent
White Collar Workers[b]	446	17.8%	124059	58.3%
Blue Collar Workers[c]	1385	55.1%	56311	26.5%
Service Workers[d]	643	25.6%	31531	14.8%
Farm Workers	37	1.5%	794	.4%
Total	2511	100.0%	212695	100.0%

[a] The data for the three census tracts in the West Side (18, 19, and 21) have been summarized for the area known as the West Side.

[b] "White Collar" includes professional and technical, managers and administrators (except farm), sales workers, and clerical workers.

[c] "Blue Collar" includes craftsmen and kindred, operatives, transport equipment operatives, and laborers.

[d] "Service Workers" includes service workers and private household workers.

Source: U.S. Bureau of the Census, *Census of Population and Housing: 1970, Census Tracts, Final Report* PHC (1) - 56, Denver, Colorado SMSA, 61, 141.

income for Chicano families in the West Side was $5,439, compared to $9,654 as median income for the city of Denver.[13] In 1970 families in Denver earned 44 percent more than Chicano residents in the West Side. This difference becomes even more accentuated when one considers that Chicano families are generally larger, and more members must survive on fewer economic resources.

Education is a variable closely related to social mobility in American society. Since the West Side is a typical barrio, we do not expect educational attainment to be high. The median level of education for Chicanos in the West Side is 8.8 years, while the median educational attainment for the city of Denver is 12.4 years.[14] At least 50 percent of all persons twenty-five years old and over in Denver have a high school diploma, whereas Chicanos in the same category for the West Side have barely completed junior high school. Without a substantial rise in median education completed by Chicanos in the near future, it is highly improbable that conditions in the barrio will change. It is the impact of socioeconomic conditions that maintains colonial community domination. As long as the colonized are kept economically powerless and educationally deprived, domination will inevitably continue. Even when decolonization is attempted, the gains achieved by the colonized are limited without changes in the basic conditions of everyday life.

External Control

Muñoz maintains that the Chicano movement ". . . has failed to develop effective mass based organizational structures which can directly challenge institutions of class and power responsible for the oppression of masses of Chicanos."[15] Moreover, Blauner observes that "though many spokesmen have advocated the exclusion of white landlords and small businessmen from the ghetto, . . . little concrete movement toward economic expropriation has as yet developed."[16] It appears that the Chicano barrio is in need of organizations that advocate reducing external control.

The Westside Coalition was created to limit outside encroachment and to decrease external control in order to preserve the neighborhood as a residential area. To these ends, the Coalition was involved in diverse activities which sought to decolonize the barrio. We shall examine some of the Coalition's major activities in an effort to understand the dynamics involved when external control is challenged.

The West Side is predominantly a residential neighborhood, but an examination of housing tenure will allow us to understand the nature of external control in a colonial situation. A substantially low number (22.9 percent) of the housing units occupied by Chicanos in the West Side are owner occupied; more than three-fourths (77.1 percent) of the housing units are renter occupied.[17] The city assessor's records reveal that most of the homes are owned by absentee landlords. The fact that most Chicanos in the West Side do not own their own homes puts them at an economic disadvantage when the community protests encroachment policies.

Absentee ownership was a major factor in the condition of homes in the West Side. In the summer of 1971, the Community Renewal Program for the City and County of Denver conducted a study of exterior conditions of housing structures to determine major structural flaws in the foundations, walls, and roofs of West Side homes. Secondary structural elements such as porches, windows, and doors were evaluated; site environment characteristics (alleys, parking problems, refuse accumulation, and drainage) also were noted. A point system for classification of housing structures was constructed, and structures were classified as to their conditions (see Table 3).

In this 1971 survey, only 5 percent of the housing structures were found to be in standard condition. Most of the housing units (70 percent) were classified as having minor exterior defects, but 25 percent were found to

Table 3
West Side Neighborhood Exterior Condition Survey of
Housing Structures, 1971

External Conditions	Number	Percent
Standard	146	5%
Minor Exterior Defects	2109	70%
Major External Defects	742	24%
Critical	36	1%
Total Structures	3033	100%

Source: *Westside Summary of Conditions and Neighborhood Improvement Plan*, Denver Community Renewal Program (December 1972), 38.

have major defects or to be in critical condition. Past findings of the Denver Urban Renewal Authority indicate that interior conditions were generally worse than exterior conditions.[18] Thus, the conditions of homes were probably more acute than the survey indicated.

Often the investment of capital in the maintenance of older single-family homes is discouraged because higher-density development is anticipated in the area. The West Side, as an internal colony, was economically controlled by outsiders who saw economic advantages in keeping the area zoned as a business and commercial area and who resisted any attempts to rezone the area for residential purposes. For example, "Ed Horton, vice president of Midland Federal Savings Board of Directors and a landowner in the area, contended property owners stand to lose the $100,000 an acre potential value instead of the $28,000 an acre present value."[19]

It was evident that Chicanos in the West Side did not own the economic base of their community—the land. As Fanon wrote, "For a colonized people the most essential value, because the most concrete, is the land . . . ."[20] The West Side was a barrio in the inner city where many Chicanos presently lived, but it was primarily owned by outside interests.

The nature of the limitations imposed by external control was best exemplified by the activities of the Westside Coalition on several community issues. The Coalition had its roots in neighborhood opposition to the proposed Auraria Higher Education Complex, which was to be built in the northern area of the neighborhood. West Side residents opposed a $6 million city bond issue for the Auraria urban renewal project because: 1) the land value in the West Side would rise, forcing many low-income renters to move; 2) further displacement of residents adjacent to the complex would not be compensated; and 3) residents were fearful that the neighborhood would become student and business oriented. A precursor of the Westside Coalition, the Committee to Preserve the West Denver Community, approached Lt. Governor Mark Hogan with a two-thousand-signature petition of residents opposed to the Auraria site.[21] Since the interests of West Side residents were secondary to citywide interests, the bond issue was approved by Denver voters.

While state and class elites control, guide, and administer programs for "growth," the barrio was removed section by section in the name of "progress."[22] The decision to construct the Auraria Complex in a significant area of the West Side was externally planned and imposed. Thus, West Side residents saw part of their neighborhood being destroyed by outside interests but were not sufficiently organized to prevent outside expansion into their residential neighborhood.

The Westside Coalition was also involved in an attempt to rezone high-density areas (apartment and business areas) into low-density residential areas.[23] Rezoning is one of the few avenues available to residents who wish to preserve the quality of their communities and insure community control. If the West Side neighborhood wished to remain residential, it had to 1) fight against the granting of zoning variances that would allow expansion for non-residential uses, and 2) seek zoning amendments that would be more consistent with residential living.[24]

The Westside Coalition submitted an application to the City Council for an amendment to the zoning map. The Coalition wanted a twenty-six-block area to be rezoned and submitted its application to the Denver Planning Board. The application was approved unanimously by the Planning Board and the mayor of Denver, and *The Denver Post* endorsed the plan.

The Coalition conducted a door-to-door survey of 275 homes (80 percent of those in the area) and found that 92 percent were in favor of rezoning.[25] But not everyone supported the Coalition's position. The Denver Planning Office issued a statement arguing that "Absentee landlords and speculators, not concerned with residential aspects, are probably looking forward to raising [*sic*] the houses because apartment buildings return a greater income."[26] The major opponents of the rezoning amendment were a group of landlords who testified against the proposed amendment at a City Council meeting. As a result of the landlords' position, the City Council voted against rezoning the area, and even the councilman who represented the West Side voted against rezoning.

The causes for the Westside Coalition's defeat on the rezoning issue were twofold: economic and political. The economic causes stemmed from the fact that most West Side residents were not homeowners. When residents spoke for the rezoning issue, city councilmen asked them to specify their resident status. Most were renters, and their status as non-owners greatly influenced the City Council's decision. The political causes are directly related to a lack of Chicano political representation on the City Council. As long as Chicanos in the West Side were represented by an Anglo who sided with the interests of land speculators, West Side residents would be powerless to improve their neighborhood.

Though the Westside Coalition was never in favor of Colorado hosting the 1976 Winter Olympics, the Coalition felt that, should the Olympics come to Colorado, the poor should benefit in some way. The Coalition proposed that the Olympic Press Village (fifteen hundred housing units) be built on the West Side, and that after the Olympics ended the buildings be converted into low- and moderate-income family housing. The plan to host the Olympics was defeated in a statewide ballot, but the federal commitment for the housing project had already been secured. However, Denver's African American community organized to acquire the housing money ($6 million) for a predominantly black neighborhood—Denver's East Side. On January 5, 1973, the Denver City Council chose the East Side as the site for the housing project.[27]

The Coalition's defeat on this issue was primarily politically based. Though blacks made up 9.1 percent of Denver's population, two blacks represented them on the City Council. Chicanos made up a larger percentage of the population (16.8 percent), yet there were no Chicanos on City Council. As was expected, black city councilmen represented the interests of their community while the Anglo city councilmen representing the West Side abstained on the issue of where the housing project would be built. Without an aggressive city councilman representing the interests of Chicanos, the West Side was at the mercy of external control in the political sphere.

The Westside Coalition also worked to secure fair treatment of Chicanos by the Denver police. In particular, the Coalition protested treatment of Chicanos by police at Curtis Park ("Mestizo Park") on April 14, 1970.[28] Five Chicanos were arrested, and two of them were brutally treated by the police. One alleged that he was clubbed and sprayed with mace while handcuffed, and that the other Chicano was shoved, kicked, and beaten while handcuffed in the detention room of the police.[29] The complainant involved was a youth services counselor for the Denver Youth

Services Bureau and was a well respected member of the community with no previous arrest record. Westside Coalition members met with the City Council and demanded that the police chief be fired for allowing such actions to occur and that the policemen involved be suspended while an investigation into the complaint was underway.

The mayor promised an investigation but saw no need for a civilian review board since the safety manager was a civilian. During the investigation the Chicano youth counselor even took a polygraph test and passed it on all questions asked about the policemen's actions at the detention room.[30] However, the safety manager's investigation cleared the officers of the brutality charge. The only significant result was the safety manager's resignation.

It was increasingly evident that Chicanos did not control the actions of the police who patrolled their neighborhoods. Even when complaints were filed by responsible Chicanos, very little justice resulted. Since Chicanos did not have representatives who could monitor and review the actions of the police, the community increasingly felt that the police were agents of the ruling class.

The extent of external control was also evident in conflicts between the Westside Coalition and external agencies involved in the barrio. The Democratic Party hired a Chicano, who was later very active in the Westside Coalition, to recruit Chicanos to run for public office. However, enemies were made with the party when a Chicano ran against a Democratic incumbent in the West Side. In addition, Chicanos in the Westside Coalition alienated the Democratic Party by attempting to organize a political machine in the West Side. There were plans to run Coalition members for the City Council, the Colorado State House of Representatives, and the Colorado Senate. It appeared that the Democratic Party wanted Chicanos to register with the party, but it did not want Chicanos running against incumbents. Furthermore, it appeared that the party was opposed to Chicanos building a political machine in West Denver.

In the West Side neighborhood, Community Action Program (CAP) agencies were headed by Anglos. In fact, most of the social service agencies in the West Side were not only headed by Anglos, they were administered by individuals who did not live in the community. Many of these agencies saw the Westside Coalition as taking over their services domain. As a result, petty criticism undermining the Coalition evolved. In addition, many well intentioned Coalition board representatives became opposed to the Coalition due to leadership conflicts.

Although the Westside Coalition was involved in many successful endeavors,[31] we shall not review these because they do not adequately exemplify the limitations imposed by external control. Most of the Coalition's defeats stemmed from economic and political control by outsiders. External control in the economic sphere was exemplified by the large number of Chicanos who were not homeowners, and in the political sphere by the lack of political representation.

Intraethnic Conflict

"Intraethnic conflict" refers to the internal conflict generated by organizations or members within a given ethnic group. Barrera et al. would classify this internal struggle as "divide and conquer," a mechanism of political domination in a colonial situation.[32] Fanon's analysis of violence in the colonies would classify such conflict as "violence turned inward."[33] We maintain that intraethnic conflict operates as an effective mechanism of colonial community domination because it results from competition for differential rewards produced by socioeconomic powerlessness. In turn, internal divisions facilitate external control. We will examine two types of intraethnic conflict which were detrimental to the development of the Westside Coalition.

Conflicts internal to the organizational structure of the Coalition greatly affected its unity. Resistance toward banding together existed from the outset. Though Chicano groups saw the advantages of forming a coalition, many organizations viewed the Coalition as a threat to their own organizational autonomy. Since the concentration of power "spotlighted" the Coalition, many groups saw it as undermining their position as "spokespersons" for the West Side.

Intraethnic conflict at the external level involved conflict between the Westside Coalition and a powerful, nationally recognized Chicano organization known as the "Crusade for Justice," which gained prominence in the late 1960s. The Coalition and the Crusade differed in basic philosophical orientations. The Coalition was more reform oriented, and the Crusade endorsed more activist perspectives. While the Crusade had abandoned working within existing political party structures and strongly supported La Raza Unida Party (an independent Chicano political party in Colorado), the Westside Coalition used the Democratic Party as a vehicle to get Chicanos elected in the West Side.

Though the Crusade for Justice was unable to get Chicanos elected to public office, it used its political party status as a forum for social activism, such as nationalism. Such an ideology put the Crusade in direct opposition to the Coalition. Since the groups had different constituencies, their philosophies created community frictions.

Thus, the Westside Coalition experienced intraethnic conflict at two levels: internal and external. The internal conflicts were generated by competition of Chicano organizations within the Coalition for the role of "spokesperson." Unity was undermined by organizations which wanted to be "the representative" of the West Side. In addition, external conflicts were evident in the Crusade for Justice's efforts to project its ideology as the major perspective of the community. Such conflicts eroded the effectiveness of the Westside Coalition.

Conclusion

We have presented a theoretical perspective of the dynamics involved in the domination of an internal colony. We specified three major mechanisms of colonial community domination: 1) socioeconomic powerlessness, 2) intra-ethnic conflict, and 3) external control. Furthermore, we postulated a primary order of effect in which socioeconomic powerlessness had the greatest effect on colonial community domination. If the cumulative effects of this domination were to be reversed, the key mechanism was socioeconomic powerlessness.

The Westside Coalition was discussed as a contemporary Chicano community organization that attempted to reduce colonial community domination. It focused on reducing intraethnic conflict by forming a coalition of Chicano organizations and neighborhood residents. It also sought to reduce external control by challenging outside encroachment. However, the pervasiveness of intraethnic conflict reduced the Coalition's effectiveness, and many of its decolonizing efforts met systemic barriers, which were economically based and politically grounded.

The Westside Coalition did not directly focus on reducing socioeconomic powerlessness. Instead, it chose to reduce the effects of colonial community domination by focusing on the other major mechanisms. Such a focus was probably a practical move, because socioeconomic powerlessness as a mechanism of domination is the most rigid to change. It is the sustenance of the colonial relationship between the colonizer and the colonized. Thus, the Coalition's efforts to decolonize the barrio were greatly limited.

Perhaps, colonialism and reform efforts are contradictory. As long as the colonizer controls the social system in which the internal colony depends for its survival, the limits of reform will be predefined by the colonizer. Decolonization, as a nonviolent process, might be destined to fail in totally reversing colonial domination. Fanon argued that decolonization was always a violent process,[34] but he was referring to colonial situations in which revolution was a possibility because the colonized were a numerical majority. Since Chicanos in the United States are a numerical minority, the possibility of social change through revolution can be seriously questioned.

The Westside Coalition sought change through the only means available—the democratic process. Undoubtedly, it was waging an impossible revolution in a situation that begged for change. The Coalition was a threat to the colonial structure because it heightened the contradiction of reform strategies. However, its existence was short-lived. By 1975 the Coalition had met its demise. Its dissolution resulted from myriad forces which converged to render it powerless. Though it no longer exists, the *espíritu* of the Westside Coalition in Denver, Colorado, remains as a model for Chicano community control.

Notes

1
For readings on Chicano community organizations, see: Salvador Alvarez, "Mexican American Community Organizations," *El Grito* 4, no. 3 (Spring 1971), 68-77; Kaye Briegel, "The Development of Mexican-American Organizations," *The Mexican Americans: An Awakening Minority*, Manuel P. Servin, ed. (Beverly Hills: Glencoe Press, 1970), 160-78; Ralph Guzman, "Politics in the Mexican American Community," *Chicanos: The Evolution of a People*, Renato Rosaldo, Robert A. Calvert, and Gustav L. Seligmann, eds. (Minneapolis: Winston Press, 1973), 413-23; Armando Navarro, "The Evolution of Chicano Politics," *Aztlan* 5, nos. 1 and 2 (Spring and Fall 1974), 57-84; Paul Sheldon, "Mexican American Formal Organizations," Mexican Americans in the United States, John H. Burma, ed. (Cambridge: Schenkman Publishing Co., 1970), 267-72; Miguel David Tirado, "Mexican-American Community Political Organization," *Aztlan* 1, no. 1 (Spring 1970), 53-78.

2
Alvarez, "Mexican American Community Organizations," 72.

3
George Rivera, Jr., and Joseph Andres Gavaldon, "The Crusade for Justice: An Alternative in Chicano Community Organization" (Paper presented at the Southern Political Science Association Meeting, Atlanta, Georgia, November 1972).

4
Robert Blauner, *Racial Oppression in America* (New York: Harper & Row, Publishers, 1972), 84.

5
For an analysis of the Colonial Model as applied to Chicanos see: Tomas Almaguer, "Toward the Study of Chicano Colonialism," *Aztlan* 2, no. 1 (Spring 1971), 7-21; Mario Barrera, Carlos Muñoz, and Charles Ornelas, "The Barrio as an Internal Colony," *People and Politics in Urban Society*, Harlan Hahn, ed. (Beverly Hills: Sage Publications, 1972), 465-98; Guillermo Flores, "Race and Culture in the Internal Colony: Keeping the Chicano in His Place," *Structures of Dependency*, Frank Bonilla and Robert Girling, eds. (Stanford: Stanford Institute of Politics, 1973), 189-223; and Ronald Bailey and Guillermo Flores, "Internal Colonialism and Racial Minorities in the U.S.: An Overview," in Bonilla and Girling, *Structures of Dependency*, 149-60.

6
Frantz Fanon, *The Wretched of the Earth* (New York: Grove Press, Inc., 1968), 84.

7
Pablo Gonzalez-Casanova, "Internal Colonialism and National Development," *Latin American Radicalism*, Irving L. Horowitz, Josue de Castro, and John Gerassi, eds. (New York: Random House, 1969), 126.

8
Blauner, *Racial Oppression in America*, 84.

9
The Denver Post, January 4, 1970.

10
Tomas Almaguer, "Historical Notes on Chicano Oppression: The Dialectics of Racial and Class Domination in North America," *Aztlan* 5, nos. 1 and 2 (Spring and Fall 1974), 43.

11
Flores, "Race and Culture," 198.

12
Barrera et al., "The Barrio," 481.

13
U.S. Bureau of the Census of Population and Housing: 1970, Census Tracts, Final Report PHC (1) - 56, Denver, Colorado SMSA, 91, 141.

14
Ibid., 31, 132.

15
Carlos Muñoz, Jr., "The Politics of Protest and Chicano Liberation: A Case Study of Repression and Cooptation," *Aztlan* 5, nos. 1 and 2 (Spring and Fall 1974), 120.

16
Blauner, *Racial Oppression in America*, 95-6.

17
U.S. Bureau of the Census of Population and Housing: 1970, Census Tracts, Final Report, H-70.

18
Westside Summary of Conditions and Neighborhood Improvement Plan (Denver: Denver Community Renewal Program, December 1972), 36.

19
Rocky Mountain News, October 29, 1969.

20
Fanon, *The Wretched of the Earth*, 44.

21
The Denver Post, October 29, 1969.

22
Flores, "Race and Culture," 198.

23
The Denver Post, November 19, 1971.

24
Westside Recorder, October 1971.

25
Rocky Mountain News, April 1, 1972.

26
Ibid., November 17, 1971.

27
Ibid., June 9, 1973.

28
The Denver Post, April 17, 1970.

29
Ibid.

30
Rocky Mountain News, April 30, 1970.

31
The major successes of the Westside Coalition were less threatening to the economic and political structure and, thus, were allowed to occur. The Coalition's successes included: 1) preventing a one-way system through the neighborhood; 2) stopping a Greyhound Bus terminal from being built; 3) closing an x-rated movie house on a business strip that bisects the community; 4) getting a new health center and a new recreation center built in the

neighborhood; and 5) preserving green belt areas as mini-parks.

32
Barrera et al., "The Barrio," 489.

33
Fanon, *The Wretched of the Earth*, 18, 54.

34
Ibid., 35.

The Life History of Diana Velazquez:
La Curandera Total

Ramon Del Castillo

ABOUT THE AUTHOR

Ramon Del Castillo is a journalist, poet, and educator who is on staff in the Chicano Studies Department at Metropolitan State College of Denver. His poetry books depict the plight of the Chicano/a in American society. He is a former columnist for the *Rocky Mountain News* and is currently a columnist for *El Semanario*, a statewide bilingual newspaper.

IANA VELAZQUEZ is a *curandera* who practices the art of *curanderismo* in Denver. During her thirty-six-year career, she has weathered changes in the community's perception of curanderismo, "a holistic approach to physical, psychosocial, and spiritual conditions used . . . by contemporary Chicanos despite the predominance of 'modern' medical science."[1] Velazquez is the only "bona fide" curandera in the state of Colorado who practices curanderismo within a formal institution. She is thus a unique example of a nontraditional medical practitioner who continually crosses cultural bridges.

As part of the multicultural revitalization movement occurring in American society, particularly with its changing demographics, it is important to give credence to longstanding sociocultural elements that have not received formal recognition or respect. Curanderismo has played a major role as one pragmatic method of healing on a continuum of mental health practices; however, it has not received proper recognition from mainstream society.

Recent research by members of the psychiatric community in the United States has unveiled various methods of physical, emotional, mental, and spiritual healing practices throughout the world.[2] Researchers have concluded that "psychiatric imperialism" exists in American society, and that "curanderismo and modern medicine assume complementary roles at the present time, at least in the minds of the medical professionals of the area."[3]

Definition and History of Curanderismo

Stemming from the Spanish verb *curer*, to cure, the term *curandera* translates as a healer or curer.[4] The specific techniques comprising curanderismo vary geographically and have different cultural labels attached to them. These include Mexican-American healing practices and rural folkloric medicine. Bobette Perrone, who studies women's folk healing, defines *curanderismo* as

> . . . a set of folk medical beliefs, rituals, and practices that seem to address the psychological, spiritual and social needs of traditional . . . people. It is a complex system of folk medicine with its own theoretical, diagnostic and therapeutic aspects. Curanderismo is conceptually holistic in nature, no separation is made between the mind and the body, as in western medicine and psychology. Curanderismo, simply, is the art of Hispanic healing.[5]

Importantly, researchers separate curanderismo into specific categories. The *adivina* is a diagnostician who does not treat any disease. The *alboria* is an herbalist. The *médica* relies on *mágica* for psychotherapeutic treatment. The *mágica* combines herbs and spiritualism in treatment techniques.[6] A *curandera total* is all of these. Diana Velazquez states simply, "Curanderismo is what in English would be called the art of healing."[7]

Curanderismo is a blend of colonial Spanish and traditional Indian healing practices which later incorporated some Western scientific knowledge. Part of its philosophy stems from Greco-Roman tradition and Catholic beliefs.[8] It was transported throughout the Southwest by conquistadors, Franciscan friars, and female healers known as curanderas, who traveled with Spanish colonial expeditions that came to settle the "New World." While curanderas have traditionally been women, men have performed these roles as well.

Curanderas were "the repository of ancient folk-healing knowledge and seemed to know exactly how to treat complicated afflictions by using a variety of herbs and healing plants that they carried with them."[9] With teaching from the indigenous healers, the colonial curanderas enhanced their knowledge of plants that they encountered in the New World and subsequently combined it with their previous knowledge to form a branch of medicine and healing that has persisted over time.

The Role of the Curandera

As a general practitioner who has the gift, the curandera assists patients in the healing process for a variety of physical and psychological maladies. She must work within the hierarchical structure of curanderismo to balance patients' complaints with a combination of intra-cultural approaches.

Curanderas include a variety of specialists such as *sobador*, or massager, and others who treat sprains and strained muscles; *yerbero*, herbalist; *médica*, medical healer; *partera*, midwife; and *bruja*, witch. *Señoras* are known for their knowledge and intervention in mild *remedios* (remedies) and for their ability to intervene in mild ailments. As well, curanderas are known for their work in manipulating the supernatural and physical world. Hierarchies exist among healers. There is overlap and specialization, as well as regional distinctions. The universally skilled *curandera total* is usually ranked first and seen as the most powerful healer.[10]

Religion, culture, and family are important contexts in healing Mexican people. Curanderas usually practice a culturally specific form of family therapy. They always work in consultation with family members in order to establish a diagnosis and the specific techniques to be utilized in the healing process.[11]   Depending on the malady being treated, the rituals asked of the patients may include activity by various members of the nuclear and extended family. The role of family members is integral to the overall healing that takes place.

Research indicates that some curanderas believe they have acquired a "divine power from God" that allows them to be used as Christian instruments of healing. Others believe that "this divine power comes from a vision, a calling or dream."[12]   Studies have shown that the majority of Mexican curanderas were highly religious; many were raised in a strict Catholic background.[13]

In short, the curandera adopts the functional role as "balancer or restorer to homeostasis."[14] The curandera performs rituals, prayers, incantations, and an assortment of culturally specific remedies that assist the client in becoming whole and balanced again.

Diana Velazquez: *La Curandera Total*

Diana Velazquez was born in Lockhart, Texas, on March 11, 1939, into a family of female healers. She was practically destined to fulfill the role at birth. Her great-grandmother and Grandmother Chona were considered strong healers in their respective communities. Her grandmother died while giving a *curación*, "the healing":

> A young person, about twenty-two years of age, needed to be cured. My grandmother . . . was about sixty-three, which, at that time, you were elderly. She weighed her life against the life of a young person and figured that it was worth saving because . . . if she was gone that was fine because then this person had a long life to live. . . . So she went into battle and she lost. The young person lived.[15]

Diana's grandmother was considered a primary physician within the hierarchy of healers. She was instrumental in the application of curanderismo and referrals to the networking system of curanderas who lived in her Lockhart, Texas, barrio. Networking is vital for the curandera because of the large number of clients and the various maladies she must contend with in the barrio. However, legally speaking, the work of curanderas was considered a form of medical malpractice and kept underground.

For some, the process of becoming a curandera begins with a revelation, a vision, or a dream.[16] Diana's was initiated in the womb. The sounds of her voice crying in the womb before actual birth, witnessed by family and community members, was an Indian/Mexican cultural sign that another healer was coming to life.[17]

Velazquez began training at an early age to enhance her gift, accompanying her grandmother throughout the community. She was present at many of the cultural healing rituals her grandmother performed and was aware even at a very young age of what was going on around her:

> I remember being in an orange crate in a pink blanket. . . . And I heard what was going on, and described what was going on . . . . I remember talking to the person who had been healed at a later time in life. I know her name, Virginia, because that is what I heard them call her and she was married to a man who worked in a hospital. They found Virginia, maybe thirty years ago. They found her through an aunt who had a mutual friend. They asked her if she knew Chona Reyes. "Oh ya, *la curandera*, ya did I know her. I went to her. The *curación* was so difficult that it had to be done outside so we went to the chicken coop in the back, and that is where we went to get the *curación*."[18]

Diana began practicing curanderismo at the tender age of eight. With inborn power and abilities, and through the counseling, mentoring, and guidance of her grandmother, she began to perform healing rituals with barrio women. She remembers:

> My grandmother, when I was eight, would say, "So-and-so is sick. That is what is wrong with her. Get what you need and go take care of them." As a child, it did not occur to me to say, "Well, what if I don't know? What if I fail? I've never done this before." I went. I picked up what I needed: the herbs, the eggs, the lemon, the charcoal, and I went and said, "Chona told me to come." They said, "O.K.," and I did what I was supposed to do. I went back home, didn't report to anybody or was never asked, "How did it go?" I assumed that lady was going to get well. I did everything I was supposed to. And she did get well.[19]

Diana was promised in marriage to Cecilio Velazquez at the age of twelve. She defines her arranged marriage as a "marriage of convenience." Cecilio, a Yaqui Indian, had been sent on a mission to find another healer to join the family. The Velazquez clan had a family tradition of curanderismo; however, a generation had passed, and there were no signs that a healer existed among that particular generation. It was Cecilio's cultural duty to find a curandera who would become part of their family and continue the cycle of curanderismo.

As promised, Diana married Cecilio Velazquez at the age of fifteen. They moved to Sonora, Mexico, where she was embraced and mentored by Cecilio's father, Herman Velazquez (Don Chito), a well-known healer. While in the Yaqui village, Diana played the role of a *partera* (midwife) and a nurse. Here she encountered the "real" local doctor, who also mentored her and allowed her to treat Indian patients.

During her time in the village, she delivered six hundred twelve babies and provided pre- and post-natal care for the mothers. She emphasized the traditional curandera method of delivery. In particular, the role of the father and the relationship between humankind and nature was of paramount importance in the birth process.[20]

The teachings of Don Chito were geared toward the development and enhancement of her power as a healer. From him, she learned culturally significant rituals, common sense, and powerful life lessons. One such lesson required her to find the solution to a problem based on a fire she built according to Don Chito's specifications:

> After sorting through the amber and the ashes, it finally came to me . . . so he said, "Did you find the solution in the amber or the fire?" "No," I said. "Was it in the ashes or in the stick?" "No," I said. So I pointed to my head and heart and said, "That is where the answer is at." "Ah," he said. That was his highest compliment. He was teaching me that I did not need a crystal ball; I didn't need anything to find the solutions that I had to trust what I already knew, that I had to trust . . . myself.[21]

Diana's relationship with Don Chito allowed her to learn the philosophy of curanderismo, with its inherent traditions passed down for generations by Yaqui ancestors who had lived in Mexico. He became her mentor, friend, and ally, not merely her father-in-law.

It was through this series of teachings under the cover of the moon and the stars and with spiritual guidance that Velazquez gained confidence and trust in her ability to heal. The significance of her work, because of its uniqueness and the lack of mentors in the United States, required her to build and maintain self-confidence. She knew that once she returned to the United States to practice, it would be difficult to receive adequate mentorship.

Velazquez grasped the importance of training as central to the curandera's successful practice. Her training with Don Chito was a blessing because of his knowledge, strength, and ability to understand the concept of power. In particular, the use, versus the abuse, of power was critical to her training and it was something that she learned quickly. She states:

> The first thing I learned from Don Chito was how to channel that power for myself—how to inwardly heal myself spiritually. He taught me how to go off to a mountaintop or to the desert by myself, sweat out a lot of things, and concentrate on how [for] anything bad that happened something good was going to come out of it.[22] It's important for that middle step of your learning: how to use your psychicness, your own power, the cleansing, the purification, the getting together with that higher spirit. And when that is missing you use the only resources you have—your own energy—and it burns out quick.[23]

As Carlos Castaneda shows in *The Teachings of Don Juan*, it is the responsibility of the healer to learn all aspects of power. Castaneda, an anthropologist who studied with Don Juan, a sorcerer from the state of Sonora, Mexico, whom some considered a powerful healer, once stated to his mentor that power is both a friend and an enemy. Don Juan responded: "Power is the strongest of all enemies. And naturally the easiest thing to do is to give up; after all, the man is truly invincible. He commands; he begins by taking calculated risks; and ends in making rules, because he is a master. Power will turn him into a cruel, capricious man."[24]

In 1974 the Velazquez family returned to San Antonio, Texas, where Diana continued her practice. Until she reached the age of thirty-five, her work was typical of most curanderas; other curanderas helped her through an "underground" networking system. Because this kind of healing art had not been accepted by the medical establishment, its practice was confined to Mexican barrios, where clients entered treatment through word of mouth.

Velazquez earned her "credentials" when she proved her healing skills to the community. Essentially, the *curandera total* earns her credentials via her reputation and through an informal training curriculum. Her reputation flourishes as a result of actual work accomplished, in contrast to traditional Western practice, where one must certify theoretical competence before being allowed to practice. Undoubtedly, folk curers are not professionals in the sense that they receive formal training in the art of medicine or make a living by clinical practice. They are, however, "regarded as specialists because they have learned more of the popular medical lore of their culture than have other barrio people."[26]

In 1972 the Velazquez family moved to Denver. For Diana, breaking into the field of mental health was either an aberration or an act of God, leading her down a path that was meant for her. Diana stated that she had to be a curandera. She could play multiple roles in her life, but being a curandera was her greatest calling.

But suddenly, she was diagnosed with cancer. She decided to seek counseling to help her deal with the ensuing depression. Paradoxically, she chose a modern psychiatric counseling center, Centro de las Familias, a bilingual, bicultural mental health clinic located in southwest Denver.

Velazquez believes that her admission to the clinic was part of her destiny. At the time, the psychiatric team was looking for a secretary, and Velazquez was hired for the job. It was during a psychiatric case consultation that they became aware of her healing abilities. "My role," she stated, "was to take notes. However, I felt compelled to intervene." When she finished her assessment, the team leader asked her how she had known what to do. "I am a curandera," Velazquez responded. "I have been working with our people for a long time."[27]

The team leader, Ernesto Alvarado, applied for funds to implement curanderismo as a specialized kind of mental health treatment. Following her initiation into the field of modern psychiatry, Velazquez was able to grasp many of the concepts of community mental health that were already a part of her repertoire of skills, but from an Indian/Mexican/Chicano perspective. In the counseling profession it is often referred to as "transcultural psychiatry."

After joining Centro de las Familias, Diana's curanderismo work began to be recognized, appreciated, and validated by both the institution and the community. Through her teachings, her presence became known. As a result, demands for her services began. She describes one of her most vivid experiences in healing a hexed client, in this case a child:

> I said hello to her, and I asked her if she knew who I was. I thought maybe they had told her they were bringing a curandera. And she said, "No, I don't know who your are. But somehow I feel that you are the one that is going to help me." So I figured I'm halfway home. And I asked for a room that I could work with her, and right away they wanted to videotape it and all that stuff. And I said no, that I did not approve of that, that this was something that was sacred . . . . So I went in there and entered the room. . . . I had a set of beads, they are round like a sunburst and they have like three different kinds of heads and seeds. And this is something that my father-in-law made for me, so that when I worked with a child, it's almost like a condenser, that the right

energy would flow to her as opposed to an adult. So I took the beads and swept her with them, and we prayed the Our Father which she was familiar with, and I prayed the way I do. And when we had finished the prayer, I said to her, "Now I want you to move this finger [pointing to her index finger]," and she very slowly . . . did it. And I said "Now I want you to move your other fingers," and she did. So, "Now let's move your whole hand," and she opened both hands and she was able to extend them. And that took about twenty-five minutes. So I wheeled her out, and the doctors said, ". . . Is there anything you are going to be able to do to help us?" And I said, "Well, I think so." And I said, "Lisa, would you shake hands with your doctor?" So she extended her hand . . . and then she waved with the other one.[28]

Velazquez stated that this was her "first miracle." The professional staff had mixed emotions about this experience: some were in awe, others were in doubt, and some were even angry. Nonetheless, the word permeated the local psychiatric community that a healer had performed a miracle. This set the stage for an influx of requests from the Chicano community for her services.

Cultural Diagnostics and Treatment Methods

Velazquez utilizes cultural diagnostics in order to determine her clients' disorders and/or needs. This provides the basis for an effective treatment plan suited to each individual.

She defines *trisia* as "a *tristeza* [depression] that goes not only from the body but into your soul." It appears that this particular diagnostic fits categorically into what Western psychologists call depression, or perhaps melancholia, except that it manifests itself in the spirit and the soul as well. Beyond the textbook definition, Diana adds,

Trisia means that down to the very core of your soul there is this sadness . . . this deep depression. . . . The other thing that I see is a lot of men who carry a lot of guilt and are exhibiting it through bad luck or illness that they can't diagnose. Guilt such as having killed somebody, having incested their daughter or sister, and even guilt of having come to the United States from Mexico, promising to support their mothers and fathers, and not following through—whether it's because they can't afford it or it's because they have given money to women or whomever it is. . . . They have that feeling. So they come in exhibiting symptoms of what you might call a hex.[29]

Velazquez treats people with these maladies through the use of cultural rituals, prayer, and empowerment. She believes that God has given her power to heal, and that through her He transmits healing energy to clients. Her techniques are culturally specific, laden with the values that Chicanos and Mexicans carry as part of their cultures.

Her insight and ability to "know" her clients is a key factor in diagnosing and treating them. Her direct approaches in dealing with clients gain her a position of respect from them. Psychologically she blends common sense with a variety of culturally responsive methods.

Mal de oio, or "evil eye," is a common occurrence in the Mexican-American community. Generally, it is associated with children.[30] Certain people are believed to have "a very strong or hot vision capable of harming another person. If a person with this powerful vision happens to desire or admire a person for any reason, a supernatural force is projected onto that person who then becomes ill."[31] Noted researcher Ari Kiev suggests that *mal de oio* "is an expression of guilt and anxiety being projected onto another person (usually a stranger)."[32] According to Velazquez, "children are more susceptible to this illness because of their lack of social interaction skills and are not aware of transmitted energy, positive or negative."[33] Prevention of *mal de oio* is achieved through a simple touch by the person projecting the energy. Curanderas are trained to diagnose and treat this malady.

Tools of the Trade

Velazquez uses several natural elements in her practice. Salt is one such tool. It is viewed as a pure element, and Velazquez sees it as a precious commodity: "In ancient times, they didn't pay with coins, they paid with salt. It comes from the sea, and it's natural. It helps people to ground better." She expects clients to bathe in it, with the use of other elements such as candles and prayers. Candles often embellish the treatment process. Velazquez describes their importance in her therapy:

> I have always used color, heat, and light. Candles represent all of the above. I think all three, from a color to a candle. I get a color, I can get the heat, I can get the light, and then the saint is thrown in for good measure. So the significance is that, if you are a Catholic person, which most of my clients are, they are very attached to praying to the saints. I am aware of what saint is good for what. San Ramon, believe it or not, is good for something. San Ramon is the saint that people claim to, that women claim to, when their husbands are starting to stray from the family home.[34]

Velazquez has deviated from typical Catholic curanderismo in that she offers services to clients regardless of their religious beliefs. She is familiar with many religions and uses appropriate cultural/religious symbols in dealing with each client individually.

Mysticism is highly valued in the treatment process. Velazquez believes that Chicanos and Mexicans, in the modern Catholic church, have lost a sense of the unknown. Many times they seek out rituals, designed with a specific purpose in mind, only to discover that the mystical significance has been obliterated. It is no longer practiced due to the changing structure of the church. As Velazquez states, "nuns who used to be dressed in mystic black are now dressed like the rest of us. Mysticism has been lost."[35]

Oils are also an integral element of Velazquez's treatments. She believes that oil is very sacred: "It was what Jesus Christ used for anointing, for healing."[36] Her knowledge of the various oils available allows her to concoct specific oil blends based on the needs of individual clients. Oils are combined with rituals as another part of the treatment process.

Eggs are used because they represent innocence. According to Velazquez:

> Eggs are very ritualistic for us because they represent new life, rebirth; they are pure. They have never been touched by human hands. . . . Why do we have Easter eggs? Because it represents resurrection. So we use eggs internally, externally, and we use them to cleanse the body, and to cure *empacho*. *Empacho* is a folk illness. Eggs are used in the diagnostic procedures and to treat it.[37]

Differently colored ribbons signify particular moods of the human condition. Sometimes Velazquez will tie knots in the ribbons in order to remind clients that protection is near.

> I use ribbons a lot. I tie seven knots in a row, then I go along with the patient and say, "O.K., this knot is for your son, or this knot is for that neighbor that doesn't love you, and this knot is for God to bless you, and this knot is for God to prosper you." . . . Each of the knots is named and blessed. Whenever that person feels threatened . . . or scared in a business situation . . . at school, or wherever, but they feel a fear, then what they do is they take their hand and put it in one of the knots, and I tell them to take a deep breath and become centered again.[38]

Part of the philosophy of curanderismo is geared toward being in touch with the universe. Velazquez times many of her rituals to coincide with the position of the moon and the stars, and she blends many of her teas and herbs at specific times. She uses quassia (a tropical tree or shrub, also known as bitter wood) "depending on the situation, whether it is a man or a woman and what the need is; [I] will set it out early in the morning from certain hours to certain hours, and if it is for a man I will put it out at night, and usually whenever the moon cycle of his birth is."[39]

Velazquez describes her practice as holistic medicine. She believes that everything used for healing is God-given. This belief permits the use of modern physicians, nurses, and other types of healers. She is able to work with doctors who are puzzled about a particular client's condition. By the same token, she freely refers clients to doctors when she feels that the client has a particular malady she cannot treat.

Velazquez plays multiple roles as a curandera. As a holistic healer, she deals with the spiritual aspect of a person. This is not general psychiatric practice in this country but rather is usually reserved for priests and other clergy. Therefore, she often is seen as a spiritual healer.

Religious persons of various denominations have contacted her because someone in their particular parish was *embruiada*, or "bewitched." She responds by performing consultative services via the community mental health center. Her other complementary roles include *médica*, psycho-therapist, and herbalist. Velazquez adheres to "affective neutrality," that is, the notion that doctors in this society are expected to remain effectively neutral toward the client. However, as a healer, she also becomes involved in the personal and spiritual lives of her clients. She attends rosaries, funerals, and other cultural and religious functions with them. This adds credibility to her status and demonstrates her genuine compassion for her clients.

Velazquez's status also allows her entry into the private and highly valued family structure traditional within Mexican society. Anyone admit-ted into the "business of the family" must be a special person. From the perspective of the family, her reputation and her interaction on a personal basis enable this penetration to occur. The importance of the family is central to the existence of Mexican-American culture. Family allegiance, loyalty, and obligation are primary values, and to step outside of these prescribed boundaries is considered disloyal. Curanderismo "provides a mechanism to avoid or relieve situations involving conflict between Mexican and American values."[40]

Velazquez blends the Western view of medical practice, based on the relationship of the physician to the client, with a culturally specific role as determined by Indian/Mexican/Chicano culture. This multicultural process allows patients of diverse acculturation levels to fulfill their expectations of a "doctor" while satisfying other culturally specific expectations. It also enables Velazquez to alleviate her clients' anxiety over the treatment process. She describes one instance in which a client refused to take psychiatric medication because she insisted that she was "not *loca* [crazy]." Through rituals Velazquez designed, the client agreed to take a tea mixed with a psychiatric medication. Because the client's ritualistic needs were met, she was willing to take the antipsychotic.

In the case of curanderismo, Velazquez validates the client's illness by acknowledging the hurt and pain. This enables the healing process to begin immediately. Noted transcultural psychiatrist E. Fuller Torrey describes a concept that he refers to as the "Rumpelstiltskin" principle: giving a name to a disorder automatically relieves the patient's anxiety.[41] Additionally, by validating a client's illness, Velazquez sets the tone for a respectful and healthy client-healer relationship—the most important criterion for evaluating curanderismo, whether or not the client responds to the treatment.

Integration into Psychiatric Care
The practice of curanderismo has met with mixed reactions from the psychiatric community. Many psychiatrists have explored the concept, while others have remained solidly within their traditional boundaries as Western healers. Even among staff at Centro de las Familias, curanderismo has received mixed reviews. Velazquez recalls:

> They presented a case of a woman who believed she was hexed. A social worker commented, "well, maybe if I wear a long black robe and get some feathers, and make some noises, she'll think she got well." I became very upset about that. . . . I confronted the person. I told the person that this was nothing to laugh about. . . . This was a turning point in my life.[42]

Currently, the Colorado State Division of Mental Health is aware of curanderismo and sanctions it as a viable form of transcultural psychiatry. According to Velazquez, her record-keeping is scrutinized by both the Division and the internal quality assurance team at the mental health center. Her *remedios* and treatment plans must be approved by the staff psychiatrist, particularly when used in conjunction with special teas and concoctions. This acceptance factor enables the Chicano community's psychiatric needs to be met without the violation of any medical or psychiatric treatment.

Velazquez has worked at Centro de las Familias for nineteen years. She has advanced from the position of secretary to clinical supervisor and manager, and is well versed in all aspects of community mental health and their relevant applications. She works with staff psychiatrists who are interested in cross-cultural psychology and healing methods. As a clinical supervisor, with a staff of seven, she is also responsible for the care of approximately two hundred fifty clients.

From a psychiatric perspective, curanderismo is viewed as a culturally specific modality of treatment, like many of its counterparts such as behavior therapy and psychodynamics. Velazquez offers these treatments to anyone whom she feels might respond to them. She also serves as a consultant to several local, regional, and national psychiatric facilities, providing assistance in diagnostic assessments and clarifying cultural diagnostics and the ways curanderismo might benefit clients. She has addressed groups of psychiatric professionals interested in curanderismo and the role it plays within the context of the Indian/Mexican/Chicano community's mental health.

The Importance of Transcultural Psychiatry

Diana Velazquez can be classified as a transcultural psychiatrist: she has the cultural knowledge to heal within a particular sociocultural framework. A leading authority argues that the etiology of mental disorders is culturally specific and cannot be transposed from culture to culture.[43] Many disorders and forms of mental illness do not fit into the categories defined by Western psychology. Therefore, treatment that is not culturally specific may not assist the Chicano client in the healing process. Because transcultural psychiatrists are aware of culturally laden values, behaviors, symbols, traditions, and conflicts, they can treat a malady within the existent cultural framework.

Velazquez plays a specific role when interacting with patients. Her status within the patient-client relationship is an ascribed one, in contrast to one that is earned through competency training. Though she was trained by an expert *curandero* (Don Chito) before she could enter formal training, particular cultural signs had to be present; she possessed those traits at birth. In other words, she had the basic qualifications for this role within her culture, while she also experienced mentoring that enhanced her abilities.

Many clients who request Velazquez's services feel they must "play the role" of the client. In American society, a sick person has to play a "sick" role.[44] This relinquishes them from performing the responsibilities and expectations that our society defines. At times, based on the expectations of the diagnostic model, the identified client must present symptoms that reflect an illness. In the field of psychology, those clients whose symptoms are only present in the mind are often diagnosed as having a psychosomatic disorder.

Blending Western Psychiatry and Curanderismo

Modern psychiatry would benefit from further research related to the notion of incorporating enthnopsychiatrists into the field of community mental health. It would provide culturally specific mental health services to clients who would not, under normal circumstances, respond to approved forms of treatment.

As American health costs soar, it might behoove public administrators to investigate today's indigenous physical and mental health practices. Many times, they can be less costly and more beneficial and can complement contemporary medical and psychological practices. It could easily be argued that this healing art form can be seen as a threat to modern medicine and psychiatry because of the "stranglehold" that many professional medical associations have on the practice of medicine. Breaking through the barriers of acceptance will be difficult at best. Traditional and modern medicine complement each other, and when traditional indigenous healing develops legitimacy in the eyes of modern medical practitioners, nontraditional healing can be viewed as a culturally competent modality of treatment for those who seek it out.

Furthermore, an ethical issue is at stake. Denying taxpayers culturally relevant mental health services, especially if one believes that he or she can respond effectively to these treatment techniques, reinforces the notion of "psychiatric imperialism."

The life and experiences of Diana Velazquez clearly demonstrate that, with proper guidance, nurturing, and understanding from the psychiatric community, cross-cultural psychology, in particular curanderismo, can be a viable tool in the healing processes of Indian/Mexican/Chicano clients. Velazquez has opened the doors so that other ethnic healers may leave their "underground" community domains and enter formal institutions that could train and license them in forms of innovative psychological practices and use those practices as an effective means of treatment.

Notes

1
Aileen Lucero, "A Profile of a Curandera and Her Curandera-Treated Clients: The Southwest Denver Community Mental Health Center" (Ph.D. diss., Washington State University, 1981), 1.

2
E. Fuller Torrey, *Witchdoctors and Psychiatrists: The Common Roots of Psychotherapy and Its Future* (New York: Harper and Row Publishers, 1986), 8.

3
Ibid.

4
Lucero, "A Profile of a Curandera," 3.

5
Bobette Perrone, H. Henrietta Stockel, and Victoria Kruger, *Medicine Women: Curanderas and Women Doctors* (Norman: University of Oklahoma Press, 1989), 86.

6
Torrey, *Witchdoctors and Psychiatrists*, 135.

7
Diana Velazquez, personal interview, July 23, 1993.

8
Perrone et al., *Medicine Women*, 88.

9
Ibid.

10
Ibid, 89-90.

11
Margaret Clark, *A Community Study: Health in the Mexican American Culture* (Berkeley: University of California Press, 1970); A. Kiev, *Curanderismo: Mexican American Folk Psychiatry* (New York: Free Press, 1968); W. Madsen, "Value Conflicts and Folk Psychotherapy," *Magic, Faith and Healing*, A. Kiev, ed. (New York: Free Press, 1964), 420-44; L. Saunders, *Cultural Difference and Medical Care: The Case for the Spanish Speaking People of the Southwest* (New York: Russell Sage Foundation, 1954); E. Fuller Torrey, *The Mind Game: Witchdoctors and Psychiatrists* (New York: Bantam Books, 1972).

12
Lucero, "A Profile of a Curandera," 6.

13
D. Alegria, E. Guerra, C. Martinez, Jr., and G. G. Meyer, "El Hospital Invisible: A Study of Curanderismo," *Archives of General Psychiatry* 34 (1977), 1354-7.

14
C. S. Scrimshaw and E. Burleigh, "The Potential for the Integration of Indigenous and Western Medicines in Latin America and Hispanic Popu-lations in the United States of America," *Modern Medicine and Medical Anthropology in the United States: Mexico Border Populations*, B. Velimirovic, ed. (Washington, D.C.: Pan American Health Organization, 1978), 36.

15
Velazquez, personal interview.

16
George M. Foster, "Relationships between Spanish and Spanish American Folk Medicine," *Journal of American Folklore* 66 (1953), 201-17; Madsen, "Value Conflicts and Folk Psychotherapy"; O. I. Romano, "Charismatic Medicine, Folk-Healing, and Folk-Sainthood," *American Anthropologist* 67 (1956), 1151-73.

17
Perrone et al., *Medicine Women*, 92.

18
Velazquez, personal interview.

19
Ibid.

20
Lucero, "A Profile of a Curandera," 15.

21
Velazquez, personal interview.

22
Ibid.

23
Lucero, "A Profile of a Curandera," 14.

24
Carlos Castaneda, *The Teachings of Don Juan: A Yaqui Way of Knowledge* (Berkeley: University of California Press, 1968), 86.

25
Richard A. Kurtz and H. Paul Chalfant, *The Sociology of Medicine and Illness* (Boston: Allyan and Bacon, Inc., 1984), 144.

26
Clark, *A Community Study*, 207.

27
Velazquez, personal interview.

28
Ibid.

29
Ibid.

30
Madsen, "Value Conflicts and Folk Psychotherapy"; Kiev, *Curanderismo*; Arthur J. Rubel, "The Epidemiology of a Folk Illness: Susto in Hispanic America," *Hispanic Culture and Health Care: Fact, Fiction, and Folklore*, Ricardo Arguijo Martinez, ed. (St. Louis: The C. V. Mosby Company, 1978).

31
Lucero, "A Profile of a Curandera," 36.

32
Kiev, *Curanderismo*, 1067.

33
Lucero, "A Profile of a Curandera," 37.

34
Velazquez, personal interview.

35
Ibid.

36
Ibid.

37
Ibid.

38
Ibid.

39
Ibid.

40
Madsen, *Mexican Americans of South Texas*, 95.

41
Torrey, *Witchdoctors and Psychiatrists.*

42
Velazquez, personal interview.

43
Torrey, *The Mind Game*, 25.

44
Kurtz and Chalfant, *The Sociology of Medicine and Illness*, 74.

Cultural Landscapes and Biodiversity:
The Ethnoecology of an Upper Río Grande Watershed Commons

Devon G. Peña

ABOUT THE AUTHOR

Devon G. Peña is a professor of sociology and environmental studies at the Colorado College. He lives and works at a small farm in El Rito, Colorado. Peña is an internationally recognized research scholar and has been published in the United States, Mexico, and Europe. His most recent books include *The Terror of the Machine: Technology, Work, Gender, and Ecology on the U.S.-Mexico Border* (University of Texas Press, 1997) and *Chicano Culture, Ecology, Politics: Subversive Kin* (University of Arizona Press, 1998).

This essay has been excerpted and modified from Ethnoecology: Situated Knowledge, Located Lives, *edited by Virginia D. Nazarea, to be published in 1999 by the University of Arizona Press. Published by permission.*

HIS ESSAY DESCRIBES the agroecology of Chicano family farms in the San Luis Valley of southern Colorado. Chicano farming systems are authentically multicultural, as they incorporate elements from three different continents: the *acequia* irrigation tradition with roots in North Africa; the riparian long-lot land use pattern from the Franco-Iberian villages of the Pyrenees; field crops from Native American and Mexican sources; and livestock and orchard crops from Mediterranean Europe.

The agroecology of Chicano farming systems promotes biodiversity through a variety of practices: acequia irrigation ditches create biological corridors and vital habitat; the riparian long-lot preserves multiple life zones and ecotones; and the conservation and use of native land races as family heirlooms preserves the genetic diversity of rare and endangered crops.

At the heart of these farming systems are the commons (*ejidos*) of the Spanish-Mexican land grants. This cultural landscape links watershed ecosystems of the high mountain peaks with farms and ranches in the bottom lands. The watershed is traditionally and historically treated as a common property resource. The restoration of traditional usufructuary rights to the commons is thus of pivotal importance in the preservation of these rare and endangered cultural landscapes.[1]

Introduction

The Upper Río Grande watershed is a thirty-four thousand square mile area stretching from the Rocky Mountains in southern Colorado and northern New Mexico to the Juarez Valley, across the border from El Paso, Texas.[2] The northernmost one-third of the watershed encompasses a seven-county area in northern New Mexico and southern Colorado with a predominantly Chicano (Spanish-Mexican origin) population.[3] This area is the principal headwaters bioregion of the Upper Río Grande but includes important tributaries of the Arkansas watershed. It consists of a series of high-altitude valleys that drain forested, snow-covered mountains.[4] At the end of the sixteenth century, coming north from Mexico, a diverse people began to settle in the intermontane valleys of the watershed.[5] The settlers established agropastoral villages that have been widely praised as examples of sustainable human adaptation to high-altitude, arid environments.[6] At the heart of these farm and ranch communities is the watershed commons. The high mountain peaks provide water, timber, pasture, medicinal plants, and wildlife for use in common by the villagers.

Watersheds have traditionally defined the boundaries of self-governing communities in the Upper Río Grande. This invention of political jurisdiction as derivative from a type of hydrographic unit was probably first described by John Wesley Powell in 1890. Writing on the possibilities for sustainable human settlement in the arid intermountain West, Powell observed:

> The people of the Southwest came originally, by the way of Mexico, from Spain, where irrigation and the institutions necessary for its control had been developed from high antiquity, and these people well understood that their institutions must be adapted to their industries, and so they organized their settlements as pueblos, or "irrigating municipalities," by which the lands were held in severalty while the tenure of the waters and works was communal or municipal. . . . [The goal of this irrigation tradition was] to establish local self-government by hydrographic basins.[7]

The organization of acequia-based farms and ranches of the Chicano upland villages of northern New Mexico and southern Colorado is an important example of this watershed commonwealth form of self-governance. The association of acequia members (*parciantes*) is a community of irrigators with shared responsibility in the care, maintenance, and use of the ditch networks. The irrigating municipality is a deeply rooted tradition for effective, local self-management of water and land. The ultimate responsibility of the acequia associations is the management of water rights and stewardship of the watershed commons. This tradition of local self-governance only recently has been recognized as a viable alternative in the debate over the future of the commons in the intermountain West.[8] Moreover, acequias are themselves innovations on the rhythms and patterns of the watershed, a type of disturbance ecology that, like beaver works, increases biodiversity by creating wildlife habitat.[9]

Ethnoecology of the Culebra Microbasin
The San Luis Valley in southern Colorado is a high-altitude, cold desert environment. The valley is topographically and climatically similar to the high steppes of central Asia. The valley has an average elevation of eight thousand feet above sea level and is surrounded by the fourteen-thousand-foot peaks of the Sangre de Cristo Mountains to the east and the San Juan Mountains to the west. The bioregion receives very little rain (with average annual precipitation of seven to eight inches). However, the high

mountain peaks on average receive more than one hundred inches of snow during the long seven-month winter season. The moisture from the snow-pack is what makes agriculture possible. The valley is the northernmost headwaters basin of the Río Grande, collecting stream flow from some fifty tributary creeks of the river that originate in the high peaks. One of these tributaries is the Río Culebra with headwaters in the Culebra Range, the southernmost extension of the Sangre de Cristo Mountains in Colorado.[10]

The Culebra Microbasin. The Culebra microbasin is home to the oldest agricultural communities in the state of Colorado. The Chicano villages of the Culebra were settled between 1850 and 1860 by *pobladores* (village colonists) invited by the heirs of the Sangre de Cristo land grant (issued in 1844).[11] The microbasin includes nearly every major life zone in North America, from alpine tundra above timberline (at twelve thousand feet and higher) to Upper Sonoran cold desert (at eight thousand feet and lower). Montane and subalpine fir forests located at nine to twelve thousand feet are the heart of the watershed. The forest canopy protects the winter snowpack. During the spring and summer the gradual melting of the snow is the primary source of water for irrigation in the microbasin.

Acequias. The irrigation system in the Culebra microbasin is based on the acequia or gravity ditch system. This irrigation tradition has independent roots in three continents: Africa, Europe, and North America.[12] The term *acequia* derives from the Arabic word, *asSaquiya*, the "water bearer" or "water carrier." Acequia irrigation systems are renowned around the world as culturally and ecologically sustainable technologies. They are notable for several reasons:

1) a renewable use of water maintains the equilibrium of the local hydro-logical cycle (through aquifer recharge and return to in-stream flows);

2) a renewable use of energy relies on the force of gravity to move water;

3) a network of earthen-work ditches increases biodiversity by creating wetlands and woodlands that serve as wildlife habitats and biological cor-ridors;

4) these woodlands and wetlands help control soil erosion and maintain water quality;

5) the collective community management of the acequia ditches provides a cultural foundation and an established institutional tradition for local self-governance and the reproduction of conservation ethics from one generation to the next.[13]

To work effectively, acequias rely on the gradual melting of winter snowpack in the mountains. Any disturbance of the watershed ecology can result in serious problems for acequias. For example, deforestation can lead to excessive sediment in the ditches, *arroyo* cutting, flooding, or lack of sufficient water during the irrigation season.[14]

In the Culebra microbasin, twenty-three historical acequia associations are represented by *mayordomos* (ditchriders) for each ditch.[15] These acequias hold the oldest water rights in Colorado under the doctrine of prior appropriation (see Table 1). For example, the San Luis People's Ditch, which has the first priority, was constructed in 1852, decreed in 1862, and adjudicated in 1889. The acequias are collectively organized under the umbrella of the Costilla County Conservancy District (CCCD) established in 1976.

The CCCD has played a major role in Colorado environmental politics. During the 1970s, the district led the opposition in successfully defeating a plan by the San Marcos Pipeline Company to mine the local groundwater aquifer to operate a coal slurry line. Repeatedly since the 1980s, the CCCD has been a major force lobbying against the reclassification of farmlands by the Colorado state legislature. These legislative initiatives would change the tax structure so that small farm properties (for example, with less than twenty acres or five thousand dollars in annual sales) would lose their status as agricultural land. These initiatives have been thrice opposed by the CCCD because the proposed reclassification would undermine the ability of Chicano smallholders to continue the sustainable tradition of subsistence agropastoralism in the San Luis Valley. In the late 1980s and early 1990s the acequias, through the CCCD, led the opposition to the Battle Mountain Gold (BMG) strip mine and cyanide leach mill.[16] As a result of the BMG struggle, the CCCD played a major role in a 1993 campaign to reform the Colorado Mined Land Reclamation Act (MLRA). Most recently, the CCCD has played a critical role in the establishment of La Sierra Foundation of San Luis, a community-based organization seeking the return of the Culebra Mountain Tract through a national fundraising campaign for a community land trust.[17]

Table I
Original Acequias, Culebra Microbasin

PRIORITY/DITCH	CONSTRUCTION DATE
1. San Luis People's Ditch	April 1852
2. San Pedro Ditch	April 1852
3. Acequia Madre Ditch	1853
4. Montez Ditch	August 1853
5. Vallejos Ditch	March 1854
6. Manzanares Ditch	April 1854
7. Acequiacita Ditch	June 1855
8. San Acacio Ditch	April 1856
9. Madriles Ditch	April 1856
10. Chalifu Ditch	April 1857
11. Cerro Ditch	November 1857
12. Francisco Sanchez Ditch	March 1858
13. Mestas Ditch	May 1858
14. San Francisco Ditch	May 1860
15. Trujillo Ditch	May 1861
16. Little Rock Ditch	1873
17. Garcia Ditch	1873
18. Torcido Ditch	May 1874
19. Abudo Martin Ditch	May 1874
20. Guadalupe Vigil Ditch	March 1880
21. Jack J. Maes Ditch	March 1881
22. Antonio Pando Ditch	April 1881
23. Guadalupe Sanchez Ditch	November 1882

The Culebra Mountain Tract. The Sangre de Cristo land grant originally encompassed approximately one million acres. But the traditional commons of the Culebra bottom land villages consists of a 77,754-acre tract that locals know as *la sierra*. The Culebra Mountain Tract includes one peak over fourteen thousand feet and eight over thirteen thousand feet in elevation. Until 1995, the area was relatively undisturbed and roadless. However, since 1995, some thirty-four thousand acres of montane and subalpine forests on *la sierra* have been logged by transnational timber companies under contract with the Taylor Family Estate.[18] The tract is apparently within the historic range of nesting pairs of the endangered Mexican spotted owl (*Strix occidentalis*), and its creeks are stocked with the native Colorado cutthroat trout (a rare and threatened species).[19] Most of the tract consists of montane and subalpine conifer forests with a mix of ponderosa, Douglas fir, and spruce. The higher elevations are characterized by alpine tundra, krummholz, and windswept rock lands that are under snow eight to ten months out of the year. Wet montane meadows and marshlands, aspen groves, piñon-juniper woodlands, riparian cottonwood and willow stands, and semidesert sagebrush prairies complete the variety of plant communities in the Mountain Tract.

Headwaters and Agroecology. An important feature of the ethnoecology of this microbasin is the relationship between the alpine and montane headwaters of the Culebra and the farms and ranches located below in the riparian bottom lands. Most local people strongly support the protection of wildlife and its habitat.[20] Local farmers and ranchers are particularly strong in their support of wildlife conservation through habitat protection because they recognize that the conditions optimizing wildlife habitat also help maintain watershed integrity and water quality.[21] The processes that destroy wildlife habitat and disrupt the watershed are seen to negatively affect farming and ranching. These farms and ranches are notable for their reliance on acequias, use of perennial polycultures, preference for rare native land races (regionally-adapted family heirloom crop varieties), and the clustering of wildlife habitats and farming landscapes. These farms and ranches are sustainable agroecosystems. A unique cultural-watershed landscape is endangered by industrial development and extractive activities affecting the ecosystem.[22]

Damage to the watershed presents a definite threat to the ecological basis of these farms and ranches. For example, a timber operation destroys wildlife habitat and reduces biodiversity. But it also creates soil erosion and channel aggradation, diminishes water quality, and causes problems with sedimentation for downstream acequias. Deforestation creates flood-control problems with the potential to irreversibly damage the acequias. Deforestation also accelerates the rate at which snowpack melts into stream flow.[23] Too much water comes down too fast at the wrong time. The entire agro-hydrological cycle is thrown off balance.

In the case of the Culebra watershed, limited storage rights for the acequias and overextended storage capacity in structurally unsound reservoirs create the conditions for a hydrological crisis. In other words, farmers and ranchers would not be able to manage the runoff and, lacking storage rights, most of the water for acequias would be lost to in-stream flows before the start of the irrigation season. The lack of sufficient water during the three- to four-month irrigation season would destroy the basis for sustainable agriculture in the microbasin.[24] A longstanding local struggle to restore communal ownership and use of the Culebra Mountain Tract stems from a desire by the irrigating community to prevent this sort of catastrophic damage.[25]

Chicano Agroecosystems: An Ideal Type

Agroecology provides an interdisciplinary framework for the study of farming communities in environmental and sociohistorical contexts.[26] Agroecology begins with an elegant, simple, and seemingly paradoxical premise: Agriculture is, above all else, a human artifact, yet the farming system does not end at the edge of the field. The primary tenet of agroecology is that the farm is itself an ecosystem and part of a larger ecosystem (it is located within a broader bioregional context). Proceeding from the basic recognition of the ecological context of agriculture, this research tradition emphasizes four foundational principles. Agroecology:

1) recognizes sense of place as a factor in the co-evolution of culture and nature and in the adaptation of agroecosystems to the physical and biological nuances of localities (ontological dimension);

2) values the preservation of local indigenous knowledge over the imposition of universal mechanistic knowledge and recognizes the sustainability of traditional agroecosystems (epistemological dimension);

3) privileges the production strategies of traditional polycultures over modern monocultures as a way to correct inequities in agricultural research and extension services (ethical dimension);

4) empowers traditional farmers by favoring local self-management of the natural conditions of production and promoting local control of political economic institutions (policy dimension).[27]

Agroecological approaches have not been used in the study of Chicano farming systems. And yet, Chicano agriculture provides a living laboratory for the study of the interactions between cultural, social, economic, political, and ecological systems in a context characterized by limited resources and relatively low levels of mechanized technology. Our preference for the agroecological approach is based on our concern for understanding these practices in a more holistic manner. We also want to endorse an ethically grounded political perspective that supports local initiatives for land reform and democratization of impinging market and state institutions.

Given current debates over the future of agricultural policy in the rural intermountain West, the nature of alternative and sustainable models must be made more salient. We must redefine the terms of this debate by outlining a comprehensive and interdisciplinary perspective of Chicano agricultural systems and studying their continuing evolution in contemporary practices.

The sustainability and dynamic character of Chicano agropastoralism is an intriguing possibility as both a historical legacy and a viable future option. But Chicano agriculture, as a set of living cultural ecological practices, has until now remained relatively unstudied at the level of specific historical research sites.[28] The remainder of this essay is the first in a series of reports focusing on multigenerational Chicano family farms and ranches that we have designated as historical research sites for an ongoing, long-term study of the cultural and environmental history of the Greater Río Grande watershed.[29] We chose these farms and ranches because they have remained in the same families for at least five or more generations and continue to be operated as profitable commercial agricultural enterprises.

Chicano agroecosystems in the Culebra microbasin are characterized by several prominent features that are hallmarks of sustainable and regenerative agriculture:

1) a riparian long-lot cultural geography characterized by multiple life zones and ecotones;

2) the use of acequia irrigation systems;

3) the clustering of wildlife habitats and farming landscapes;

4) a tradition of local and regional land races (native heirloom crop varieties);

5) the use of natural pest and weed controls with beneficial effects for soil fertility and erosion control;

6) the simultaneous production of row crops, forage crops, pastures, and livestock, and hence an integrated approach to soil conservation and range management;

7) a preference for polycultures and rotational intercropping;

8) the adoption of new soil, pasture, and water conservation practices;

9) a low level of mechanization and a preference for human and animal power;

10) the increasingly common practice of restoration ecology (to repair damaged lands);

11) a tendency towards autarkic prosumption (production for use and exchange);

12) the maintenance of access to traditional common lands for wood harvesting, hunting, fishing, limited rotational pasturing, and wildcrafting;

13) an increasingly self-organized and complex set of relationships with a variety of market and governmental institutions.

We present these as characteristics of an ideal-type. Note that we are not calling this "traditional" agropastoralism. Our point of view is that many changes have occurred in Chicano agriculture and that these thirteen features embrace both traditional and more modern practices. Nor are we suggesting that all Chicano agropastoralists are engaged in these practices. Many are not, but these features are prominent enough in most Upper Río Grande microbasins (both historically and contemporaneously) to warrant their inclusion in an ideal-type model. Where possible we have sought to compare and contrast Chicano agroecosystems with mechanized agroindustrial monocultures in order to highlight the sustainability of the agropastoral model.

1) *Riparian Long-Lot Cultural Geography.* Agropastoralism in this bioregion depends on a unique and endangered cultural landscape known as the riparian long-lot (see figure 1). After passage of the Land Ordinance of 1785, the United States established a national land survey program based on the township-and-range system. This system "divided the country from the Appalachian Mountains to the Pacific Coast into a rigid grid of square parcels one mile on a side, subdivided into quarter sections of 160 acres."[30] The square-grid system is incompatible with the topographical features and hydrographic boundaries of ecosystems in the intermountain West; it is inconsistent with the lay of the land, water, and native human communities. Anglo Americans, coming from the east to settle in this region, adopted the square-grid topography of the 1785 ordinance. This land use pattern homogenized natural and cultural landscapes by requiring the removal of woodlands, forests, wetlands, and other natural and cultural

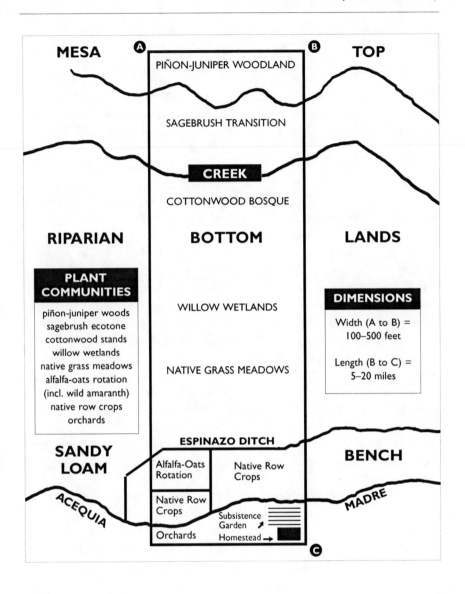

Figure 1.
THE RIPARIAN LONG-LOT

features that were considered obstacles to the mechanized economies-of-scale favored by Anglo Americans.

Instead of the square-grid settlement pattern adopted by temperate neo-European farmers and ranchers, Chicanos utilized the upland Franco-Iberian (and ultimately Roman) tradition of the riparian long-lot.[31] The long-lot represents a type of cultural landscape compatible with the bio-geographical properties of high-altitude arid environments. The cultural and ecological advantage of the long-lot is that it provides every family with access to most of the life zones in the locality. Ideally, every family has access to the piñon-juniper woodlands on the mesa tops and foothills for fuelwood and construction; dry land grass prairies for pasture; riparian bottom lands for access to water, fish, cottonwoods, and wetlands; and irrigated bench land meadows for the planting of row crops, pastures, orchards, and subsistence gardens. The riparian long-lot is not just a boundary-setting tradition. It is an ecosystem with multiple life zones and ecotones (transition zones). Many observers have commented that this agricultural settlement pattern is ecologically sustainable and well-adapted to the arid conditions of the Upper Río Grande watershed.[32]

In Spanish, this agricultural landscape is known as an *extensión*. In some areas of the Upper Río Grande it is called a *vara* strip, and in other areas it is known as a *tira*.[33] In the Lower Río Grande Valley of South Texas the long-lot is called a *porción*. The riparian long-lot is a ribbon-like strip of land that extends many miles through varied topographical and biotic zones. The size and shape of a long-lot can vary tremendously, depending on microbasin topography, socioeconomic class standing of owner(s), patterns of inheritance within families, and effects of enclosure of local common and private lands. The width of a long-lot can range from a little less than one hundred to as many as five hundred *varas* (one vara is equal to 33.3 inches).[34] The length of the long-lot is the significant factor in this cultural landscape. Estimates on the traditional length of long-lots vary from five or six miles to as many as twenty.[35]

2) Acequia Irrigation Systems. As we have seen, acequias (gravity-driven, earthen-ditch irrigation systems) are an integral part of rural Chicano communities, but they are also part of complex agroecosystems. In addition to delivering water to the irrigated fields and pastures, acequias fulfill a variety of ecological functions. What is most striking about the ditches is that they fulfill human objectives while simultaneously meeting the needs of wild plants and animals. This is an intrinsic conservation feature of Chicano agroecosystems that is often mistaken by water engineers and environmentalists as an inefficient and wasteful use of water.[36] Because the earthen ditches leak water into the land around them, they are associated with the water-loving phreataphytes (trees and shrubs with extensive root systems like cottonwoods and willows). This means that acequias increase biodiversity by contributing to the creation of wildlife habitats and biological corridors.

From the vantage point of agricultural energy systems, acequias are perhaps the most efficient of all arid land irrigation technologies.[37] Compared to the mechanical center-pivot sprinkler systems favored by agribusiness monocultures, the gravity-ditch systems do not require fossil fuel inputs. Mechanical irrigation systems utilize more energy inputs on a yearly basis, mostly in the form of diesel fuel to power the deep-well pumps that deliver groundwater to the sprinklers. Annual fuel costs for these mechanized systems can run as high as ten thousand dollars. In contrast, annual fuel costs for acequias are close to zero.

Another aspect of energy comparison is the nature of trophic and nutrient cycles. The combination of the riparian long-lot with the acequia system contributes to the maintenance of the trophic complexity of the ecosystem by encouraging an optimum mix of relationships among livestock, wildlife, crops, weeds, trees, shrubs, insects, and pathogens. The mechanized system, in contrast, disrupts the trophic webs by homogenizing the landscape and eliminating habitat niches and biological corridors. The acequias actually enhance the flow of energy circuits through the expanded interaction of land, water, flora, and fauna. Mechanized irrigation interrupts these trophic circuits by imposing uniform monocultures on naturally diverse landscapes. Finally, the long-lot/acequia complex also reduces energy inputs by relying on relatively self-enclosed nutrient cycling—that is, all nutrient requirements are met by in situ components of the soil and biota. The mechanized irrigation systems are characterized by open-nutrient cycling—that is, they require high inputs in the form of agroindustrial chemical supplements such as fertilizers, herbicides, and pesticides.

3) Clustering of Wildlife Habitats and Fanning Landscapes. The riparian long-lot cultural landscape is characterized by an extraordinary level of biological diversity. The landscape itself, because it includes different life zones, is supportive of an incredible variety of wild plants and animals. In this form, the vara-strip agricultural landscapes serve as wildlife habitats and biological corridors linking diverse habitat islands in a given microbasin. One characteristic of Chicano agroecosystems is the existence of amorphous boundaries between natural and cultural landscapes. The boundaries between pastures and wildlife habitat are less definite in this system. In contrast, mechanized monocultures reduce biodiversity because they homogenize and separate the natural and cultural landscapes.

The significance of this landscape-clustering feature of Chicano agroecosystems is implied in observations made by a variety of conservation biologists. For example, Reed Noss, a key figure in the field of island biogeography, notes that:

> The only success stories in real multiple-use conservation are a handful of indigenous peoples who have somehow been able to coexist with their environments for long periods without impoverishing them. Some indigenous cultures have even contributed to the biodiversity of their regions . . . suggesting that humans have the potential to act as a keystone species in the most positive sense. The beaver provides a good model of how humans could contribute to native biodiversity by creating habitats used by many different species.[38]

We would like to suggest that Chicano agroecosystems, based as they are on the riparian long-lot/acequia complex, constitute one such example of an indigenous cultural practice that contributes to biodiversity through the protection of the natural landscape integrity of the watershed ecosystem.

4) Heirloom Crops: Native Land Races. Chicano agroecosystems are also characterized by the farmers' preference for native land races (indigenous, locally-adapted crops). Few Chicano farmers produce hybrid crops. There is an extraordinary range of land races grown. These are usually family heirloom crop varieties: the seed stocks have been in the same families for many generations. The use of heirloom land races means that Chicano farmers are conserving the genetic diversity of food crops and encouraging the adaptation of these varieties to local climatic conditions. This also means that Chicano farmers do not have to utilize high-cost inputs like agroindustrial chemical fertilizers, herbicides, or pesticides. These native plant species are naturally resistant to pathogens and, in some cases, drought. Moreover, because the plants produce fertile seeds, the farmers do not have to rely on seed merchants for their annual seed stocks. The average Chicano farm has a considerable amount of native crop biodiversity (see Table 2). This biodiversity eliminates the need for chemical inputs, provides for natural pest and weed controls, and encourages intercropping practices that are beneficial to the soil and its nutrient cycles.

In contrast, the agroindustrial monocultures rely on sterile hybrids for their seed stocks (which makes them dependent on seed merchants and suppliers). Hybrids typically require high inputs to attain higher yields; these inputs include agricultural chemicals (pesticides, herbicides, and fertilizers) and considerable quantities of water for irrigation.[39] The use of hybrids also tends to be associated with the erosion of crop genetic diversity. And there are usually additional impacts involving higher rates of soil erosion, salinization, and compaction.

Some of the heirloom land races characteristic of Chicano agroecosystems include: *chicos* (white roasting corn), *bolitas* (a beige-colored bean related to the pinto), *habas* (horse beans), a wide variety of *chiles* (hot green peppers), and *calabacita* (Mexican green squash). Chicano agroecosystems tend not to have extensive plots of land dedicated to alfalfa or other crops for livestock feeding. The Chicano farmer favors a combination of land races for row crops, native grasses for pasture, and a variety of imported hybrids and exotic land races for subsistence gardens. In addition, Chicano agroecosystems typically include orchards with both exotic fruit trees (apple, pear, plum, and cherry), native berry shrubs (for example, chokecherry), and a wild miniature plum known locally as *cirhuelita del indio* (see Table 2 for a partial list of crops grown on Chicano farms).

5) Natural Pest and Weed Controls. Given the biodiversity of crops grown in Chicano agroecosystems, it is not surprising that natural (biological) pest and weed controls are the order of the day. The primary form of weed and pest control involves careful intercropping of land race crops. Intercropping, combined with rotational plantings, creates a condition known as "allelopathy" (what the home gardener knows as "companion planting" and ecologists recognize as a chemical interrelationship between plants). For example, the traditional trinity of Indian crops—corn, beans, and squash—does more than provide a balanced diet. Together, these companion plants work to fertilize the soil (beans as legumes are nitrogen-fixers), control weeds and soil erosion (squash as a ground-cover plant reduces weed invasions and soil loss), and eliminate many insect pests (the biodiversity and adaptation of the three crops to local microclimate and soil conditions helps them resist disease and infestation).[40]

Perhaps the most important feature of the native land race complex is the crop genetic diversity it confers on the agroecosystem:

Traditional agroecosystems are genetically diverse, containing populations of variable and adapted land races as well as wild relatives of

Table 2
Domesticated Crops, Animals, and Grasses in Hispano Agroecosystems

CROPS	ANIMALS	GRASSES
bolita beans ◆	cats	black grama ◆
broccoli (3)	cattle (6)	blue fescue ◆
cabbage (2)	chickens (8)	blue grama ◆
calabacita ◆	dogs	brohme ◆
carrots (3)	ducks (5)	luna crested wheat
cauliflower	geese (3)	redtop ◆
chicos (7) ◆	goats (5)	timothy ◆
chives	guinea fowl	western crested wheat
cilantro	hogs (6)	
corn (blue) ◆	horses	
corn (yellow sweet)	rabbits	
decorative flowers	sheep (4)	
(gladiolus, etc.)		
English peas		
habas (horse beans) ◆		
lettuce (3)		
onions		
parsley		
pinto beans ◆		
potatoes (5)		
string beans		
sweet peas		
turnips		
vine tomatoes (5)		
wheat (3)		
yellow crookneck		
squash		
zucchini		
ORCHARD CROPS		
apple (2)		
cherry (2)		
chokecherry ◆		
pear		
plum (3) (1◆)		

Numbers in parentheses indicate horticultural varieties and breeds.
◆   **indicates native land race.**

crops. Land race populations consist of mixtures of genetic lines, all of which are reasonably adapted to the region in which they evolved, but which differ in reaction to diseases and insect pests. Some lines are resistant or tolerant to certain races of pathogens and some to other races. The resulting genetic diversity confers at least partial resistance to diseases that are specific to particular strains of the crop and allows farmers to exploit different microclimates and derive multiple uses from the genetic variation of a given species.[41]

Chicano agroecosystems can thus be characterized as land race polycultures that feature both species and structural diversity. They exploit the full range of micro-environments, maintain and enhance nutrient cycles and soil tilth, rely on biological interdependencies that provide pest control, rely on local resources with little mechanical technology, rely on local varieties of crops, and incorporate wild plants and animals.[42]

6) Holistic Land and Livestock Management. One of the most significant, and most often overlooked, characteristics of Chicano agroecosystems is their integration of farming and ranching. As noted earlier, Chicano agroecosystems are not just farms and not just ranches: they typically incorporate aspects of both production systems—hence the term *agropastoral*. The typical Chicano agropastoral operation produces at least four types of plant crops: row crops (corn, bean, squash, chile, etc.), forage crops (alfalfa, hay, etc.), pastures (native grasses like timothy, blue fescue, redtop, and brome), and subsistence garden crops (corn, bean, squash, chile, tomatoes, peas, broccoli, etc.). But these operations also produce livestock—typically cattle, sheep, goats, pigs, and horses. This integration of crops, forage, pasture, and livestock increases biodiversity and maintains trophic complexity. The presence of farm animals also makes a steady supply of organic fertilizer available in the form of manure. Sheep and goats can be used to control invasive noxious weeds.

Land and range management practices in Chicano agroecosystems are centered on controlling three types of problems: overgrazing, soil fertility, and soil erosion. The use of Holistic Resource Management (HRM) practices to control grazing and soil erosion is increasingly evident.[43] The HRM model involves several primary practices: rotational grazing to reduce pressures on forage and pasture crops; electrical paddocks to control livestock movements and concentrations; and intense human supervision of grazing animals.[44]

7) Polycultures and Rotational Intercropping. Chicano agroecosystems combine elements of both perennial and annual polycultures. The perennial polycultures include native grass meadows that are never tilled or cultivated. These meadows are used as rotational pastures for grazing livestock. The annual polycultures include row crops that can be intercropped (with the corn-bean-squash-chile complex being the most common). The row crop plantings usually involve minimum tillage and plowing.[45] Some Chicano agropastoralists have in more recent times adopted monoculture plantings of alfalfa and other forage and livestock crops. However, Chicanos usually avoid alfalfa monocultures and, in most cases, plantings follow eight- to twelve-year rotational sequences: for example, alfalfa-oats-barley-corn. Rotations often include a period of fallow.

8) Soil and Water Conservation. Chicano agroecosystems have historically experienced fewer problems with soil erosion compared to agroindustrial monocultures. Several features contribute to soil conservation. First, most Chicano agropastoralists practice zero or minimum tillage, particularly in the native grass meadows that predominate in the riparian bottom lands. Second, where tillage and cultivation are practiced, the combination of crop diversity and cover crops reduces soil erosion. Third, since most agropastoralists avoid large-scale mechanization, there are fewer erosive impacts from the use of heavy machinery. Fourth, most agropastoralists practice "organic" farming, with very little use of agroindustrial chemicals; organic farming practices tend to increase soil tilth and reduce soil erosion.

Other factors contribute to soil conservation on Chicano farms and ranches. Historically, since Chicanos were the first to settle in their respective microbasins, they tend to have the best land; few Chicanos have been pushed off onto marginal lands that are more erosive. Chicanos have tended to farm only in riparian bottom lands: these areas have deeper soil horizons (usually dating to Pleistocene deposition) and tend to be protected from wind erosion by the proximity of higher lands (such as mesas and foothills). Another contributing factor to soil conservation is the existence of numerous windbreaks. The acequia networks, as we have seen, create cottonwood and willow stands which double as windbreaks. Tree-lines, woodlots, orchards, and naturally occurring wetland willow and cottonwood stands provide further protection against wind erosion.

Under certain circumstances, acequia irrigation practices can contribute to soil erosion. Such circumstances nearly always involve human error: for example, flooding fields with excessive amounts of water or irrigating at too rapid a pace can contribute to soil erosion from runoff. In some cases, farmers may inappropriately try to irrigate fields with too steep a gradient. If fields are furrowed at angles parallel to the gradient, erosion may also result. However, the main cause of soil erosion in Chicano agroecosystems has been overgrazing.[46] Overgrazing became a problem only after the conquest of the bioregion by the United States: the commercialization of livestock production, the expanded demand for beef occasioned by the arrival of the railroad, and the opening of new markets were major factors in the overgrazing of these lands.[47] More recently, Chicanos have adopted a variety of strategies to control grazing (for example, HRM as noted above).

The establishment of the Soil Conservation Service (SCS) has, on the whole, proven beneficial to Chicano practices. However, the SCS has a mixed record in attending to the needs of Chicano agropastoralists. Like the Extension Service, the SCS has not always placed a high priority on the needs of Chicano agricultural regions, and in some cases the SCS encouraged Chicanos to destroy woodlands in order to expand the acreage under cultivation with alfalfa monocrops. In more recent years, the SCS (now the Natural Resource and Conservation Service, or NRCS) has increased its Chicano staff and emphasized projects in "limited resource" farming communities. Some of the more interesting projects include the introduction of regenerative and restorationist projects to assist locals in repairing damaged lands.

Water conservation is another aspect of Chicano agroecosystems. The acequia irrigation tradition has been criticized as wasteful and inefficient; this criticism is most often made by state hydrologists and environmentalists. The debate has raged for decades, with critics emphasizing the "loss" of water since most acequias are earthen works. This has led to pressure to "line" the ditches with concrete to prevent the leakage of water. But the "loss" of water is a matter of perspective: the water is lost to what legal experts call "beneficial human use." But from an ecological perspective, the leaking water is not lost. We have already noted that acequias create habitat niches and biological corridors and thus contribute to the maintenance of biodiversity. The water "lost" by leaking acequias is very much a part of the local hydrological cycle. The water returns to the cycle via evapotranspiration (the evaporation of water through plant life) and aquifer recharge. These processes can contribute to cooler and wetter local microclimates: evapotranspiration, for example, contributes to local rain cycles through convection currents that result in summer afternoon thunderstorms.

9) Low Mechanization/Human and Animal Power. Chicano agroeco-systems are characterized by low levels of mechanization. The cultural landscape of the riparian long-lot does not lend itself easily to extensive mechanization: most long-lots are too narrow for the use of large machinery like combines or center-pivot sprinkler systems. The huge capital expenditure required for large machinery further discourages mechanization on most Chicano farms and ranches. Historically, Chicano farmers and ranchers have relied on human and animal power for plowing, planting, cultivating, and harvesting. As long as family labor is available, the incentive to mechanize remains low. However, increasing mechanization is apparent on some farms and ranches. The use of tractors, moldboard plows, windrowers (swathers), and balers is not altogether uncommon, particularly among Chicanos who produce alfalfa and hay for livestock feed.

10) Restoration Ecology. Given historical problems with overgrazing and soil erosion, some Chicano farmers and ranchers have adopted regenerative and restorative agricultural practices to repair damaged lands. One practice involves the restoration (really rehabilitation) of the native dry land grass prairie ecology that was predominant in much of the bioregion before the advent of the railroad and commercial livestock raising. The native blue grama prairies were overgrazed in much of the bioregion between the 1890s and 1930s.[48] Restoration in the Culebra microbasin is becoming more common as Chicano farmers, working with the NRCS and other agencies, reestablish prairies using a combination of native and exotic dry land grasses.

11) Autarkic Prosumption. Perhaps one of the reasons Chicano farms and ranches endure is that they have always produced both for subsistence and for the market. Production for subsistence, or prosumption, has stabilized farming operations during bust cycles in the economy, insulating the small-holders against the loss of land and keeping them in agricultural production. During periods of rising market demand, Chicanos have responded by producing and delivering farm produce to the market (in this region, particularly organic produce markets in northern New Mexico). This autarkic quality has allowed Chicano agropastoralists to survive the boom/bust cycles of the economy. Moreover, when market conditions have been poor, local producers have turned to traditional bartering networks.

12) Common Property Resources. Chicano agroecosystems have traditionally relied on access to the common lands of community land grants. Access to common property resources is a critical component in the sustainability of the agropastoral tradition. The availability of common lands for limited rotational grazing, fuelwood gathering, hunting, fishing, and wildcrafting (the harvesting of edible wild plants and medicinals) has helped to stabilize Chicano agroecosystems and reduce land degradation on the private riparian long-lots. However, enclosure of these common lands has proven profoundly detrimental to the agropastoralists. In the Upper Río Grande, enclosure has been practically universal and has destroyed the ability of many families to remain in agriculture. The restoration of common lands is thus one of the most important unresolved issues facing the ethnoecology of Chicano farming communities. Restoration, in this context, is twofold: it involves both the ecological restoration of degraded common lands and the restoration of traditional usufructuary rights.[49]

13) Links to Market and Governmental Institutions. Chicano agropastoralists have always produced for the market and not just for subsistence; this is why there was a long tradition in the bioregion of constructing *carretas* (carts) to transport farm produce to the market. From 1848 through the 1970s, Chicano agropastoralists experienced discrimination in credit markets. Many were denied credit by banks and other agricultural production creditors. However, this may have proven itself to be a blessing in disguise. Since Chicanos could not gain access to credit, they avoided debt and thus the loss of land that is often associated with indebtedness to creditors. Since the late 1970s, Chicano agropastoralists have enjoyed relatively unfettered access to credit markets and have demonstrated their ability to utilize this access to their own advantage. It is not uncommon for Chicanos to make use of producer credit associations and federal and private banks to expand their operations or acquire new land.[50]

Like non-Chicano producers, Chicanos are establishing relationships with a variety of governmental agencies to improve and strengthen their agricultural operations. In addition to relationships with private and public sector creditors, Chicanos are working with a full range of governmental agencies like the Extension Service, NRCS, Agricultural Stabilization and Conservation Service, and U.S. Forest Service. Chicanos have played a key role in the establishment of soil conservation districts and are active in federal projects such as the Conservation Reserve Program, designed to protect wetlands and other landscapes that provide wildlife habitat.

Conclusion

The ethnoecology of Chicano farming systems in the Culebra microbasin is characterized by three primary elements:

1) The riparian long-lot/acequia cultural landscape. This ethnoecological complex promotes and protects biodiversity and represents a sustainable adaptation to local environmental and cultural conditions in high-altitude, arid-zone watersheds.

2) An autochthonous form of local democratic self-governance (acequias, i.e., the irrigating municipality). The watershed commonwealth serves two primary roles in the agropastoral community: "technical" (as in the maintenance and operation of the ditch networks) and "ethical" (as in the transgenerational reproduction of land and water conservation values).

3) A set of ethnoscientific practices derived from local knowledge. These agroecological practices utilize renewable energy systems, mimic natural patterns in their species and structural diversity, preserve the diversity of heirloom germplasms, contribute to a local sense of place and land ethics, and contribute to sustainable patterns for agriculture in regional political and economic context.

Cultural landscapes in Chicano agroecosystems, i.e., the riparian long-lot/acequia complex, clearly present a unique set of opportunities for the protection of biological diversity. For example, from the perspective of island biogeography we might argue that these agroecosystems serve as habitat islands and biological corridors connecting larger regional islands. Under these circumstances, farming and ranching are directly productive of biodiversity because the land use pattern encourages the protection of an optimum mix of plant and animal communities. The practices that sustain the land and water also provide stability for the agropastoral community.

The place of the Culebra microbasin within the larger context of the Upper Río Grande bioregion must also be noted. The seventy-seven thousand acre Culebra Mountain Tract is located midway between the southern and northern watersheds of the Sangre de Cristo mountain range. Until very recent times, it was essentially a roadless area, particularly at elevations in the ten to fourteen thousand foot range (the heart of the watershed). Unfortunately, since 1995, logging on the tract has resulted in the removal of more than seventy million board feet of timber. The construction of several hundred miles of new roads and thousands of skid

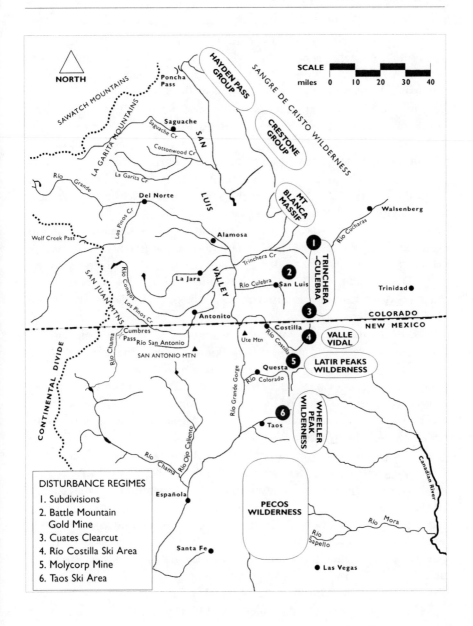

Figure 2. ISLAND BIOGEOGRAPHY
OF THE SANGRE DE CRISTO MOUNTAINS

trails have further fragmented the natural landscape and wildlife habitat of *la sierra*. An intense struggle has occurred as local ranchers and farmers join with environmental activists to stop logging damage to the Culebra watershed.[51] Despite the logging damage, the Culebra Mountain Tract remains a critical habitat and biological corridor linking the southern and northern Sangre de Cristo mountain range. Its protection and restoration are considered critical to the integrity of the southern Rockies ecosystem.

The Sangre de Cristo Mountains can be seen as comprised of two watersheds, each with several important microbasins. In the southern watershed are the Pecos Wilderness (by Santa Fe), Wheeler Peak Wilderness (Taos), Latir Peaks Wilderness (Questa), and Valle Vidal (Costilla) (see figure 2). The transitional (central) zone includes the Culebra Mountain Tract and the Forbes Trinchera. The northern watershed includes the Mount Blanca massif, the Crestone Group (lying north to northeast of the Sand Dunes National Monument), and the Hayden Pass Group—these three northern mountain groups constitute the officially designated Sangre de Cristo Wilderness Area.

There are many serious threats to the integrity of these biological island habitats. The Pecos and Wheeler Peak Wilderness areas have been severely impacted by overgrazing and excessive recreational uses (such as back-country hiking and camping). The Taos ski area presents a threat to the Wheeler Peak microbasin, while a molybdenum mine in Questa threatens the Red River and Latir Peaks areas. Battle Mountain Gold presents additional mining threats in the Rito Seco area of the Culebra microbasin, and the Forbes Trinchera with its three subdivisions threatens the watershed from real estate development and four hundred miles of roadways associated with widespread construction and timber operations. The Culebra Mountain Tract is still considered an important component of the natural landscape linkages essential for the protection of habitat for numerous wildlife species listed as rare, threatened, endangered, or endemic to the Sangre de Cristo mountain biome. Most recently, *la sierra* was identified as a "potential landscape linkage" in a map prepared for the Northern Rockies Ecosystem Protection Act (NREPA).[52]

The struggle to protect the Culebra as a biological corridor between the southern and northern Sangre de Cristos is developing in the context of a campaign for the preservation of rare and endangered cultural landscapes. The most vulnerable aspect of this ethnoecological complex is the need for a healthy, undisturbed watershed. Therefore, the most critical public policy and organizing challenges for the farming communities of the Culebra microbasin center around land reform (the restoration of a common property regime) and environmental degradation (a result of the enclosure of the commons).[53] At stake in this struggle is the preservation of a national environmental treasure and the survival of a human community that has evolved into a rare example of a human "keystone species."

Notes

Originally prepared for "Ethnoecology: Different Takes and Emergent Properties," a 1993 conference organized by the Ethnoecology and Biodiversity Laboratory of the University of Georgia, this work was supported by research grants from the National Endowment for the Humanities and the Hulbert Center for Southwestern Studies at the Colorado College. The views expressed are the sole responsibility of the author. The author gratefully acknowledges the assistance of Estevan Arellano, Bob Curry, Eric Del Balso, Malcolm Ebright, Joe Gallegos, Reyes Garcia, Bob Green, Jack Harlan, Sariya Jarasviroj, Miriam Manzanares, Maclovio Martinez, Kimberly Sanchez, and Megan Sherman.

1

Usufructuary rights in this context are defined as the rights to cultivate crops and otherwise use common-property lands as long as those lands remain protected and unharmed.

2

John Hay, "Upper Río Grande: Embattled River," *Aridity and Man: The Challenge of the Arid Lands in the United States*, Carle Hodge, ed. (Washington, D.C.: American Association for the Advancement of Science, 1963), 491.

3

This cultural "headwaters" bioregion includes the counties of Río Arriba, Taos, Mora, San Miguel, and Guadalupe in New Mexico and Costilla and Conejos in Colorado. This roughly covers the distance from San Luis, Colorado, to Española, New Mexico (approximately one hundred

thirty river miles).

4

More than 99 percent of the water supply in the Upper Río Grande comes from this headwaters bioregion in southern Colorado and northern New Mexico. Most of the water is runoff from melting snow in the high mountains. Technically, most of Mora and San Miguel counties are in the Arkansas and Pecos River watersheds, but these are also predominantly Chicano areas and share cultural and familial ties with the rest of the "Río Arriba." See Hay, "Upper Río Grande," 491.

5

The oldest Spanish-Mexican settlement in the Upper Río Grande was San Gabriel (settled in 1598). The oldest existing settlement is Santa Fe (settled in 1610).

Most of the settlers who came to work on the land were mestizos (the offspring of Indian and Spanish mixtures). The Spanish-speaking peoples of the Upper Río Grande are thus primarily the descendants of indigenous mestizos and not full-blooded Spaniards. We prefer to use the term "Chicano" (instead of "Spanish-American" or "Hispanic") in order to acknowledge the diverse character of the mestizo culture, which has roots in Mexican, Native American, Iberian, and Moorish (North African) cultural traditions. See Devon G. Peña, ed., *Chicano Culture, Ecology, Politics: Subversive Kin*, Society, Place, and Environment Series (Tucson: University of Arizona Press, 1998).

6
The agropastoral upland village is based on the integration of farming and livestock raising. For more on the cultural ecology of Chicano agro-pastoralism see John R. Van Ness, "Hispanic Land Grants: Ecology and Subsistence in the Uplands of Northern New Mexico and Southern Colorado," *Land, Water, and Culture: New Perspectives on Hispanic Land Grants*, Charles L. Briggs and John R. Van Ness, eds. (Albuquerque: University of New Mexico Press, 1987), 141-216; Devon G. Peña, "The 'Brown' and the Green': Chicanos and Environmental Politics in the Upper Río Grande," *Capitalism, Nature, Socialism* 3 (1, 1992), 79-103; Peña, *Chicano Culture, Ecology, Politics*.

7
John Wesley Powell, "Institutions for the Aridlands," *Century Magazine* 40 (May-October 1890), 112-14; see also Donald Worster, *An Unsettled Country: Changing Landscapes of the American West* (Albuquerque: University of New Mexico Press, 1994), 1-28.

8
See Charles H. Wilkinson, *The Eagle Bird: Mapping the New West* (Tucson: University of Arizona Press, 1988); Charles H. Wilkinson, *Crossing the Next Meridian: Land, Water, and the Future of the West* (Washington, D.C.: Island Press, 1992).

9
See Reyes Garcia, "A Philosopher in Aztlan: Notes toward an Ethno-meta-physics in the IndoHispano (Chicano) Southwest" (Ph.D. diss., University of Colorado, Boulder, 1989); Peña, "The 'Brown' and the 'Green'"; Peña,

Chicano Culture, Ecology, Politics. See also the intriguing commentary by Reed Noss in "A Sustainable Forest Is a Diverse and Natural Forest," *Clearcut: The Tragedy of Industrial Forestry*, Bill DeVall, ed. (San Francisco: Sierra Club, 1994), 33-8.

10
Technically, the Culebra microbasin is not considered tributary to the Río Grande. Since the turn of the century, when EuroAmerican farmers con-structed reservoirs in the watershed, the Río Culebra does not normally reach the Río Grande, twenty miles west, as a surface flow. However, the watershed is still connected to the Río Grande via groundwater aquifers.

11
The villages of the Culebra include: Viejo San Acacio (settled temporarily in 1850 and permanently in 1853), San Luis (1851), San Pablo (1852), San Pedro (1852), San Francisco (1854), Chama (1855), and Los Fuertes (1860?). On the settlement of the Sangre de Cristo land grant, see Arnold A. Valdez and Maria A. Valdez, "The Culebra River Villages of Costilla County: Village Architecture and Its Historical Context, 1851–1940," unpublished manuscript (Denver: Office of Archaeology and Historic Preservation, 1991); and Marianne Stoller, "The Settlement History of the San Luis Valley," unpublished manu-script (Colorado Springs: Department of Anthropology, Colorado College, 1992).

12
Devon G. Peña, "Acequias and Chicana/o Land Ethics" (Paper pre-sented at the Thirty-fifth Annual Conference of the Western Social

Science Association, Corpus Christi, April 1993).

13
See Peña, "Acequias and Chicana/o Land Ethics"; Peña, *Chicano Culture, Ecology, Politics.*

14
Revenue Potential and Ethical Issues in the Management of the Culebra Mountain Tract as a Common Property Resource, prepared by Robert Green and Devon Peña (San Luis, Colo.: Costilla County Conservancy District, 1993); Robert Curry, *State of the Culebra Watershed I: The Southern Tributaries*, technical report (San Luis, Colo.: Costilla County Conservancy District, 1994).

15
In addition to the twenty-three acequias with original nineteenth-century water rights, another forty-five acequias in the Culebra microbasin have more junior surface water rights.

16
See Devon G. Peña and Joseph Gallegos, "Nature and Chicanos in Southern Colorado," *Confronting Environmental Racism: Voices from the Grassroots*, Robert Bullard, ed. (Boston: South End Press, 1993), 141-60.

17
See Devon G. Peña and Maria Mondragon Valdez, "The 'Brown' and the 'Green' Revisited: Chicanos and Environmental Politics in the Upper Río Grande," *The Quest for Ecological Democracy: Movements for Environmental Justice in the United States*, Daniel Faber, ed. (New York: Guilford Press, 1998); *A Proposal for the Establishment of a Community Land Trust Based on the Principles of Environmental Justice* (San Luis, Colo.: La Sierra Foundation of San Luis, 1995).

18
In addition, the BMG strip mine and cyanide leach vat processing mill are located on land abutting the Mountain Tract in the Rito Seco watershed; see Peña and Gallegos, "Nature and Chicanos."

19
Bruce Webb, "Distribution and Nesting Requirements of Montane Forest Owls in Colorado, Part IV: Spotted Owl (*Strix occidentalis*)," *Colorado Field Ornithologists Journal* 17 (1, 1983), 2-8; Richard T. Reynolds, "Distribution and Habitat of Mexican Spotted Owls in Colorado: Preliminary Results," unpublished report (Laramie, Wyo.: Rocky Mountain Forest and Range Experiment Station, 1990).

20
Devon G. Peña, Ruben Martinez, and Louis McFarland, "Rural Chicana/o Communities and the Environment: An Attitudinal Survey of Residents of Costilla County, Colorado," *Perspectives in Mexican American Studies* 4 (August 1993), 45-74.

21
Revenue Potential and Ethical Issues.

22
Ibid.; Peña, *Chicano Culture, Ecology, Politics.*

23
Flooding is especially a problem during the "rain on snow" events characteris-

tic of the area during the wet months of spring through early summer. Rain accelerates the rate at which snowpack melts, especially in exposed cut block areas.

24
For a scientific study of the impact of timber operations on the Culebra watershed, see Curry, *State of the Culebra Watershed I*.

25
For more on the land rights struggle in San Luis, see: Marianne Stoller, "La Sierra y la Merced," *La Cultura Contante de San Luis*, R. Tweeuwen, ed. (San Luis, Colo.: San Luis Museum and Cultural Center, 1985); *A Proposal for the Establishment of a Community Land Trust*; Peña and Mondragon Valdez, "The 'Brown' and the 'Green' Revisited"; Peña and Gallegos, "Nature and Chicanos"; Peña, *Chicano Culture, Ecology, Politics*.

26
For an overview of the principles of agroecology, see Miguel Altieri, Susanna Hecht, and Richard Norgaard, *Agroecology: The Scientific Basis of Alternative Agriculture* (Boulder, Colo.: Westview Press, 1987).

27
For further discussion see Altieri et al., *Agroecology*.

28
Much of previous research has been done at the level of regions, communities, or land grants and not specific farms and ranches. Moreover, previous research is based on cultural/ecological and not ethnoecological principles.

29
This research was funded by a four-year grant from the National Endowment for the Humanities (NEH) with matching support from the Colorado College. The views expressed herein are the sole responsibility of the author and in no manner are to be taken as indicative of the official views or policies of the NEH or the federal government.

30
Worster, *An Unsettled Country*, 12.

31
The Metis of Canada fought a war (in 1868–70 and 1885) with the British over the imposition of the square-grid land survey system. The Metis, of French-Native Canadian mixture, were one of the few other major ethnic communities, besides the Chicanos, to make use of the riparian long-lot in North America. The Metis ultimately lost this struggle, while the Chicano cultural landscapes endure through the present. See John Wesley Powell, *Report on the Lands of the Arid Region of the United States* (Cambridge: Belknap Press of Harvard University Press, 1962), 34, note 7; Joseph Kinsey Howard, *Strange Empire* (New York: Morrow, 1952).

32
The first to make this argument was John W. Powell ("Institutions for the Aridlands," 111-16); see also Van Ness, "Hispanic Land Grants," and Peña, "The 'Brown' and the 'Green.'"

33
In the San Luis Valley, the long-lot is called a *vara* strip or *extensión*; in the

Embudo-Velarde-Alcalde region it
is called a *tira*. The author thanks
Estevan Arellano for this clarification
on the regional nuances of the local
vernacular terms used to describe this
cultural landscape.

34
The *vara* is a unit of measurement used
in the ancient metes and bounds system; one vara is approximately 33.3
inches wide. The vara measures width
and not length. In the IberoAmerican
system, length is measured by leagues
(*leguas*). See John R. Van Ness and
Christine M. Van Ness, eds., *Spanish
and Mexican Land Grants in New
Mexico and Colorado* (Manhattan,
Kans.: Sunflower University Press,
1980), 9.

35
The traditional length of long-lots is
five or six miles as suggested by Chris
Wilson and David Kammer,
*Community and Continuity: The
History, Architecture and Cultural
Landscape of La Tierra Amarilla*
(Santa Fe: New Mexico Historic
Preservation Division, 1990); fifteen to
twenty miles according to Marianne
Stoller, "Preliminary Manuscript on
the History of the Sangre de Cristo
Land Grant and the Claims of the
People of the Culebra River Villages on
Their Lands" (Colorado Springs:
Department of Anthropology,
Colorado College, 1993); or ten miles
as per Alvar Ward Carlson, "Rural
Settlement Patterns in the San Luis
Valley," *The Colorado Magazine* 44
(2, 1967), 111-28.

36
See Devon G. Peña, "A Gold Mine, an
Orchard, and an Eleventh Command-
ment," in Peña, *Chicano Culture,*

Ecology, Politics; Joseph Gallegos,
"Acequia Tales," ibid.

37
A. Hall, G. H. Cannell, and H. W.
Lawton, eds., "Agriculture in Semi-
Arid Environments," *Ecological
Studies* 34 (Berlin: Springer-Verlag,
1979), 29-44.

38
Noss, "A Sustainable Forest," 37.

39
We studied records in the State
Engineer's Office in Denver and found
that center-pivot sprinkler systems use
three to five times as much water as
traditional acequia systems in the San
Luis Valley.

40
For further discussion see Altieri et al.,
Agroecology; see also Jose Barreriro,
ed., "Indian Corn of the Americas:
Gift to the World," *Northeast Indian
Quarterly* 6 (1-2, 1992), 4-96.

41
Altieri et al., *Agroecology*, 89; see also
Jack R. Harlan, "Genetic Resources in
Wild Relatives of Crops," *Crop Science*
16 (3, 1976), 329-33.

42
See also Altieri et al., *Agroecology*, 88.

43
On HRM see Allan Savory, *Holistic
Resource Management* (Washington,
D.C.: Island Press, 1988).

44
This aspect of ranching activity has
benefited from the simple technological
addition of the truck. With a truck,
one person can easily supervise a herd of

two hundred to five hundred animals.

45

For example, during a soil survey conducted in July 1994, Robert Curry (staff watershed scientist) found that the soil horizon at the Corpus A. Gallegos Ranches in San Luis yielded an "A" horizon at least five feet deep. The only evidence of a "plow pan" was a half-inch-thick clay lens at about two feet in one of the corn *milpas*. See also Devon G. Peña, *Progress Report: Research Findings from the Upper Río Grande Hispano Farms Study, Vol. I, Summary of Environmental History Research Modules,* June 1994–May 1995 (Colorado Springs: Río Grande Bioregions Project, 1995).

46

For more on the problem of overgrazing in Chicano farming communities, see Devon G. Peña, "Pasture Poachers, Water Hogs and Ridge Runners: Archetypes in the Site Ethnography of Local Environmental Conflicts" (Paper presented at the Thirty-sixth Annual Conference of the Western Social Science Association, Albuquerque, April 1994).

47

See Peña, "The 'Brown' and the 'Green'"; Peña, "Pasture Poachers."

48

See Peña, *Progress Report.*

49

For further discussion see Peña, "A Gold Mine"; *A Proposal for the Establishment of a Community Land Trust.*

50

See Peña, *Chicano Culture, Ecology, Politics.*

51

For more on the anti-logging campaign see Peña and Mondragon Valdez, "The 'Brown' and the 'Green' Revisited." See also Mark Pearson, "La Sierra Tract: A Key Link in the Landscape of the Southern Rockies," *La Sierra* 1 (1, 1994), 7-8; *A Proposal for the Establishment of a Community Land Trust.*

52

See Center of the American West, *Atlas of the New West: Portrait of a Changing Region* (New York: W. W. Norton, 1997), 147.

53

The problem of land degradation is complicated by the complete enclosure of the common lands. See Peña, *Chicano Culture, Ecology, Politics,* especially the chapter by Peña and Martinez, "The Capitalist Tool, the Lawless, and the Violent: A Critique of Recent Southwestern Environmental History."

Selected Bibliography

Published Books, Articles, and Periodicals

Abbott, Carl, Stephen J. Leonard, and David McComb. *Colorado: A History of the Centennial State.* Niwot: University Press of Colorado, 1982.

Acuña, Rodolfo. *Occupied America: A History of Chicanos.* New York: Harper and Row, 1988.

Adams, Graham, Jr. *Age of Industrial Violence, 1910–15: The Activities and Findings of the United States Commission on Industrial Relations.* New York: Columbia University Press, 1966.

Alegria, D., E. Guerra, C. Martinez, Jr., and G. G. Meyer. "El Hospital Invisible: A Study of Curanderismo." *Archives of General Psychiatry* 34 (1977).

Almaguer, Tomas. "Historical Notes on Chicano Oppression: The Dialectics of Racial and Class Domination in North America." *Aztlan* 5, nos. 1 and 2 (Spring and Fall 1974).

_____. "Toward the Study of Chicano Colonialism." *Aztlan* 2, no. 1 (Spring 1971).

Altieri, Miguel, Susanna Hecht, and Richard Norgaard. *Agroecology: The Scientific Basis of Alternative Agriculture.* Boulder, Colo.: Westview Press, 1987.

Alvarez, Salvador. "Mexican American Community Organizations." *El Grito* 4, no. 3 (Spring 1971).

Athearn, Robert G. *The Coloradans.* Albuquerque: University of New Mexico Press, 1976.

Atkins, James A. *Human Relations in Colorado: A Historical Record,* Byron W. Hansford, ed. Denver: Colorado Department of Education, 1968.

Bailey, Ronald, and Guillermo Flores. "Internal Colonialism and Racial Minorities in the U.S.: An Overview." In Bonilla and Girling, *Structures of Dependency.*

Bancroft, Hubert Howe. *History of Arizona and New Mexico, 1538–1888.* Reprint of 1889 edition. Albuquerque: Horn and Wallace, 1962.

Barnes, Thomas C., Thomas H. Naylor, and Charles W. Polzer. *Northern New Spain: A Research Guide.* Tucson: University of Arizona Press, 1981.

Barrera, Mario, Carlos Muñoz, and Charles Ornelas. "The Barrio as an Internal Colony." In Hahn, *People and Politics in Urban Society.*

Barreriro, Jose, ed. "Indian Corn of the Americas: Gift to the World." *Northeast Indian Quarterly* 6, nos. 1 and 2 (1992).

Beck, Warren A. *New Mexico: A History of Four Centuries.* Norman: University of Oklahoma Press, 1962.

Bernstein, Irving. *The Lean Years: A History of the Worker, 1920–1933.* Boston: Houghton Mifflin Company, 1960.

Beshoar, Barron B. *Out of the Depths: The Story of John R. Lawson, a Labor Leader.* Denver: Golden Bell Press, 1942.

Blauner, Robert. *Racial Oppression in America.* New York: Harper & Row, Publishers, 1972.

Bonilla, Frank, and Robert Girling, eds. *Structures of Dependency.* Stanford: Stanford Institute of Politics, 1973.

Bradley, Emma J. "Narrative of Elfido Lopez." *Trinidad Chronicle-News,* June 19, 1937.

Briegel, Kaye. "The Development of Mexican-American Organizations." In Servin, *The Mexican Americans.*

Briggs, Charles L., and John R. Van Ness, eds. *Land, Water, and Culture: New Perspectives on Hispanic Land Grants.* Albuquerque: University of New Mexico Press, 1987.

Brown, John. *The Mediumistic Experiences of John Brown, the Medium of the Rockies.* Des Moines: Moses Hull & Co., 1887.

Bryan, Howard. *Wildest of the Wild West.* Santa Fe: Clear Light Publishers, 1988.

Bullard, Robert, ed. *Confronting Environmental Racism: Voices from the Grassroots.* Boston: South End Press, 1993.

Burma, John H., ed. *Mexican Americans in the United States.* Cambridge: Schenkman Publishing Co., 1970.

Cabeza de Baca, Fabiola. *We Fed Them Cactus.* Reprint of 1954 edition. Albuquerque: University of New Mexico Press, 1994.

Cabeza de Vaca, Alvar Nuñez. *Castaway.* Enrique Pupo-Walker, ed., Frances M. Lopez-Morillas, trans. Berkeley: University of California Press, 1993.

Calafate Boyle, Susan. *Comerciantes, Arrieros, y Peones: The Hispanos and the Santa Fe Trade.* National Park Service, Southwest Cultural Resources Center, Professional Paper No. 54. Washington, D.C.: Government Printing Office, 1994.

Carlson, Alvar Ward. "Rural Settlement Patterns in the San Luis Valley: A Comparative Study." *The Colorado Magazine* 44, no. 2 (1967).

Castaneda, Carlos. *The Teachings of Don Juan: A Yaqui Way of Knowledge.* Berkeley: University of California Press, 1968.

Center of the American West. *Atlas of the New West: Portrait of a Changing Region.* New York: W. W. Norton, 1997.

Cerny, Charlene, and Christine Mather. "Textile Production in Twentieth-Century New Mexico." In Fisher, *Spanish Textile Tradition of New Mexico and Colorado.*

Chavez, Fray Angelico. *Origins of New Mexico Families in the Spanish Colonial Period.* Santa Fe: The Historical Society of New Mexico, 1954.

Chavez, John R. *The Lost Land: The Chicano Image of the Southwest.* Albuquerque: University of New Mexico Press, 1984.

Clark, Margaret. *A Community Study: Health in the Mexican American Culture.* Berkeley: University of California Press, 1970.

Cleland, Robert Glass. *The Reckless Breed of Men: The Trappers and Fur Traders of the Southwest.* New York: Alfred E. Knopf, 1963.

Colorado Fuel and Iron Company (Pueblo). *Blast*, 1931–1948.

Cutter, Charles R. *The Protector de Indios in Colonial New Mexico, 1659-1821.* Albuquerque: University of New Mexico Press, 1986.

Davis, W.W.H. *El Gringo: New Mexico and Her People.* Reprint of 1857 edition. Lincoln: University of Nebraska Press, 1982.

DeBuys, William. *Enchantment and Exploitation: The Life and Hard Times of a New Mexico Mountain Range.* Albuquerque: University of New Mexico Press, 1985.

Deutsch, Sarah. *No Separate Refuge: Culture, Class, and Gender on an Anglo-Hispanic Frontier in the American Southwest, 1880–1940.* New York: Oxford University Press, 1987.

DeVall, Bill, ed. *Clearcut: The Tragedy of Industrial Forestry.* San Francisco: Sierra Club, 1994.

Donner, Frank J. *The Age of Surveillance: The Aims and Methods of America's Political Intelligence System.* New York: Alfred A. Knopf, 1980.

Eastman, Max. "Class War in Colorado." *Echoes of Revolt: The Masses, 1911–1917.* William L. O'Neill, ed. Chicago: Quadrangle Books, 1966.

Ebright, Malcolm. *Land Grants and Lawsuits in Northern New Mexico.*

Albuquerque: University of New Mexico Press, 1994.

El Gallo (Denver). June 1967–January 1968.

Elazar, Daniel J. *Cities of the Prairie: The Metropolitan Frontier and American Politics.* New York: Basic Books, Inc., 1970.

Ewers, John C. *Plains Indian History and Culture: Essays on Continuity and Change.* Norman and London: University of Oklahoma Press, 1997.

Faber, Daniel, ed. *The Quest for Ecological Democracy: Movements for Environmental Justice in the United States.* New York: Guilford Press, 1998.

Fanon, Frantz. *The Wretched of the Earth.* New York: Grove Press, Inc., 1968.

Fetherling, Dale. *Mother Jones: The Miners' Angel.* Carbondale: Southern Illinois University Press, 1974.

Findley, Earl H. "Bitter War Bred under Wings of Strike." *New York Tribune,* May 10, 1914.

Fink, Walter H. "The Ludlow Massacre." In Stein and Taft, *Massacre at Ludlow.*

Fisher, Nora, ed. *Spanish Textile Tradition of New Mexico and Colorado.* Santa Fe: Museum of International Folk Art, 1979.

Flores, Guillermo. "Race and Culture in the Internal Colony: Keeping the Chicano in His Place." In Bonilla and Girling, *Structures of Dependency.*

Forbes, Jack D. *Apache, Navaho, and Spaniard.* Norman: University of Oklahoma Press, 1982.

Foster, George M. "Relationships between Spanish and Spanish American Folk Medicine." *Journal of American Folklore* 66 (1953).

Goff, Richard, and Robert H. McCaffree. *Century in the Saddle.* Denver: Colorado Cattlemen's Centennial Commission, 1967.

Goff, Richard, Robert H. McCaffree, and Doris Sterbenz. *Centennial Brand Book of the Colorado Cattlemen's Association.* Denver: Colorado Cattlemen's Centennial Commission, 1967.

Gonzales, Rodolfo. *I Am Joaquín* (Yo Soy Joaquín): *An Epic Poem.* Reprint of 1967 edition. Toronto, New York, London: Bantam Pathfinder Editions, 1972.

Gonzalez-Casanova, Pablo. "Internal Colonialism and National Development." In Horowitz et al., *Latin American Radicalism.*

Gutiérrez, Ramón A. *When Jesus Came, the Corn Mothers Went Away: Marriage, Sexuality, and Power in New Mexico, 1500–1846.* Stanford: Stanford University Press, 1991.

Guzman, Ralph. "Politics in the Mexican American Community." In Rosaldo et al., *Chicanos.*

Hafen, LeRoy R., ed. *Colorado and Its People.* New York: Lewis Historical Publishing Company, Inc., 1948.

Hahn, Harlan, ed. *People and Politics in Urban Society.* Beverly Hills: Sage Publications, 1972.

Hall, A., G. H. Cannell, and H. W. Lawton, eds. "Agriculture in Semi-Arid Environments." *Ecological Studies* 34. Berlin: Springer-Verlag, 1979.

Hammond, George P. *The Adventures of Alexander Barclay.* Denver: Old West Publishing Co., 1976.

Harlan, Jack R. "Genetic Resources in Wild Relatives of Crops." *Crop Science* 16, no. 3 (1976).

Hay, John. "Upper Río Grande: Embattled River." In Hodge, *Aridity and Man.*

Hodge, Carle, ed. *Aridity and Man: The Challenge of the Arid Lands in the United States.* Washington, D.C.: American Association for the Advancement of Science, 1963.

Hoffman, Abraham. "Mexican Repatriation Statistics: Some Suggested Alternatives to Carey McWilliams." *Western Historical Quarterly* 3 (October 1972).

_____. *Unwanted Mexican Americans in the Great Depression: Repatriation Pressures 1929–1939.* Tucson: University of Arizona Press, 1974.

Hollon, W. Eugene. *The Southwest: Old and New.* Lincoln: University of Nebraska Press, 1968.

Horgan, Paul. *Great River: The Río Grande in North American History.* 2 vols. Reprint of 1954 edition. Austin: Texas Monthly Press, 1984.

Horowitz, Irving L., Josue de Castro, and John Gerassi, eds. *Latin American Radicalism.* New York: Random House, 1969.

Howard, Donald. *The WPA and Federal Relief Policy.* New York: DeCapo Press, 1973.

Howard, Joseph Kinsey. *Strange Empire.* New York: Morrow, 1952.

Hurd, C. W. *Boggsville: Cradle of the Cattle Industry.* Las Animas, Colo.: Boggsville Committee and *Bent County Democrat*, 1957.

Hurtado, Albert L. "When Strangers Met: Sex and Gender on Three Frontiers." In Jameson and Armitage, *Writing the Range.*

Jameson, Elizabeth, and Susan Armitage, eds. *Writing the Range: Race, Class, and Culture in the Women's West.* Norman: University of Oklahoma Press, 1997.

Jensen, Billie Barnes. "Woodrow Wilson's Intervention in the Coal Strike of 1914." *Labor History* 14 (Winter 1974).

Jones, Mary. *Autobiography of Mother Jones.* Mary Field Parton, ed. Chicago: Charles H. Kerr and Company, 1925.

Kessell, John L., ed. *Remote Beyond Compare: Letters of don Diego de Vargas to His Family from New Spain and New Mexico, 1675–1706.* Albuquerque: University of New Mexico Press, 1989.

Kiev, A. *Curanderismo: Mexican American Folk Psychiatry.* New York: Free Press, 1968.

_____, ed. *Magic, Faith and Healing.* New York: Free Press, 1964.

Kurtz, Richard A., and H. Paul Chalfant. *The Sociology of Medicine and Illness.* Boston: Allyan and Bacon, Inc., 1984.

Lamm, Richard D., and Duane A. Smith. *Pioneers and Politicians: Ten Colorado Governors in Profile.* Boulder: Pruett Publishing Company, 1984.

Lecompte, Janet. *Pueblo, Hardscrabble, Greenhorn: Society on the High Plains, 1832–1856.* Norman and London: University of Oklahoma Press, 1978.

Lloyd, Rees, and Peter Montague. "Ford's Pacification Program for La Raza." *El Grito del Norte*, August 29, 1970.

Lopez Tushar, Olibama. *The People of El Valle: A History of the Spanish Colonials in the San Luis Valley.* Pueblo, Colo.: El Escritorio, 1992.

Louden, Richard. "The Military Freight Route." *Wagon Tracks: Santa Fe Trail Association Quarterly* 7, no. 3 (May 1993).

Lucero, Donald L. *The Adobe Kingdom: New Mexico 1598–1958 as Experienced by the Families Lucero de Godoy y Baca.* Pueblo, Colo.: El Escritorio, 1995.

Madsen, W. "Value Conflicts and Folk Psychotherapy." In Kiev, *Magic, Faith and Healing.*

Markoff, Dena S. "A Bittersweet Saga: The Arkansas Valley Beet Sugar Industry, 1900–1979." *The Colorado Magazine* 56, nos. 3 and 4 (Summer and Fall 1979).

Marsh, Charles S. *People of the Shining Mountains.* Boulder, Colo.: Pruett Publishing Co., 1982.

Martinez, Ricardo Arguijo, ed. *Hispanic Culture and Health Care: Fact, Fiction, and Folklore.* St. Louis: The C. V. Mosby Company, 1978.

McGovern, George S., and Leonard F. Guttridge. *The Great Coalfield War.* Boston: Houghton Mifflin Company, 1972.

Meketa, Jacqueline Dorgan. *Legacy of Honor: The Life of Rafael Chacon, a Nineteenth-Century New Mexican.* Albuquerque: University of New Mexico Press, 1986.

Meyer, Marian. *Mary Donoho: New First Lady of the Santa Fe Trail.* Santa Fe: Ancient City Press, 1991.

Muñoz, Carlos, Jr. "The Politics of Protest and Chicano Liberation: A Case Study of Repression and Cooptation." *Aztlan 5*, nos. 1 and 2 (Spring and Fall 1974).

Nabokov, Peter. *Tijerina and the Courthouse Raid.* Albuquerque: University of New Mexico Press, 1969.

Nash, Gerald D. *The American West in the Twentieth Century: A Short History of an Urban Oasis.* Englewood Cliffs: Prentice-Hall, Inc., 1973.

Navarro, Armando. "The Evolution of Chicano Politics." *Aztlan 5*, nos. 1 and 2 (Spring and Fall 1974).

Noss, Reed. "A Sustainable Forest Is a Diverse and Natural Forest." In DeVall, *Clearcut.*

O'Neill, William L., ed. *Echoes of Revolt: The Masses, 1911–1917.* Chicago: Quadrangle Books, 1966.

Pearson, Mark. "La Sierra Tract: A Key Link in the Landscape of the Southern Rockies." *La Sierra 1*, no. 1 (1994).

Peña, Devon G. "The 'Brown' and the 'Green': Chicanos and Environmental Politics in the Upper Río Grande." *Capitalism, Nature, Socialism 3*, no. 1 (1992).

_____. "A Gold Mine, an Orchard, and an Eleventh Commandment." In Peña, *Chicano Culture, Ecology, Politics.*

_____, ed. *Chicano Culture, Ecology, Politics: Subversive Kin.* Society, Place, and Environment Series. Tucson: University of Arizona Press, 1998.

Peña, Devon G., and Joseph Gallegos. "Nature and Chicanos in Southern Colorado." In Bullard, *Confronting Environmental Racism.*

Peña, Devon G., and Ruben Martinez. "The Capitalist Tool, the Lawless, and the Violent: A Critique of Recent Southwestern Environmental History." In Peña, *Chicano Culture, Ecology, Politics*.

Peña, Devon G., Ruben Martinez, and Louis McFarland. "Rural Chicana/o Communities and the Environment: An Attitudinal Survey of Residents of Costilla County, Colorado." *Perspectives in Mexican American Studies* 4 (August 1993).

Peña, Devon G., Ines Talamantez, and Vernon Kjonegaard, eds. *Subversive Kin: Chicana/o Studies and Ecology*. Special Thematic Issue. *The New Scholar* 16 (Winter 1995).

Peña, Devon G., and Maria Mondragon Valdez. "The 'Brown' and the 'Green' Revisited: Chicanos and Environmental Politics in the Upper Río Grande." In Faber, *The Quest for Ecological Democracy*.

Perrone, Bobette, H. Henrietta Stockel, and Victoria Kruger. *Medicine Women: Curanderas and Women Doctors*. Norman: University of Oklahoma Press, 1989.

Porter, Eugene D. "The Colorado Coal Strike of 1913: An Interpretation." *The Historian* 12 (Autumn 1949).

Powell, John Wesley. "Institutions for the Aridlands." *Century Magazine* 40 (May-October 1890).

_____. *Report on the Lands of the Arid Region of the United States*. Cambridge: Belknap Press of Harvard University Press, 1962.

A Proposal for the Establishment of a Community Land Trust Based on the Principles of Environmental Justice. San Luis, Colo.: La Sierra Foundation of San Luis, 1995.

Reed, John. "The Colorado Wars." *Metropolitan Magazine* 14 (July 1914).

Romano, O. I. "Charismatic Medicine, Folk-Healing, and Folk-Sainthood." *American Anthropologist* 67 (1956).

Romero-Oak, Judy. "Padre Martinez." *Spirit: Rocky Mountain Southwest* 8 (Spring 1995).

Rosaldo, Renato, Robert A. Calvert, and Gustav L. Seligmann, eds. *Chicanos: The Evolution of a People*. Minneapolis: Winston Press, 1973.

Rubel, Arthur J. "The Epidemiology of a Folk Illness: Susto in Hispanic America." In Martinez, *Hispanic Culture and Health Care*.

Ruland, Sylvia. *The Lion of Redstone*. Boulder, Colo.: Johnson Books, 1981.

Saunders, L. *Cultural Difference and Medical Care: The Case for the Spanish Speaking People of the Southwest.* New York: Russell Sage Foundation, 1954.

Savory, Allan. *Holistic Resource Management.* Washington, D.C.: Island Press, 1988.

Scamehorn, H. Lee. *Pioneer Steelmaker in the West: The Colorado Fuel and Iron Company, 1872–1903.* Boulder: Pruett Publishing Company, 1976.

Schlereth, Thomas J. "Columbia, Columbus, and Columbianism." In Thelen and Hoxie, *Discovering America.*

Schlissel, Lillian, Vicki L. Ruiz, and Janice Monk, eds. *Western Women: Their Land, Their Lives.* Albuquerque: University of New Mexico Press, 1990.

Scrimshaw, C. S., and E. Burleigh. "The Potential for the Integration of Indigenous and Western Medicines in Latin America and Hispanic Populations in the United States of America." In Velimirovic, *Modern Medicine and Medical Anthropology.*

Servin, Manuel P., ed. *The Mexican Americans: An Awakening Minority.* Beverly Hills: Glencoe Press, 1970.

Sheldon, Paul. "Mexican American Formal Organizations." In Burma, *Mexican Americans in the United States.*

Sigerman, Harriet. *Land of Many Hands: Women in the American West.* London and New York: Oxford University Press, 1997.

Silverberg, Robert. *The Pueblo Revolt.* Lincoln and London: University of Nebraska Press, 1994.

Simmons, Marc. *Coronado's Land: Essays on Daily Life in Colonial New Mexico.* Albuquerque: University of New Mexico Press, 1991.

_____. *The Little Lion of the Southwest: A Life of Manuel Antonio Chaves.* Chicago: Sage Books, 1973.

Spicer, Edward H. *Cycles of Conquest: The Impact of Spain, Mexico, and the United States on the Indians of the Southwest, 1533–1960.* Tucson: University of Arizona Press, 1986.

Stein, Leon, and Philip Taft, eds. *Massacre at Ludlow: Four Reports.* New York: Arno and the *New York Times,* 1971.

Stoller, Marianne. "La Sierra y la Merced." In Tweeuwen, *La Cultura Contante de San Luis.*

Suggs, George G., Jr. *Colorado's War on Militant Unionism.* Detroit: Wayne State University Press, 1972.

Taylor, Morris F. *Pioneers of the Picketwire*. Pueblo, Colo.: O'Brien Printing & Stationery Co., 1964.

Thelen, David, and Frederick E. Hoxie, eds. *Discovering America*. Urbana: University of Illinois Press, 1994.

Thomas, Alfred Barnaby, trans. and ed. *Alonso de Posada Report, 1686: A Description of the Area of the Present Southern United States in the Seventeenth Century*. Pensacola: The Perdida Bay Press, 1986.

Tirado, Miguel David. "Mexican-American Community Political Organization." *Aztlan* 1, no. 1 (Spring 1970).

Tjarks, Alicia V. "Demographic, Ethnic, and Occupational Structure of New Mexico, 1790." *The America* 35, no. 1 (July 1978).

Torrey, E. Fuller. *The Mind Game: Witchdoctors and Psychiatrists*. New York: Bantam Books, 1972.

_____. *Witchdoctors and Psychiatrists: The Common Roots of Psychotherapy and Its Future*. New York: Harper and Row Publishers, 1986.

Tweeuwen, R., ed. *La Cultura Contante de San Luis*. San Luis, Colo.: San Luis Museum and Cultural Center, 1985.

Twitchell, Ralph E. *The Spanish Archives of New Mexico*. 2 vols. Cedar Rapids: Torch Press, 1914.

Tyler, Daniel. *Sources for New Mexico History, 1821–1848*. Santa Fe: Museum of New Mexico Press, 1984.

Van Ness, John R. "Hispanic Land Grants: Ecology and Subsistence in the Uplands of Northern New Mexico and Southern Colorado." In Briggs and Van Ness, *Land, Water, and Culture*.

Van Ness, John R., and Christine M. Van Ness, eds. *Spanish and Mexican Land Grants in New Mexico and Colorado*. Manhattan, Kans.: Sunflower University Press, 1980.

Velimirovic, B., ed. *Modern Medicine and Medical Anthropology in the United States: Mexico Border Populations*. Washington, D.C.: Pan American Health Organization, 1978.

Viva! The Battle Cry of Truth (Denver). May-June, 1964.

Weber, David J. *The Taos Trappers: The Fur Trade in the Far Southwest, 1540–1846*. Norman: University of Oklahoma Press, 1982.

_____, ed. *Myth and the History of the Hispanic Southwest*. Albuquerque: University of New Mexico Press, 1988.

Wilkinson, Charles H. *Crossing the Next Meridian: Land, Water, and the Future of the West.* Washington, D.C.: Island Press, 1992.

_____. *The Eagle Bird: Mapping the New West.* Tucson: University of Arizona Press, 1988.

Wilson, Chris, and David Kammer. *Community and Continuity: The History, Architecture and Cultural Landscape of La Tierra Amarilla.* Santa Fe: New Mexico Historic Preservation Division, 1990.

Worster, Donald. *An Unsettled Country: Changing Landscapes of the American West.* Albuquerque: University of New Mexico Press, 1994.

Wroth, William, ed. *Hispanic Crafts of the Southwest.* Colorado Springs: The Taylor Museum of the Colorado Springs Fine Arts Center, 1977.

Unpublished Manuscripts and Papers

Bowden, J. J. *Private Land Claims in the Southwest.* 6 vols. Master's thesis, Southern Methodist University, 1969.

Bundy, William Wilson. "The Mexican Minority Problem in Otero County, Colorado." Master's thesis, University of Colorado, 1936.

Crisler, Carney Clark. "The Mexican Bracero Program with Special Reference to Colorado." Master's thesis, University of Denver, 1968.

Garcia, Reyes. "A Philosopher in Aztlan: Notes toward an Ethnometaphysics in the IndoHispano (Chicano) Southwest." Ph.D. diss., University of Colorado, 1989.

Hubbard, E. J. "Reminiscences of E. J. Hubbard." Trinidad, Colo.: DeBusk Collection, Trinidad State Junior College.

Lucero, Aileen. "A Profile of a Curandera and Her Curandera-Treated Clients: The Southwest Denver Community Mental Health Center." Ph.D. diss., Washington State University, 1981.

Peña, Devon G. "*Acequias* and Chicana/o Land Ethics." Paper presented at the Thirty-fifth Annual Conference of the Western Social Science Association, Corpus Christi, April 1993.

_____. "Pasture Poachers, Water Hogs and Ridge Runners: Archetypes in the Site Ethnography of Local Environmental Conflicts." Paper presented at the Thirty-sixth Annual Conference of the Western Social Science Association, Albuquerque, April 1994.

Rivera, George, Jr., and Joseph Andres Gavaldon. "The Crusade for

Justice: An Alternative in Chicano Community Organization." Paper presented at the Southern Political Science Association Meeting, Atlanta, Georgia, November 1972.

Scheinberg, Stephen J. "The Development of Corporation Labor Policy, 1900–1940." Ph.D. diss., University of Wisconsin, 1966.

Stoller, Marianne. "Preliminary Manuscript on the History of the Sangre de Cristo Land Grant and the Claims of the People of the Culebra River Villages on Their Lands." Colorado Springs: Department of Anthropology, Colorado College, 1993.

_____. "The Settlement History of the San Luis Valley." Unpublished manuscript. Colorado Springs: Department of Anthropology, Colorado College, 1992.

Valdez, Arnold A., and Maria A. Valdez. "The Culebra River Villages of Costilla County: Village Architecture and Its Historical Context, 1851–1940." Denver: Office of Archaeology and Historic Preservation, 1991.

Public Documents

Cabinet Committee Hearings on Mexican American Affairs: Labor Standards. El Paso, Texas: Inter-agency Committee on Mexican American Affairs, 1967.

Colorado Adjutant General. *The Military Occupation of the Coal Strike Zone of Colorado by the Colorado National Guard: Report of the Commanding General to the Governor for the Use of the Congressional Committee. Exhibiting an Account of the Military Occupation to the Time of the First Withdrawal of Troops in April, 1914* (Denver).

Curry, Robert. *State of the Culebra Watershed I: The Southern Tributaries.* Technical report. San Luis, Colo.: Costilla County Conservancy District, 1994.

Federal Bureau of Investigation. Denver field office. File 100-9290, Rodolfo Gonzales.

_____. Headquarters. File 105-176910, Rodolfo Gonzales.

Friedman, Paul D. "Final Report of History and Oral History Investigation at the Proposed Pinyon Canyon Maneuver Area." Denver: U.S. Department of the Interior, National Park Service.

Peña, Devon G. *Progress Report: Research Findings from the Upper Río Grande Hispano Farms Study, Vol. I, Summary of Environmental*

History Research Modules, June 1994-May 1995. Colorado Springs: Río Grande Bioregions Project, 1995.

Revenue Potential and Ethical Issues in the Management of the Culebra Mountain Tract as a Common Property Resource. Prepared by Robert Green and Devon Peña. San Luis, Colo.: Costilla County Conservancy District, 1993.

U.S. Congress. House. Committee on Mines and Mining. *Report on the Colorado Strike Investigation.* Made under H. Res. 387. 63rd Cong., 1915.

U.S. Congress. Senate. *Industrial Relations: Final Report and Testimony Submitted to Congress by the Commission on Industrial Relations, Created by the Act of August 23, 1912.* 64th Cong., 1st sess., 1916.

U.S. *Congressional Record.* 63rd Cong., 2d sess., April 29, 1914.

U.S. *Congressional Record.* 63rd Cong., 2d sess., July 13, 1914.

U.S. Department of Labor. *Second Annual Report of the Department of Labor.* Washington, D.C.: U.S. Government Printing Office, 1915.

West, George P. *Report on the Colorado Strike.* Washington, D.C.: U.S. Commission on Industrial Relations, 1915.

Westside Summary of Conditions and Neighborhood Improvement Plan. Denver: Denver Community Renewal Program, December 1972.

Index

References to illustrations are shown in boldface.

COLORADO HISTORICAL SOCIETY
HISPANIC ADVISORY COUNCIL 1998